NORTHWEST CHEAP SLEEPS

Recommendations for the Budget Traveler

Edited by
Stephanie Irving and Nancy Leson

SASQUATCH BOOKS
SEATTLE

Second printing 1996.

Library of Congress Cataloging in Publication Data
Irving, Stephanie, 1962-
Northwest cheap sleeps; recommendations for the budget traveler/edited
by Stephanie Irving and Nancy Leson. — [2nd. ed.]
        p. cm.
    Includes index.
    ISBN 1-57061-024-X: $12.95
        1. Hotels—Northwest, Pacific—Guidebooks. I. Leson, Nancy,
1959- . II. Title.
TX907.3.N96178 1995   94-35652
647.9479501—dc20

Interior design: Lynne Faulk
Cover design: Elizabeth Watson
Cover illustration: Laura Cook
Interior map illustrations: Karen McClinchy
Composition: Fay Bartels
Contributors: Rachel Bard, Richard Fencsak, Carrie Floyd, Joan
Gregory, Emily Hall, Heather Lockman, Sandra McKenzie, Kerry
McPhedran, Kathryn Robinson, Steven Threndyle, Cleve Twitchell,
and Kasey Wilson.

Sasquatch Books
1008 Western Avenue
Seattle, Washington 98104
(206) 467-4300

CONTENTS

ACKNOWLEDGMENTS

Many thanks to the writers who packed their overnight bags, camping gear, ski equipment, fishing rods, road bikes, AAA maps, laptops, and notebooks, jumped into their cars, and headed out in search of the best places not-a-lot-of money can buy. Traveling on the cheap is always an adventure—as everyone who toes the thin line between taking a vacation and making a buck can attest.

Thanks to Rachel Bard, Richard Fencsak, Carrie Floyd, Joan Gregory, Emily Hall, Heather Lockman, Sandra McKenzie, Kerry McPhedran, Kathryn Robinson, Steven Threndyle, Cleve Twitchell, and Kasey Wilson for taking working vacations, sleeping around for our benefit and agreeing to share their favorite finds and word-of-mouth discoveries with our readers.

Also a fond thank you to wordsmith Sherri Schultz, designer Lynne Faulk, cover designer Elizabeth Watson, cover artist Laura Cook, and art director Nancy Deahl, for refining our words and transforming them into a great-looking book.

—The Editors

INTRODUCTION

Here is a trustworthy travel guide for the everyman budget, a solution for those bemoaning the creeping costs of weekend jaunts in Oregon, Washington, and British Columbia. From the desks of the *Best Places* editors, *Northwest Cheap Sleeps* comes to you packed with recommended inexpensive lodgings as well as tips on how to get the most out of your vacation dollar. Inside you'll discover lodgings good enough for those with champagne tastes and beer pockets. We'll lead you to mountain motels, island cabins, ski bunks, and beach bungalows, where two of you will pay less than $60 U.S. In addition, you'll be clued in to hundreds of penny-pinching travel ideas: $1 movies in Portland, community lamb bakes on Saturna, discount tickets at Whistler, and even where to whale-watch on the Oregon Coast without chartering a boat. Often when you seek out smaller, lesser-known places to stay, you find yourself on a journey of unexpected delights.

We use the same policy for *Cheap Sleeps* as we do for our dependable *Best Places* guides, only in this book we're looking for the best places at bargain prices. A platoon of writers scoured the Northwest, ferreting out the best finds for the least money. *Best Places* and *Cheap Sleeps* writers always travel anonymously and pay in full. And we pull no punches in our reviews.

The first thing you'll notice about this new, second edition of *Northwest Cheap Sleeps* is the changed cover and more readable design. But this baby has had more than just a new paint job. We stripped it down and scrubbed out all of the places we could no longer recommend to a best friend. Then we polished it up with new finds, threw in additional things for you to do on the road, and topped it off with more money-saving tips. The biggest difference for me this time was that the book was in the capable hands of Associate Editor Nancy Leson, who kept the whole traveling crowd of writers moving toward the ultimate destination—a new, second edition, just in time for your next road trip.

So this book is for you—the person who travels with a light heart, who smiles at the cat curled up at the foot of the bed, who enjoys lighting a wood-fired sauna on a rocky Vancouver Island beach, or who just wants a quiet, comfortable bed (and a hearty, no frills dinner). *Northwest Cheap Sleeps* is for smart, adventurous people of all ages, those who know it's not necessary to pay top dollar to revel in a four-star experience.

—Stephanie Irving

WHAT'S CHEAP?

We did our darnedest to review only lodgings that charge less than $60 (U.S.) for two. And of those, we included only the ones we could honestly recommend. All prices are based on two people, one night. Occasionally prices crept above the limit, sometimes they remained well below, but they were always a great deal for the area. Our price ceiling in Canada was a bit higher, but a favorable exchange rate makes traveling there a real bargain for those of us with U.S. funds in our pockets. The British Columbia chapters quote rates in Canadian dollars.

Discounts

Obviously, prices for off-season visits, weeknights, and stays of three days (or more) are usually discounted. Ask for the corporate rate, which is always less than the standard rack rate. You don't need to be on the job or even look corporate; just drop the name of your company, and you'll usually be rewarded. Have an AAA card? A student ID? Don't forget to flash it for a possible discount. To save even more money, travel in groups of four or more and ask for a group discount.

Kids

In general, most of the lodgings listed welcome children. We make note of those that do not. To be sure, call ahead.

Smoking

More and more establishments either offer a choice of smoking and nonsmoking rooms or designate all as nonsmoking. When an inn is all-smoking (more the occasion than the rule), we've done our best to point it out. If you smoke and don't want to be relegated to puffing in the rain, call ahead.

Wheelchairs

Many of the listings in *Northwest Cheap Sleeps* are smaller bed and breakfasts, older motels, and remote cabins. Not all of them are easily accessible to the physically challenged. If you have special needs, please make sure to call ahead.

Pets

A surprising number of the lodgings listed here do allow pets, though there are often many "okay, buts" involved: small pets but not large, only well-mannered ones, dogs but not cats. Whenever possible, we've specified those establishments that generally welcome pets. In cases where the owners were lukewarm, charged a steep fee, or attached too many qualifications, we did not mention pet policy.

OREGON

Portland

Long overshadowed by Seattle, often mistaken for the city in Maine, and located in a state whose name is chronically mispronounced, Portland lacks the ego and cosmopolitan pretensions that one might expect from Oregon's largest city.

Civic pride is strong, however, in this tree-filled city divided east-west by the murky Willamette River and bounded to the north by the Columbia. Residents point to the serene beauty of Mount Hood rising in the east. They gaze to the west at rambling Victorians stacked upon hills blanketed in the velvety green of Forest Park—which they're quick to tell you is, at nearly 5,000 acres, the largest urban park in the nation. They relish the character of the city, from its 10 quirky bridges (which are gradually being individually illuminated) to its former mayor Bud Clark, who posed as a flasher in the well-known "Expose Yourself to Art" poster, and who not only frequently biked to work but also put the police on two wheels.

Portlanders gather at the edge of the Willamette for myriad festivals, attend free twilight concerts at the zoo, and keep downtown alive (if not exactly kicking) well into the night. And although they'd never admit it, they pride themselves on the long-awaited discovery of their city by the rest of the world—due

3

at least partially to the growing fame of local writers, artists, and filmmakers.

Despite census figures that put the local population at nearly half a million, Portland remains at heart a small town. We mean that in the kindest of ways. It's clean, it's verdant, and the mood is decidedly mellow; this is a place where networking is as straightforward as a trip to the grocery store. The lay of the land is easy to understand, and the city is so compact that you can ditch the car and stroll.

Portland is a settlement devoted to the simple pleasures of life—cafes and espresso carts can be found on just about every street, along with bookstores and brew pubs serving specialty beers. Nearly 300 parks are sprinkled throughout the city, and there's fine hiking and biking minutes from the downtown core.

ON THE ROAD

At the slightest hint of sun, sidewalk tables appear and Portland residents set out en masse, whiling away hours in the clustered "urban villages" that dot the town, rummaging through piles of castoffs at the numerous neighborhood porch sales, sunbathing in the nude on Sauvie Island, and strolling through the gardens at Washington Park.

Once winter enshrouds the city, and early morning mists and fog tangle on the hills, the locals retreat—to bookstores such as Powell's (the country's largest), to movie houses (most shows are discounted until 6pm), and to the plentiful restaurants (there are more per capita in Portland than anywhere else in the United States). And while some head to Mount Hood to ski, others simply head to bed, leaving instructions not to be roused until the rains let up.

The hotbed of urban activity throughout the summer is the grassy, river-hugging expanse known as **Tom McCall Waterfront Park**, which stretches on the west side of the Willamette from the Marquam to the Steel bridges. At its southern end is Riverplace, a mini-boardwalk of shops and waterfront restaurants claiming a view of the ships cruising upriver. The overheated douse themselves with abandon under the Salmon Street Springs fountain. And on almost any summer night, you're

Festivities

In the summer months, Portland hops with concerts and festivals. Here are the biggies, most of which are free:

Rose Festival
Portland's premier festival, along Waterfront Park and throughout the city
First three weeks of June
(503)227-2681

Your Zoo and All That Jazz
Jazz under the stars at Metro Washington Park Zoo
Wednesdays, mid-June through mid-August
(503)226-1561

Rhythm and Zoo Concerts
Blues and reggae at Metro Washington Park Zoo
Thursdays, mid-June through mid-August
(503)226-1561

Miller Genuine Draft Waterfront Blues Festival
Blues bash at Waterfront Park
First weekend in July
(503)282-0555

The Bite
Pig-out at Waterfront Park
Second weekend in August
(503)248-0600

Artquake
Theater, art, music, food, and more at Pioneer Courthouse Square, along Broadway and in the Park Blocks
Labor Day weekend
(503)227-2787

bound to discover something going on in the park; the Waterfront Blues Festival, the Oregon Brewers Festival, and The Bite are some of the big events. Just north, under the Burnside Bridge, is the site of the **Saturday Market**, where all weekend from March through December, the smell of shish kabobs hangs in the air and artists peddle everything from jewelry to jam.

In **Old Town**, indulge in the buttery croissants and satiny coffee at Le Panier Very French Bakery (71 SW 2nd Avenue, Portland; (503)241-3524), or opt for a cappuccino with a view at La Pâtisserie

(208 NW Couch Street, Portland; (503)248-9898). You can find cheap but quite decent Greek food at Johnny's Greek Villa (200 NW 3rd Avenue, Portland; (503)227-1096). Don't miss the Church of Elvis, a wacky window-front art gallery where computers talk, tell fortunes, and deliver prizes down chutes when prompted by the plunk of a quarter (720 SW Ankeny Street, Portland; (503)226-3671). A visit to McCormick & Schmick's (235 SW 1st Avenue, Portland; (503)224-7522) before 6:30pm or after 9:30pm affords you their bar-meal steal—$1.95 for a thick cheeseburger with fries, Greek salad, or macaroni and cheese.

Afterward, hop on one of the sleek trolleys that make up the city's light-rail system, affectionately called MAX (like the buses, light rail is free in the downtown core), and head to **Pioneer Courthouse Square** (SW Morrison Street at 6th Avenue), an amphitheater-style gathering place. On any sunny day of the week—but particularly at lunch hour—the square is crammed with urbanites who perch on its steps to read, take in the entertainment (which might be a symphony concert or the taping of a TV show), or simply people-watch while sipping espresso. Under Pioneer Courthouse Square, you can travel vicariously via Powell's Travel Store and snag bus schedules at the Tri-Met Information Center; (503)238-7433.

One block south is the mystifying **Niketown** (930 SW 6th Avenue, Portland; (503)221-6453), where sports facts are broadcast from the sidewalk, videos play through the floor, and running shoes swim in fish tanks. Is it a shoe store or Nike's answer to Disney World? In either case, you can find cheaper shoes if you drive to Nike's outlet store (3044 NE Martin Luther King Jr. Boulevard, Portland; (503)281-5901). And since window shopping is free, you might as well indulge your fantasies at **Pioneer**

Movie Tips

Check out the $1 movies at the McMenamins pubs and theaters: the Mission (1624 NW Glisan Street, Portland; (503)223-4031) and the Bagdad (3702 SE Hawthorne Boulevard, Portland; (503) 236-9234) in town, and the Edgefield in Troutdale (2126 SW Halsey Street, Troutdale; (503)669-8754). If you're 21 or over, you can sip on a microbrew; bring photo ID.

Cheap movies can also be found at the Hollywood Theatres (NE 41st Avenue and Sandy Boulevard, Portland; (503)248-6977), a vintage 1920s movie palace with worn velvet seats and balcony. It takes a while for just-released movies to find their way here, but heck, for a $1.50 double feature, who's complaining?

Place (SW Fifth Avenue and Morrison Street), the city's most exclusive mall, which boasts eateries, big-name shops, and Saks Fifth Avenue.

Wander along the tree-lined Park Blocks to the **Portland Art Museum** (1219 SW Park Avenue, Portland; (503)226-2811), where admission is free from 4pm to 9pm on the first Thursday of each month. PAM is also known to sponsor free lectures open to the public. The Portland Center for the Performing Arts (1111 SW Broadway, Portland; (503)248-4335) stages Shakespearean plays, symphony concerts, and an arts and lectures series. On the first Thursday of each month, join in the **city-wide art walk**: galleries stay open late and crowds jam into the Pearl District (NW 10th to NW 14th avenues between Everett and Glisan streets). Or stop by the offices of the Metropolitan Arts Commission in the Portland Building (1120 SW 5th Avenue, Portland; (503)823-5111) to pick up a guide (for a nominal fee) to the many installations of street-level art.

For **cheap eats downtown**, check out the cafeteria-style Mayas (1000 SW Morrison Street, Portland; (503)226-1946) or the healthful Macheesmo Mouse (700 SW 5th Avenue, Portland; (503)248-0917). While B. Moloch/The Heathman Bakery and Pub (901 SW Salmon Street, Portland; (503)227-5700) can be expensive for the solo diner, the large portions make it a good place to share a pizza and a couple of Widmer draft beers. For just a slice, check out the OK Cafe (222 SW Washington Street, Portland; (503)224-5477); the owners are the former managers of Hot Lips Pizza, and their pizza is reliably good.

If you're a shameless grazer, you can enjoy reasonably priced appetizers (try the roasted garlic with rosemary bread) at Pazzo (627 SW Washington Street, Portland; (503)228-1515) or shoot up 30 floors to the lounge at Atwater's (111 SW 5th Avenue, Portland; (503)275-3600), where you can drink a microbrew for the same price as any other place in town, make a meal of the lower-end appetizers ($4–$7), and get a bird's-eye view of Portland's rambling hills and bridges.

Nightlife revolves around the Lotus Cafe and Card Room (932 SW 3rd Avenue, Portland; (503)227-6185), where between 4:30pm and 7:30pm, the pool tables are free and food and drinks are discounted; the disco in back is free if you arrive before 10pm. Despite renovations, the place retains a shady air that attracts some of Portland's sleaziest men and, for some reason, some of its loveliest women.

Brew pubs are big in Portland. Some of the faves: Bridgeport (1313 NW Marshall Street, Portland; (503)241-7179), Portland Brewing Company (1339 NW Flanders Street, Portland; (503)222-3414), and B. Moloch/The Heathman Bakery and Pub (see address above).

Late-night dancing to a reggae beat rocks the back room at the Red Sea Restaurant on Thursday nights ($3 cover charge); $2 on Friday or Saturday buys you calypso, world beat, or disco music (318 SW 3rd Avenue, Portland; (503)241-5450). The recently face-lifted Brasserie Montmartre (626 SW Park Avenue, Portland; (503)224-5552) is a fun late-night place to listen to **jazz** while sipping on one of the Bra's famous steamers; from 11pm to closing you can munch on Eggs Benedict ($5.25) or scrambled eggs with smoked salmon ($5).

In the east side's **Hawthorne District**, you can grab a coffee at one of the area's many coffeehouses or cafes. We like Cup and Saucer (3566 SE Hawthorne Boulevard, Portland; (503)236-6001), Starbucks (3639 SE Hawthorne, Portland; (503)234-1757), and Coffee People (3500 SE Hawthorne, Portland; (503)235-1383). At Thanh Thao, you can treat yourself to some of the best Vietnamese food in the city without hurting your pocketbook (4005 SE Hawthorne, Portland; (503)238-6232). Any visit to the east side is reason enough to check out the fare at Jarra's (1435 SE Hawthorne, Portland; (503)230-8990), which serves Ethiopian food on the traditional injera, a spongy bread that doubles as fork and plate.

The Hawthorne area has a handful of excellent bookstores where you can spend the afternoon browsing; find cheap thrills at Murder by the Book (3210 SE Hawthorne, Portland; (503)232-9995) and an occasional good deal on used or remaindered cookbooks at Powell's Books for Cooks (3739 SE Hawthorne, Portland; (503)235-3802).

Try some late-night falafel at Garbonzos (2074 NW Lovejoy Street, Portland, (503)227-4196, or 3433 SE Hawthorne, Portland, (503)239-6087), which stays open until 1:30am on weekdays and 3am on weekends. To get a taste of what **Chinatown** was like in the days when opium dens were the draw and the underground shanghai tunnels were in active use, go late at night to the dark and tiny Temple Lounge at Hung Far

Coffee

From Portland to Seattle, drinking coffee and hanging out has become a regional pastime, and why shouldn't it be? After all, a cup of coffee won't set you back too much, and hang time is free. Here are some of Portland's best coffeehouses: Torrefazione Italia (838 NW 23rd Avenue, Portland; (503)228-2528), Coffee People (533 NW 23rd Avenue, Portland; (503)221-0235), The Pied Cow (3244 SE Belmont Street, Portland; (503)230-4866), and Common Grounds Coffee House (4321 SE Hawthorne, Portland; (503)236-4835).

🍷 Happy Hour

"Happy hour" sometimes seems to be an expression of the past, but with a little sleuthing you can still find good deals on food and drink. If you stop by Casa-U-Betcha between 2:30pm and 6:30pm, for instance, you can make a meal out of one of the $2.25 happy-hour choices—veggie or black-bean quesadillas, tacos, or tamales (612 NW 21st Avenue, Portland, (503)222-4833, or 700 NE Broadway, Portland, (503)282-4554). Between 4pm and 7pm, the Gypsy (625 NW 21st Avenue, Portland; (503)796-1859), run by the same people who own the downtown Lotus, serves half-price appetizers such as pot-stickers, steamed clams, and nachos, as well as 95-cent pints of domestic beer. And on Thursdays and Saturdays at the Virginia Cafe (725 SW Park Avenue, Portland; (503)227-0033), drinks are just $1.50.

Low (112 NW 4th Avenue, Portland; (503)223-8686), where the drinks are cheap and the atmosphere is mysterious.

Literary types should scan the "Words" column in the free *Willamette Week* to see which national authors are giving **free readings** at Powell's (1005 W Burnside Street, Portland; (503)228-4651). Even if no readings are scheduled, you can easily spend an evening (or even days) wandering through the sprawling bookstore. Settle into the adjoining Anne Hughes Coffee Room with your stack of reading material and a cup of java.

The **NE Broadway** neighborhood offers some tasty diversions. Have lunch or afternoon coffee at Ron Paul Charcuterie (1441 NE Broadway, Portland; (503)284-5347), stop into Great Wine Buys (1515 NE Broadway, Portland; (503)287-2897) for a glass of wine at the wine bar, or venture into Merchant of Venice (1432 NE Broadway, Portland; (503) 284-4558) for an evening meal of pasta with garlic bread and salad for $6.

To understand Portland's hamlet nature, travel through its urban villages. The most popular is **Nob Hill**, more commonly called "northwest" or "23rd" by locals, where throngs pack the sidewalks from Burnside to Pettygrove and the liveliness spills over to NW 21st Avenue. Get bagels to go at Kornblatt's Deli (628 NW 23rd Avenue, Portland; (503)242-0055) or some of the city's finest cookies at Coffee People (533 NW 23rd Avenue, Portland; (503)221-0235). The pumpkin muffins at Gabriel's Bakery (2272 NW Kearney Street, Portland; (503)227-4712) are heavenly.

Carnivores' needs are well attended to at the Foothill Broiler (31 NW 23rd Place, Portland; (503)223-0287), where the burgers come in assorted sizes. Or treat yourself to the chicken skewers at the dueling shish kabob stands at Phil's Uptown Meat Market (17 NW 23rd Place, Portland; (503)224-9541) and West Coast Bento (2340 NW Westover Street, Portland; (503)227-1779). And while you're there, cruise through Elephant's Deli (13 NW 23rd Place, Portland; (503)224-3955) and make a list of all the gourmet foods you're going to buy when you return to town as a millionaire. There's a provocative selection of magazines at Rich's (706 NW 23rd Avenue, Portland; (503)227-6907) and a thoughtful one at 23rd Avenue Books (1015 NW 23rd Avenue, Portland; (503)224-5097).

Across Burnside and up Vista (warning: it's steep) is **Washington Park** (4001 SW Canyon Road, Portland; (503)226-1561). Stroll through the International Rose Test Garden, where local novelist Katherine Dunn was inspired to write *Geek Love*; the Rhododendron Gardens; and the wondrous Japanese Gardens—recently proclaimed by the Japanese ambassador to be the world's loveliest this side of Japan (spendy at $6, but well worth it). After wandering through the **Hoyt Arboretum** (4000 SW Fairview Boulevard, Portland; (503)228-TREE), take a hike on the Wildwood Trail.

Those in need of a vigorous **bike ride** should pedal up the inclines of Portland's dormant volcano, Mount Tabor, or through Forest Park on the unpaved Leif Erickson Trail. If you're in the mood for a run or a leisurely stroll, go under the Thurman Bridge to lovely McCleay Park, which leads to the Audubon Society, Pittock Mansion, and ultimately Washington Park. And, across town, **ice-skate** at the Lloyd Center Ice Pavilion (953 Lloyd Center, Portland; (503)288-6073). The whole family skates for only $7.

CHEAP SLEEPS

Portland offers so many great opportunities for the bargain-conscious that we were surprised to find a dearth of cheap sleeps. Here are a few. Let us know if you come across others.

Carriage Inn
2025 NW Northrup Street, Portland, OR 97209 • (503)224-0543

With its wood paneling and many shades of beige, this place is the ultimate deal for two ($49). The elevator feels as if it won't ascend even 3 inches (although it does manage to climb the three floors), but the rooms are spacious (stove, oven, fridge, dishwasher, and private bath with tub and shower). It's seconds away from the stores of northwest Portland and restaurants of Nob Hill. Stop by Pastaworks (735 NW 21st Avenue, Portland; (503)221-3002), where they cut the pasta in front of you, and grab some of their puttanesca sauce to make your own meal. McCleay and Washington parks are a 20-minute stroll.

The Imperial Hotel
400 SW Broadway, Portland, OR 97205 • (503)228-7221
or (800)452-2323

Located in the heart of the urban bustle, the Imperial is comfortable in a tired sort of way. An ongoing renovation to this old hotel has edged it toward the category of "almost cheap." The least expensive room is $60; it's a single and, of course, is not renovated. What you get is a tiny room in Early Aunt Bertha decor, complete with her paintings. But you also get what the fancy hotel next door sells for three times the price—location. Valet parking is free (as are local calls), the staff is friendly (even to your dog), and the trendy Pazzo is out the door and to the left. Two blocks from Pioneer Courthouse Square (where you can pick up MAX) and one block from the Transit Mall, the Imperial affords easy access to all that lies in—or out—of downtown.

The Mallory Hotel
729 SW 15th Avenue, Portland, OR 97205 • (503)223-6311
or (800)228-8657

Owned by the same folks who run the Imperial, the Mallory is a bit more stately in quieter surroundings. Located between downtown and Nob Hill, the hotel offers easy access to both as well as a quiet neighborhood and free parking. The rooms are fine (a few might even steal a view) and the most inexpensive singles can be had for $55, while the cheapest doubles are only $5 more. Shade your eyes when you open the door; some of the carpet is as green as Astroturf. The lobby and dining room are charming; the dark, '50s-style Driftwood Room draws theater types and anyone else who considers the free goldfish crackers a full meal.

Mark Spencer Hotel
409 SW 11th Avenue, Portland, OR 97205 • (503)224-3293
or (800)548-3934

From the outside, this U-shaped, yellow-brick hotel looks pretty worn, but the remodeled interior is very clean and pleasant. Once considered a place strictly for longer stays, the Mark Spencer is now quite a find for the short-term guest, too. The bedroom studios have kitchenettes and cost $57 for two. If you plan to stay for a month, the standard room will cost you $28 a night.

Portland Guest House
1720 NE 15th Avenue, Portland, OR 97212 • (503)282-1402

The best deal in this charming bed and breakfast near the Broadway neighborhood is the back room on the second floor: it's small and cozy, a door leads out to a shared balcony, and the bathroom—also shared—is right next door. At $45 for a single ($55 for a double), it books quickly, so call well in advance to reserve. Owner Susan Gisvold encourages a come-and-go-as-you-please philosophy (when you check in, you'll be given keys for both the front door and your room). Each room has its own phone and is tastefully furnished with white carpet and antique linens and furniture. Gisvold doesn't live in the Guest House, but she drops in each morning to serve a fine breakfast of fresh fruit, scones, and perhaps a basil omelet. When the weather is warm, the brick courtyard out back is a pleasant place to while away the morning.

YWCA
1111 SW 10th Avenue, Portland, OR 97205 • (503)223-6281

The Y has gone to great lengths to improve its lodgings for budget-minded overnight guests. The floors have been buffed up and the rooms rearranged so that residents are on a separate floor. Currently only three guest rooms are available; a single with a private bath costs $28 (you pay even less if you opt for a room with a bathroom down the hall). If you stay in the hostel and bring your own bedding, the cost is $11; for another couple of bucks, you get linens too. There are plans to remodel the hostel in the future—verify the status when you call. A week's advance registration is recommended. Maximum six-night stay. Women only.

ACCESS

The Portland International Airport is 20 minutes from downtown on I-84. By cab, it can cost $20 or more, but a one-way ride is $7 on the Raz Downtowner, which picks up and drops off every half hour at major downtown hotels; (503)246-3301. Amtrak pulls into Old Town's Union Station with destinations north-, south-, and eastbound; (503)273-4865. Next door is Greyhound; (503)243-2316 or (800)231-2222. From there, you can walk a block to the Transit Mall and ride a bus into downtown at no charge; (503)238-7433.

Seventy-one bus lines and the light-rail system, MAX, make it exceptionally easy to get around the city without a car. Most buses run at 15- to 30-minute intervals throughout the week, with express service during rush hour on some routes. Many of the buses are wheelchair-accessible. Travelers in the downtown area ride free anywhere in the 300-block Fareless Square. The square extends from Interstate 405 on the south and west to Hoyt Street on the north and the Willamette River on the east. Otherwise, fares are $1.00 for travel in two zones and $1.30 for three. All-day tickets are $3.25. If you're going to be in town several days and plan to travel via Tri-Met a lot, buy a book of tickets; you'll save 10 cents a ride. You can purchase tickets at Tri-Met at Pioneer Courthouse Square or pay cash on board buses (exact change), but MAX tickets are available only from ticket machines at each stop along the line. For more information, visit the Portland Transit Mall (SW 5th and 6th avenues) along Pioneer Courthouse Square, the location of Tri-Met's Customer Assistance Office; (503)238-7433.

Willamette Valley

This is the real Oregon, the Oregon of small, sleepy towns and slow-talking farmers in battered pickups, the Oregon that's reserved and uncertain about strangers at first but that warms up once folks get to know you. This is the Willamette Valley, the first region settled by those who found their way west on the Oregon Trail.

Some rural towns here look much as they did 100 years ago, with covered bridges, tidy farms, and orchards that could have been transplanted from Vermont or southern England, and vineyards that evoke images of Alsace or Burgundy. Mountains frame the valley and give it a warmer, drier climate than the coast. Just about anything grows here: apples, peaches, plums, filberts, walnuts, grapes, hay, mint, corn, peas, potatoes, cherries, strawberries, blueberries, and raspberries. From June to October, you can always find some fresh U-pick vegetables or fruit if you pull off onto the side roads.

Wine is the main attraction of the region for today's visitors. In just a couple of decades, more than 50 wineries and many more vineyards have sprung up in the valley. Most are small, family-run businesses. Many sell their wines only locally. Some are making world-class wines. The area's best grapes are pinot *noir, the grape used for the fabulous (and unbelievably expensive) red Burgundies of France, and pinot gris, a grape almost unknown in California but one of the staple grapes of France's Alsace region, which produces a dry but full-bodied, fruity white wine. Sparkling wine may be the next hot item.*

It's easy enough to zip out of Portland and visit some of the larger wineries along the main roads; however, the real adventure lies in searching the country roads for out-of-the-way wineries, some with stunning natural settings, and talking with the vintners themselves. It's wine touring with a personal touch, the kind you could do in Napa and Sonoma 30 years ago. Given the rapid growth in the local wine industry, who knows how much longer it will last here—so go now.

ON THE ROAD

Most people whiz from Portland to Eugene on I-5, which heads straight down the middle of the Willamette Valley. A more interesting route is Highway 99W, which parallels I-5 a little to the west and imparts a much better flavor of rural, small-town western Oregon and the valley's **wineries**. Two excellent wineries are 20 minutes west of downtown Portland: Ponzi Vineyards (14665 SW Winery Lane, Beaverton; (503)628-1227) and Cooper Mountain (9480 SW Grabhorn Road, Beaverton; (503)649-0027). Ponzi is one of the oldest and best wineries in the state and turns out particularly fine, muscular pinot noir. Cooper Mountain is much smaller but has excellent pinot gris and good pinot noir.

Farther west, around **Forest Grove**, is another cluster of wineries. Tualatin (10850 NW Seavey Road, Forest Grove; (503)357-5005) makes some of the best chardonnays in the state. Elk Cove (27751 NW Olson Road, Gaston; (503)985-7760) has one of the most stunning sites in the valley, perched on a narrow ridge; pinot noir and late-harvest riesling are the top wines here.

The primary wine territory starts off down Highway 99W with **Newberg**, just 30 minutes from Portland. McMinnville is wine-touring headquarters, having proximity to both wineries and numerous eateries. Be sure to pick up the annual Oregon Winegrowers' Association brochure

---

🍷 *Prime Wine Time*

September and early October are ideal times for a visit to the wine country. The weather is still warm and dry, the grapes are ripening, and tourist spots are more relaxed. It's also crush time, one of the more interesting occasions in the winemaking year. Crush time, when the harvested grapes are pressed to extract their precious nectar, may take place anytime from the end of September to the beginning of November. It's a frantically busy period, so it's best to call ahead. Of course, you can always volunteer to help pick grapes—it's back-breaking labor, but it's certainly rewarding.

"Discover Oregon Wineries." This comprehensive touring guide is available at most wineries, or call (503)228-8403. In the Newberg area, right on the highway, you'll find Rex Hill Vineyards (30835 N Highway 99W, Newberg; (503)538-0666), which has not only a fancy Napa Valley-style tasting room, but also terrific pinot noirs from a variety of vineyards.

Down the road in **Dundee** are several places worth visiting. Argyle (691 Highway 99W, Dundee; (503)538-8520), on the main drag, specializes in top-notch sparkling wine. Knudsen Erath (Worden Hill Road, Dundee; (503)538-3318 or (800)KEW-WINE) and Sokol Blosser (5000 Sokol Blosser Lane, Dundee; (503)864-2282 or (800)582-6668), both just off the highway, are among the older wineries in the state and produce a wide range of wines, including fine pinot noir. **Little Crabtree Park**, near Knudsen Erath, makes a good picnic stop. Lange Winery (18380 NE Buena Vista, Dundee; (503)538-6476), in the hills above Dundee, is literally a basement operation; the pinot gris here is especially good. Stop for lunch in Dundee; the tiny Red Hills Cafe (976 Highway 99W, Dundee; (503)538-8224) serves excellent housemade soups, sandwiches (the meat loaf is delectable), and desserts.

South of McMinnville on 99W in **Amity**, Amity Vineyards (18150 Amity Vineyards SE, Amity; (503)835-2362) is another of the modern pioneers in Willamette winemaking. The pinot noir and gewürztraminer are excellent. Don't miss the gamay noir, from the true grape of Beaujolais. Bethel Heights (6060 Bethel Heights Road NW, Salem; (503)581-2262) offers good pinot noir and chenin blanc from its commanding position on a hilltop.

Around **Rickreall**, just west of Salem, are a few more wineries, including Eola Hills Wine Cellars (501 S Pacific Highway W, Rickreall; (503)623-2405), a young winery making promising cabernet sauvignon and chenin blanc. Once past Rickreall, you're out of the richest part of the wine country. Still, there are some good stops. Airlie (15305 Dunn Forest Road, Monmouth; (503)838-6013) and Serendipity Cellars (15275 Dunn Forest Road, Monmouth; (503)838-4284) are side by side, southwest of downtown **Monmouth**; there's good Müller Thurgau at Airlie and an unusual red, Marechal Foch, at Serendipity.

Seven miles south of downtown **Corvallis** is Tyee (26335 Greensberry Road, Corvallis; (503)753-8754), which produces some of the best gewürztraminer in the state. Broadley Vineyards (265 S 5th, Monroe; (503)847-5934), in Monroe, makes powerful pinot noir. To the west, Alpine Vineyards (25904 Green Peak Road, Monroe; (503)424-5851) makes a consistently good cabernet.

A couple of state parks provide pleasant respites from the road (as well as inexpensive places to camp, if you're so equipped). **Champoeg State Park** (pronounced "shampooey") is a small park on the banks of the Willamette, just off I-5 and a few miles from the heart of the wine country, with fishing, boating, nature trails, and a playground. It's also a great place for bikes. **Silver Falls State Park**, one of the crown jewels of the well-maintained state park system, is farther off the beaten path but worth the detour. Go east from Salem on Highway 22 to 214. This immense park, set in the forested foothills of the Cascades, has everything: sparkling waterfalls, miles of biking trails and horse trails, hiking trails, picnic and camping facilities, and even a gorgeous conference center. (Beware of summer holiday weekends; they can be a zoo.) Call the Campsite Information Center for campsite availability and reservations ($15–$17 a night); (800)452-5687).

Biking in the valley is excellent. Once outside the ring of hills that surrounds Portland, you can ride a straight, flat shot down the valley by following (roughly) the Willamette River along the web of small roads that spreads between I-5 and Highway 99W. At the southern end of the valley, Eugene is a motorist's nightmare of blocked-off streets, but it's heaven for cyclists.

CHEAP SLEEPS

Flying M Ranch
23029 NW Flying M Road, Yamhill, OR 97148 • (503)662-3222

The setting, at the end of the road in the Coast Range, is terrific. The motelish bunkhouse is no bargain, but if you're in a party of 4 to 10, the cabins make economic sense. They have their own kitchens but no phones or TVs. Prices drop every night after your first. For a really large group (up to 20), check out the remote lodge on Trask Mountain (the highest peak in the Coast Range), a somewhat-primitive shelter often used as an overnight spot for trail riders. For $10 a night, campers have access to all the recreational opportunities the ranch offers its guests: ponds for swimming and fishing, and miles of trails for hiking or horseback riding. The restaurant and Western bar keep 'em content.

Safari Motor Inn
345 N Highway 99W, McMinnville, OR 97128 • (503)472-5187

The Safari is right in the heart of the wine country. Accommodations here are far better than your basic bed-in-a-box: rooms are spacious and quiet, and the beds are comfortable. The former motel pool is now pushing up daisies, so if you want to cool off on a hot afternoon, head a quarter mile south on 99W to McMinnville's excellent Aquatic Center; (503)434-7309. Here you can frolic in a large pool for just a couple of bucks.

Thre'pence Bed and Breakfast
27175 SW Frys Lane, Sheridan, OR 97378 • (503)843-4984

Sheridan, less than a half hour from McMinnville, is halfway between Portland and the coast. Its cheap sleep is an 1885 Italianate farmhouse plunked down in the middle of fields that stretch to the horizon and offer views of both the Cascades and the Coast Range. Bill and Frieda Jarvis are California refugees who have remodeled their house extensively, adding a huge kitchen-dining area and a deck in back. There are only two guest rooms, both with bath.

Howell's Bed and Breakfast
212 N Knox Street, Monmouth, OR 97361 • (503)838-2085

Don't ask what's going on in Monmouth. Instead, enjoy its location, convenient for hitting Polk County and Salem area wineries or for launching a tour of the southern Willamette wine region. The Boylans and their four sons took a run-down 1891 rooming house and stripped off a century of changes (they even tore off the modern porch and replaced it with a Victorian one). The interior is full of richly detailed wallpapers and period antiques; there's an old coal stove, too. The immaculate high-ceilinged rooms may be small, but the breakfasts aren't.

B & G's Bed and Breakfast
711 W 11th Avenue, Eugene, OR 97402 • (503)343-5739

There's only one room for rent in the main house, but a sauna in the backyard has been turned into a tiny but bright and airy cottage for two, with a queen-size futon, bathroom, skylight, and French doors that open out onto a small private garden. Owner Barbara Koser takes advantage of Eugene's plethora of natural-food stores, using mostly organic ingredients in the full breakfast she prepares each morning.

McKenzie River Inn
49164 McKenzie River Highway, Vida, OR 97488 • (503)822-6260

In the heart of one of Oregon's most beautiful river valleys, this simple bed and breakfast, about 35 miles east of Eugene, should satisfy your longing for peace and quiet. A small orchard separates the riverfront house from the highway. Comfortable, dark furniture gives a '40s feel. Choose from one of the three bedrooms or the cottage next door, which has its own kitchen. The river runs swiftly past the doorstep; you can virtually fish from your window. For intrepid boaters, there's a public boat launch a few miles downstream.

Northern Oregon Coast

The northern Oregon Coast epitomizes the eternal struggle between water and land. From Astoria to Yachats—from the mouth of the Columbia River to Cape Perpetua—this rugged coastline is embossed with a series of headlands holding out against Neptune's fury, separated intermittently by expanses of sand. Numerous rivers sever the Coast Range and, finally, widen into estuaries just before emptying into the blue Pacific.

Showing considerable foresight, the state of Oregon has decreed public access to all beaches sacrosanct. Many stretches of coastline, still in pristine condition, are preserved as state parks. Between some of the parks, however, development persists. Astoria, the largest city on the north coast, has a relatively stable population of 10,000 inhabitants, but other areas, such as Seaside and the stretch between Lincoln City and Newport, are bulging with resort hotels and related tourist concessions. Fortunately, these towns are the exceptions. Most coastal towns are hamlets of just a few hundred people.

Fishing and logging dominate the coastal economy, although tourism is quickly encroaching. Realizing this, many of the residents—an eclectic mix of artists, retirees, upwardly mobile surfers, fishermen and loggers, and entrepreneurs trying to escape *city life—are seeking a consensus on the appropriate amount of development. There is little agreement, except on two counts: that the coast's population will continue to grow, and that it rains a lot—70 to 80 inches annually.*

ON THE ROAD

The Oregon beach begins at **Fort Stevens State Park**, 10 miles southwest of Astoria. But first, consider Astoria—the first permanent American settlement west of the Rockies, founded in 1811. Restored Victorian residences dot the steep hillside that extends up from the Columbia River. The Columbia River Maritime Museum is the finest such museum on the West Coast; admission includes a visit aboard the lightship *Columbia*. For a sweeping view of the city and the 4-mile-wide estuary of the Columbia, head up to the **Astoria Column** atop Coxcomb Hill. Hiking, running, and mountain-bike trails fan out in various directions from the parking lot.

Sea lions and seals are usually found down at the river park at the foot of 6th Street, particularly during the winter months. The viewing pier at the foot of 14th Street shares space with the Brix Maritime tugboat fleet. Here's a good place to watch the Columbia River bar and river pilots get on and off oceangoing vessels just a stone's throw away in the river channel.

The best chow in town is available at the Columbia Cafe (1114

Coastal Critters

Plan a trip to the Jewell Elk Refuge (26 miles southeast of Astoria on Highway 202; (503)755-2264), where some of the larger mammals in the Lower 48 cavort on thousands of grassy and forested acres. But drive slowly; sometimes the elk take over the roadway. Closer in, the Twilight Creek Eagle Sanctuary (8 miles east of Astoria, off Highway 30 on Burnside Road) is home base for approximately 50 bald eagles, plus numerous other winged species. You might spy one of these magnificent birds boldly swooping into the Columbia, ensnaring a fish in its talons, or—with the help of binoculars—watch while a mom feeds her young in a nest that can weigh as much as 2 tons.

Marine Drive, Astoria; (503)325-2233), a '60s throwback that purveys scrumptious vegetarian cuisine and seafood. The place is always crowded, though, and the service can be painstakingly slow. Lee's Kitchen (225 14th Street, Astoria; (503)325-9141) serves toned-down but hearty Korean fare. Astoria's intelligentsia frequent Ricciardi Gallery (108 10th Street, Astoria; (503)325-5450), which offers pleasing local and regional art, high-octane espresso, and *The New York Times*. Astoria Coffee Co. (1154 Commercial Street, Astoria; (503)325-7173) is the place for local chitchat and great joe. Parnassus Books (234 10th Street, Astoria; (503)325-1363) is a good browse.

Seaside has become Oregon's most crowded beach town, with all the expected tourist accoutrements. Surfers head for "The Point" at the south edge of town to catch the finest left-handed waves north of Santa Barbara. Cleanline Surf Company (719 1st Avenue, Seaside; (503)738-7888) is a good source for ocean playthings. Miguel's (412 Broadway, Seaside; (503)738-0171) serves decent Tex-Mex chow, while the Little New Yorker on Broadway (604 Broadway, Seaside; (503)738-5992) doles out hearty meatball sandwiches.

South of Seaside, a 7-mile trail winds over Tillamook Head, high above the water—part of **Ecola State Park** (primitive camping facilities only)—and ends at Indian Beach and (farther still) Ecola Point. Beware of incoming tides and plan your water-level hikes accordingly. Sunset Empire Park and Recreation District, headquartered at Sunset Pool (1140 E Broadway, Seaside; (503)738-3311) offers $2.25 lap swims.

Whale Watch Week

Each year, gray whales log 12,000 miles on their round-trip voyage (which occurs between late October and early April) from the nutrient-rich feeding grounds in the Bering Sea to the subtropical breeding lagoons in Baja. For one week in March, Oregon State University stations about a hundred volunteers at 19 different sites along the coast; (503)867-0100. Their mission? To count whales, observe their behavior, and educate visitors on the leviathans' life and migration. Don rain gear, sweaters, boots, and binoculars and hike to the farthest tip of a headland or promontory (be aware of slippery surfaces and loose rocks). The lucky and the patient may witness a breach, three spy hops, or a courtship. Some of the best vantage points for land-based whale watching are from lighthouses, which are sometimes outfitted with viewing platforms or trails leading out to the best perch.

Tip for a Tailwind

Every year almost 10,000 bicyclists pedal the Oregon Coast. If it's your turn to bike Highway 101, choose September for your trip. You'll enjoy the coast's sunniest weather, warmest days, and least amount of traffic. You'll also have a tailwind (northwest winds are prevalent from mid-June through the end of September). Bikes & Beyond (1089 Marine Drive, Astoria, OR 97103; (503)325-2961) is an excellent source for on- and off-road bicycle routes, great places to carbo-load along the way (ask the owners), and free Oregon Coast bike maps. Call or write the Bicycle/Pedestrian Program Manager (Oregon Department of Transportation, Room 210, Transportation Building, Salem, OR 97310; (503)378-3432) for additional info.

Cannon Beach has become the Carmel of the Northwest. The main attraction is still the wide-open, white-sand beach with its silhouette of Haystack Rock, a massive monolith that presents an excellent opportunity for low-tide exploration. Less crowded stretches of sand are located at Chapman Point, at the north end of town (although parking is limited), and at Tolovana Park Wayside, at the south end. At low tide, you can walk all the way to Arch Cape, 5 miles south. Always carry a local tide table (available at many stores in town), and be aware of tides on the return trip. The Cannon Beach Energy-Conservation Project operates a free, natural gas-powered shuttle in the Cannon Beach–Tolovana Park area year-round.

The Lazy Susan Cafe (126 N Hemlock Street, Cannon Beach; (503)436-2816) serves reasonably priced breakfasts (try the waffles topped with fresh fruit and yogurt) and lunches. Always hopping, the kitschy, dineresque Midtown Cafe (1235 S Hemlock Street, Cannon Beach; (503)436-1016) offers an eclectic and unbelievably delicious mix of breakfast and lunch choices.

Cassandra's (60 Laneda Avenue, Manzanita; (503)368-5593), purveyor of the coast's tastiest pizza and a haven for boardheads, bicyclists, and tourists, is newly located right near the beach. There's beachcombing galore on either the ocean or the Nehalem Bay side of the Manzanita Peninsula. Summer winds from the northwest afford excellent windsurfing conditions. Learn more at Manzanita Surf & Sail (150 Laneda Avenue, Manzanita; (503)368-7873). Manzanita News and Espresso (500 Laneda Avenue, Manzanita; (503)368-7450) is a good bet for a coffee jolt and take-out snacks.

Four miles south, Nina's (Highway 101, Wheeler; (503)368-6592) serves up hearty marinara-based lunches and dinners. Bay City's Downie's Cafe (9320 5th Street, Bay City; (503)377-2220) offers ample burgers, deep-fried fresh halibut or cod, and old-fashioned milkshakes. Just down the block, Artspace (9120 5th Street, Bay City; (503)377-2782) exhibits unusual paintings and sculpture, and serves great grilled oysters. Ask here for advice about where to buy the freshest 'sters. Bear Creek Artichokes (11½ miles south of Tillamook, Hemlock; (503)398-5411) features a first-class selection of fruits, veggies, and herbs.

Tillamook Bay and the surrounding countryside provide outstanding fishing opportunities. Anglers routinely haul 30-plus-pound Chinook from the Ghost's Hole section of the bay. The Kilchis, Wilson, Tillamook, and Trask rivers are superb salmon and steelhead streams, although more fish are taken from the Nestucca River than from any comparably sized stream in the state. The Nestucca is accessible from Highway 101 between Beaver and Pacific City. Fishing licenses are required and can be purchased at many sporting goods stores. Be aware that ever-more-restrictive regulations may prevent you from wetting your hook at certain times of the year.

The 22-mile **Three Capes Scenic Drive**, which begins west of Tillamook, affords spectacular vistas from atop Capes Meares, Lookout, and Kiwanda. It's also an excellent but hilly bicycle route, although

Off on Your Own

Wander off the beaten path of Highway 101 and you'll discover unlimited—and uncrowded—opportunities for two-footed and two-wheeled adventure. The coastal mountains are laced with logging roads that make excellent passageways into primitive terrain featuring dense second-growth forests, sparkling-clean creeks, and raging waterfalls (great places to take a quick—'cause it's always cold—dip). Some logging roads have been gated and are off-limits, but many more are open to folks on foot or on all-terrain bikes. Unless a road is signed "No Trespassing," it's probably okay to enter. When in doubt, use common sense, and don't enter areas that are being actively logged. All of the headlands and capes (Tillamook Head, Falcon, Lookout, Foulweather, Yaquina, and Perpetua) offer hiking, running, and off-road biking. (For north coast information, contact the Oregon Forestry Department, Route 1, Box 950, Astoria, OR 97103; (503)325-5451.)

shoulder space is minimal. All three headlands have hiking trails. South of Cape Meares, in the picturesque village of Oceanside, you can imbibe Northwest microbrews and enjoy high-calorie desserts (spoon up the Toll House pie and Tillamook ice cream) at Roseanna's (1490 Pacific Avenue NW, Oceanside; (503)842-7351). Pacific City's Grateful Bread Bakery (34805 Brooten Road, Pacific City; (503)965-7337) offers tempting breads and muffins and scrumptious sweet treats, as well as hearty breakfast and lunch fare.

Another majestic sea-and-weather-sculpted promontory is **Cascade Head**, just south of Neskowin. Two obscure trails take off from the highway on the north and south sides of the headland, traversing rain forests, meadows, and rocky cliffs. In the summer, the Sitka Center for Art and Ecology presents diverse workshops, concerts, and exhibits; (503)994-5485. A few miles east at the Otis Cafe (Highway 18 at Otis Junction, Otis; (503)994-2813), you can chow down on beefy burgers, sumptuous soups, and legendary plates of hash browns, onions, peppers, and melted cheese.

Once termed the "20 miracle miles," the distance from **Lincoln City to Newport** is hardly a wonder; however, there are a few finds along this strip of almost-continuous development. On the north end of Lincoln City, Road's End Dory Cove (5819 Logan Road, Lincoln City; (503)994-5180) serves a monster half-pound burger, clam chowder, and housemade pies. Lincoln City has more tourist accommodations than any other Oregon Coast city. In the winter, when the place isn't as crowded, you can usually find a discounted motel room. Come summer, prices jump into the stratosphere. About halfway through town, Café Roma (1437 NW Highway 101, Lincoln City; (503)994-6616) provides a worthwhile respite and light grub.

Farther south, in **Newport**, the Whale's Tale (452 SW Bay Boulevard, Newport; (503)265-8660) is a good escape on the touristy bay front. Try the poppyseed pancakes or the fisherman's stew. Rogue Ale, the local microbrew, is available down the block at the Bayfront Brewery (746 SW Bay Boulevard, Newport; (503)265-3188). On the ocean side of town, in hip **Nye Beach**, check out the Cosmos Cafe & Gallery (740 W Olive Street, Newport; (503)265-7511) for espresso, desserts, and art. Or chow down on pizza and seafood lasagne at Don Petrie's Italian Food Co. (613 NW 3rd Street, Newport; (503)265-3663).

The **Hatfield Marine Science Center** (2030 S Marine Science Drive, Newport; (503)867-0100) offers free marine-life displays, films, and field trips, especially in the summer. Nearby, the **Oregon Coast Aquarium** (2820 SE Ferry Slip Road, Newport; (503)867-3474) exhibits a splendid collection of finny, furry, and feathery creatures.

Beyond Newport, the coast opens up again. **Waldport** is a town in coastal limbo, overshadowed by its larger, better-known neighbors—Newport to the north and Yachats to the south. Not to worry, as Waldport has much to recommend, including the lovely Alsea River estuary, untrampled beaches at either end of town, and a city center unspoiled by tourism. Bumps and Grinds Coffeehouse (225 SW Maple Street, Waldport; (503)563-5769) is a good stop. Pick up a free copy of *Inkfish Magazine* (it's published in town and is available at coffee shops and markets) for more info about local goings-on.

The beach in **Yachats** is rocky and rife with tide pools and whooshing geysers. Yachats itself is another Cannon Beach-type hip arts community with an interesting mix of aging counterculturalists, yups, and tourists. It's also a prime area for harvesting sea-run smelt (savory sardine-like fish) when they congregate near the shore during mating season (April through October). The New Morning Coffeehouse (373 Highway 101 N, Yachats; (503)547-3848) offers excellent baked goodies, a laid-back ambience, a wood stove in the winter, and, of course, a solid selection of coffee. Catch some grilled fish or chowder at the Yachats Crab & Chowder House (131 Highway 101, Yachats; (503)547-4132). Orca Wholefoods (84 Beach Avenue, Yachats; (503)547-4065) sells tempting salads and fresh-squeezed juices.

CHEAP SLEEPS

Clementine's Bed and Breakfast
847 Exchange Street, Astoria, OR 97103 • (503)325-2005

A reasonably priced addition to Astoria's burgeoning bed and breakfast scene, Clementine's is an 1888 Italianate Victorian located on the edge of downtown, partway up hyper-steep Eighth Street. Your hosts, Judith and Cliff Taylor (she's a master gardener and a cooking instructor; he's into boats) are enthusiastic and very knowledgeable about north coast happenings. Five nicely decorated rooms reflect the Taylors' attention to detail; breakfast reflects their ability to satisfy. All the rooms have private baths and are appointed with fresh flowers from the garden. A "vacation rental" sleeps six and fetches $85 (breakfast not included).

Rosebriar Hotel
636 14th Street, Astoria, OR 97103 • (503)325-7427 or (800)487-0224

At the turn of the century the Rosebriar was a private residence. It next became a convent and then a halfway house for the mentally ill. Now, in its finest reincarnation, the place is a rambling 11-room inn. All guest rooms are small but beautifully furnished and meticulously clean, and include private baths. Rates begin at $49 (including a full breakfast). The common rooms are spacious and homey, and the grounds offer a garden-like setting with a view of the Columbia River.

Riverside Inn Bed and Breakfast

*430 S Holladay Drive, Seaside, OR 97138 • (503)738-8254
or (800)862-6151*

The Riverside continues to be Seaside's best bargain for traditional-style lodging. It's comfortable, spacious, and clean, with adjacent cottages. While the front faces bustling Holladay Drive, the rear recedes gracefully to the Necanicum River. A large riverfront deck provides opportunities for fishing, semisecluded sunbathing, or relaxing. The beach is just 3½ blocks away.

Seaside Inn and International Hostel

930 N Holladay Drive, Seaside, OR 97138 • (503)738-7911

It was only a matter of time before resort-minded Seaside welcomed a European-style hostel. This reconverted motel, which opened in summer 1994, features traditional dormitory-style sleeping quarters (45 beds), shared bathroom facilities, and a large, well-equipped communal kitchen. There's an in-house espresso bar and outside decks, and the Necanicum River flows past the backyard. In the summer, you can expect to meet travelers here from all over the world, and intermingling is encouraged. Unlike traditional hostels, you don't have to leave during the day (the place remains open) and no curfew is imposed. Dorm rates are $12 (for AYH members); private rooms with their own baths, kitchenettes, and TVs run $45–$55.

Cannon Beach Hotel

*1116 S Hemlock Street (PO Box 943), Cannon Beach, OR 97110
(503)436-1392*

Most lodgings in Cannon Beach are priced somewhere west of Pluto, but the nine-unit Cannon Beach Hotel (originally a boardinghouse) is a pleasantly sized, quiet, reasonably priced respite from the sprawling, costly "luxury" motels located nearby. Clean, comfortable rooms are available for $49 (though you pay more if you choose a spa-and-fireplace room). A complimentary light breakfast is served. The cozy lobby is a nice place to get involved with a good book, and the adjacent J.P.'s restaurant is a worthwhile dining option.

Some of the finest scenery on the Oregon Coast can be seen from the state parks. As long as the weather's good, consider camping. Rates are generally the same throughout the park system, beginning at $16 for an improved campsite with a parking space. The best deals (and sometimes the prettiest locations) are the rugged sites reserved for hikers and bicyclists; $4.50 buys a space as well as a hot shower (not available in all state parks). State parks can fill up during the summer season, particularly on weekends, but hiker-biker sites are usually available. Three parks you shouldn't miss:

• **Fort Stevens** (10 miles southwest of Astoria; (503)861-1671) is the largest in the state park system, with 605 campsites, a military museum and historical area, miles of paved bike paths and off-road single-track, and hiking and running trails. The South Jetty lookout tower is a prime whale- and storm-watching spot. Surf fishing can be productive off the jetty (no license required unless you're salmon fishing), and razor clamming is good on the vast expanse of the mostly empty beach (check with park officials concerning clamming regulations). Nearby Trestle Bay offers choice windsurfing conditions when the wind is blowing (which is most of the time).

• **Oswald West** (11 miles south of Cannon Beach; (503)238-7488) offers scenic beauty unsurpassed in the Northwest. The Oregon Coast Trail winds its way through the park. You can pick it up about a half mile south of the Arch Cape Tunnel on the west side of Highway 101. Hike the 5 miles over Cape Falcon to Short Sands Beach, a picture-perfect cove with a creek emptying into the ocean, a waterfall, and steep, forested hillsides extending down to water level. Another option is Neahkahnie Mountain Trail, which leads to the 1,600-foot summit, offering the north coast's finest view. Oswald West's camping area (no reservations accepted) is situated a half mile down a paved trail from a parking area adjacent to Highway 101, where wheelbarrows are available for your gear.

• **Cape Lookout** (8 miles west of Tillamook on Three Capes Scenic Drive; (503)842-3182) lays claim to some of the largest old-growth cedar and hemlock in the world. A steep trail leads up from water level to the top of the cape and then hugs the headland to its tip, high above the crashing Pacific. During whale migration season, you might observe gray whales scraping off troublesome barnacles against offshore rocks. On either side of Cape Lookout, the uncrowded beach extends for miles.

Anchorage Motel
6585 Pacific Avenue (PO Box 626), Pacific City, OR 97135
(503)965-6773

Blue-shingled with white trim, and a little off the beaten path, the Anchorage is a blue-collar kind of place. There's no luxury here, just quiet, clean accommodations. You're three blocks from the Nestucca River estuary and four blocks from the ocean, but you can see neither from your $35 room.

Camp Westwind
c/o YWCA, 1111 SW 10th Street, Portland, OR 97205 • (503)223-6281
(ask for camp programs)

During June, July, and August, Camp Westwind, just south of Cascade Head and 5 miles north of Lincoln City, operates as a YWCA camp. The rest of the year, the 500-acre grounds are available for small or large groups. "Small" means no more than 5; "large" means more than 40. Anything in between doesn't work. Small groups get the Wy'East cabin, warmed by a stone fireplace and overlooking the mile or so of private beach. Large groups stay in the main lodge, where a wood stove and a couple of fireplaces keep the cold at bay. You must bring your own bedding, towels, and food. Don't plan on eating out, because you need to cross the Salmon River via barge just to reach the camp. No cars.

Brown Squirrel Hostel
44 SW Brook Street, Newport, OR 97365 • (503)265-3729

It's a given that hostels don't offer all the comforts of home, but the Brown Squirrel is a (dare we say?) quaint stopover in tourist-mad Newport. The place can accommodate 22 visitors in five dorm rooms. The proprietor isn't exactly the outgoing type, but hey, you're here for a cheap bunk (bring your own sleeping bag) and the chance to meet like-minded travelers. Rates are $10 a night, whether or not you're an AYH member. Private rooms for couples or families fetch $25 and are available only in the off season (September through June).

Sylvia Beach Hotel
267 NW Cliff, Newport, OR 97365 • (503)265-5428

Goody Cable and Sally Ford's well-known rambling ocean-front hotel, dedicated to literary types, is not on most lists of cheap sleeps. Indeed, the acclaimed Agatha Christie and Mark Twain rooms are not bargains; however, the third-floor dormitory ($21 per bunk) is the ideal beach-bunk find. Besides, most of your time will be spent on the beach (right outside the hotel) or in the fireplace-warmed library on the top floor. None of the rooms have TVs, radios, or phones (so you're not deprived of anything except privacy—and literary whimsy—in the dorm room). Interaction with other guests is de rigeur, particularly in the well-stocked library, where hot mulled wine is served at 10pm. There's an ample breakfast every morning.

The Vikings

729 NW Coast Street, Newport, OR 97365 • (503)265-2477 or (800)480-2477

This place offers some of the sweetest deals on the coast. Thirteen rustic cottages sit on an ocean-front bluff, while a steep but sturdy staircase leads to an untrampled beach below. All cottages have color TVs; some have fireplaces and kitchens. Off-season, the primo bargain (at $60) is room 10, the romantic, wood-paneled "crow's nest"; it's a second-story studio with double bed, kitchen, private bath with shower and an unbeatable Pacific panorama.

Edgewater Cottages

3978 SW Pacific Coast Highway, Waldport, OR 97394 • (503)563-2240

The Edgewater, located 2½ miles south of town, sits on an ocean-front bluff with easy beach access. All nine cottages feature attractive wood interiors, ocean-facing sun decks, fireplaces, TVs, and kitchens ($45 and up). Larger families should rent the unit known as the Rustic. Alas, there are some strings attached (a four-night minimum stay in the summer; no one-night reservations any time of the year), but the hassles are worth wading through. Make certain you call in advance, and leave your credit card at home.

Wayside Lodge

5773 N Highway 101, Yachats, OR 97498 • (503)547-3450

Located a couple of miles north of town, the Wayside is a low-lying, ocean-blue structure nestled in a thicket of shore pines, nicely sheltered from Highway 101. There's a grassy area out back just above the beach, and even though houses are situated on either side, a feeling of privacy prevails. The best deal here is the beach-accessible studio ($45 at peak season). All rentals have kitchens and an ocean view.

Southern Oregon Coast

Along large sections of the southern Oregon Coast, life goes on the way it always has—slowly. Here, miles of untouched coastline outnumber fast-paced commercial strips. From Yachats south to the California border, only a few towns of any size break up the 160-mile stretch of mostly wild seashore. A long succession of state parks and 50 miles of the Oregon Dunes National Recreation Area ensure that this paradise will not be subjected to the over-development that has ravaged sections of the northern coast.

Small tribes of Native American hunter-gatherers first settled along this coast more than 5,000 years ago. European contact began in the late 16th century, when, most historians believe, English mariner Sir Francis Drake sailed as far north as the Oregon Dunes area and became the first non-native to lay eyes on the northwest coast of North America. In his wake came other European and American seafarers led, initially, by the Spanish. Capes Ferrelo, Sebastian, and Blanco, as well as Heceta Head, are geographical reminders of these explorers' maritime forays to this area.

The Columbia River, and the Strait of Juan de Fuca farther north, became the focal points for further exploration and subsequent settlement, while the south coast remained relatively *undeveloped. Perhaps because of this isolation, the folks who live here now are fiercely independent. With the exception of the stretch between Yachats and Coos Bay (a one-day, round-trip drive from Eugene), the south coast is a long way from any urban center; it remains a wild place with singular sense of openness.*

ON THE ROAD

Driving through the **Cape Perpetua Scenic Area**, a 2,700-acre slice of the Siuslaw National Forest, is an exhilarating roadside journey, jam-packed with spectacular panoramas carved out of the rocky cliffs that abut the ever-charging Pacific. Three miles south of Yachats is the Cape Perpetua Visitor Center (PO Box 274, Yachats, OR 97498; (503)547-3289), a good place to gather information and soak up the scenery. Trails with stunning views take off from here. Some lead down to the rocky shoreline, while others, such as the Cummins Creek Loop, head up into the hills, traversing old-growth forests along the way.

The next headland to the south is Heceta (say e-THEY-ta), named after an 18th-century Spanish explorer who sailed up the Northwest coast from Mexico. **Heceta Head Lighthouse** is the Oregon Coast's most powerful beacon and perhaps the most photographed lighthouse on the West Coast (*the* photo op is located about 1 mile south; look for the parking pullouts alongside Highway 101). Situated just off Highway 101, the lighthouse itself isn't open to the public, although the former light-keeper's quarters are.

Florence has transformed itself during the last 20 years from a sleepy fishing village to a tourist mecca. The revitalized **Old Town** has become visitor-oriented without selling out to schlock. At the Old Town Coffee Company (1269 Bay Street, Florence; (503)997-7300), you can scope out the Old Town scene and pick up local gossip. Try the inexpensive fish—from shrimp and crab cocktails, to chowder, to full-course meals— at the International C-Food Market (1498 Bay Street, Florence; (503)997-9646). It's located right on the Siuslaw River, so you can watch the fleet unload before you eat. Or take your treats to the **public fishing dock**; you can park a few blocks west on Bay Street. South of the Siuslaw River Bridge on Highway 101, Morgan's Country Kitchen (85020 Highway 101 S, Florence; (503)997-6991) serves hearty breakfasts and specials such as chicken-fried steak and biscuits 'n' gravy. Florence's sea lion caves (91560 Highway 101, Florence; (503)547-3111)

🚲 Oregon Coast Trail

Challenging mountain biking abounds along sections of the Oregon Coast Trail, especially at Humbug Mountain State Park and along the vertical slopes of Cape Sebastian. Steep up-and-down single-track traverses rocky cliffs and mountain meadows before diving down through lush lowlands; logging roads head off into the rugged hills along the east side of Highway 101. When you ride, always respect the rights of private-property owners, and be aware that some trails within Oregon's state parks are off-limits to mountain biking. Ask for info at Moe's Bike Shop (1397 Sherman Avenue, North Bend; (503)756-7536), or stop at the Chetco Ranger District (555 5th Street, Brookings; (503)469-2196).

are a fun stop. For $5.50, you can descend 21 stories to a peephole into a natural cave swarming with hundreds of sea lions.

The caves are just a peekaboo stop, though; the real draw along this section of the coast is the 53-mile-long **Oregon Dunes National Recreation Area** (855 Highway Avenue, Reedsport, OR 97467; (503)271-3611). Because you can catch only glimpses of this sandy wilderness from the highway, plan to stop and explore the dunes. Good departure points include the Clearwox Lake area of Honeyman State Park; the Westlake area; Threemile Road, just north of Gardiner, which leads to the north spit of the Umpqua River; North Eel campground, which has a trailhead leading to the Umpqua Scenic Dunes area; and the Horsfall Dunes area, just north of North Bend.

The **numerous lakes** in the Oregon Dunes make refreshing warm-water (in season) swimming holes, and the larger lakes, such as Siltcoos, Tahkenitch, and Tenmile, are great for freshwater angling and boating. Be advised that large portions of the dunes are open to off-road recreational vehicles. Check a map to find out who's allowed where.

South of the dunes, **North Bend and Coos Bay** combine to form the largest urban area on the Oregon Coast. You can view the revitalized Coos Bay waterfront from the public pier and boardwalk adjacent to Highway 101. Nearby, the Blue Heron Bistro (100 Commercial, Coos Bay; (503)267-3933) purveys an inexpensive, eclectic selection of the south coast's finest chow. Don't miss the fish specials and the apple pie. On the south edge of town, right on the main drag, Kum-Yon's (835 S Broadway, Coos Bay; (503)269-2662) is a worthwhile Chinese-Japanese food stop. **33**

Wilderness with an Ocean View

Three designated wilderness areas lie on the southern Oregon Coast between Yachats and the California border. The 9,173-acre **Cummins Creek Wilderness** is easily accessible from Highway 101 and the Cape Perpetua Scenic Area, south of Yachats. It includes the 6.2-mile Cummins Ridge Trail, which winds through the last remaining virgin stands of Sitka spruce, western hemlock, and Douglas fir along the Oregon Coast. Elevations range from 100 feet to 2,400 feet. For information, contact Waldport Ranger District, 1049 SW Pacific Coast Highway, Waldport, OR 97394; (503)563-3211; or Cape Perpetua Visitor Center, 2400 Highway 101 S, Yachats, OR 97498; (503)547-3289.

The **Grassy Knob Wilderness** is a patch of extremely rugged, wild land just behind Port Orford. It's approachable via Elk River Road (Highway 208) or Grassy Knob Road (which intersects Highway 101 1 mile south of the Sixes River), where the lone trail begins. You may encounter deer, elk, eagles, black bear, and cougars in this remote section of coastal wilderness, but you'll probably be one of the only humans around.

Farther south, the equally remote **Kalmiopsis Wilderness** lies deeply entrenched in the Siskiyou Mountains, between Gold Beach and Brookings. You can gain access by a number of unimproved roads, and the wilderness is crisscrossed with numerous trails.

For information concerning Grassy Knob or Kalmiopsis Wilderness, contact Gold Beach Ranger District, 1225 S Ellensburg Avenue, Box 7, Gold Beach, OR 97444; (503)247-6651; or Chetco Ranger District, 555 5th Street, Brookings, OR 97415; (503)469-2196.

For an exhilarating side trip and a gorgeous sunset, drive west about 10 miles to Charleston and the beach. **Sunset Bay State Park**, with year-round camping, has a bowl-shaped cove with 50-foot-high cliffs on either side—a good spot to dip your feet or even take a swim; (503)888-4902. The water in the protected cove is perpetually calm, even during midwinter sou'westers, when a colossal surf rages a few hundred yards offshore.

Just down the road at **Shore Acres State Park**, the colorful botanical gardens complex, containing a restored caretaker's house and an impeccably maintained display of native and exotic plants and flowers, is worth visiting; (503)888-3732. At the park, there's also an enclosed shelter where you can view winter storms and watch for whales. Bring your binoculars to windy Cape Arago, which overlooks the Oregon Islands National Wildlife Refuge. The **Oregon Coast Trail** winds through all three parks. The road ends here, so double back and take Seven Devils Road south to Highway 101 more than halfway to Bandon (a good bicycling route).

The **South Slough National Estuarine Research Center Reserve** (4 miles south of Charleston; (503)888-5558) is headquartered at an interpretive center, a good source for information and free maps. Get a glimpse of the wetlands exhibits, too. Hikers, canoeists, and kayakers (no motor boaters) can experience an environment that is still untouched by civilization.

Three miles north of Bandon, **Bullards Beach State Park** occupies an expansive area crosscut with hiking and biking trails leading to uncrowded, driftwood-and-kelp-cluttered beaches. The 1896 Coquille River Lighthouse (open to the public) is located at the end of the park's main road. Good windsurfing beaches abound on the river and ocean side of the park; (503)347-2209.

The town of **Bandon**, a self-proclaimed storm-watching hot spot and cranberry capital, looks—and feels—newly painted, freshly scrubbed, and friendly. Head for Old Town, where you can take a coffee or meal break at Andrea's Old Town Cafe (160 Baltimore, Bandon, (503)347-3022), or buy fish 'n' chips at Bandon Fisheries (250 SW 1st Street, Bandon; (503)347-4454) and take it down to the public pier, adjacent to the harbor. Sugar freaks can score at Cranberry Sweets (501 1st Street, Bandon; (503)347-9475), where the staff is generous with free samples. When leaving town, take Beach Loop Road (good for biking); it parallels the ocean in view of weather-sculpted offshore rock formations with names such as Devil's Kitchen and Face Rock, and it's a good alternative to Highway 101.

South of Bandon, myrtlewood factories and their adjacent retail shops flourish. The landscape then opens to reveal sparsely forested yellow and brown hills dotted with thousands of grazing sheep. **Boyce-Cope Country Park** is the site of the large, freshwater Floras Lake, popular with boaters, anglers, and board sailors. The park also features an extensive trail system suitable for hiking and mountain biking (take the hike to isolated Blacklock Point).

Cape Blanco Lighthouse, situated in Cape Blanco State Park (6 miles west of Highway 101; (503)332-6774), is the most westerly lighthouse—on the westernmost piece of coastline—in the Lower 48. The lighthouse, closed to the public, is approached via a windy, narrow, and potholed road (definitely not for motor homes). On the west side of the light station, a path through the grass leads to the end of the cape—the edge of the continent. The vista here is surely one of the world's more breathtaking seascapes, with its Canada-to-Mexico panorama. Blanco is the windiest station on the coast, so if the view doesn't claim your breath, the wind will.

Port Orford, Oregon's oldest coastal town, is a premier whale-watching location (occasionally, single whales or small groups spend all year in the quiet, kelp-protected coves found here). It's a town far removed from big-city nuances yet hip in its own way, especially considering the seasonal proliferation of board sailors and surfers, who head for Battle Rock and Hubbard's Creek beaches. Fishing fanatics should visit the Elk and Sixes rivers for the salmon and steelhead runs. For the best eats in town, stop by the Truculent Oyster (236 6th Street, Port Orford; (503)332-9461), which features fresh oyster shooters and savory soups. And—bonus of bonuses!—Port Orford marks the beginning of Oregon's coastal "banana belt," which reaches to the California border. This stretch enjoys the Northwest's warmest winter temperatures, along with a considerably earlier spring and more sunshine than other coastal areas.

The final 60 or so miles of Oregon's shore is a can't-miss section of coastline loaded with desolate black-sand beaches, uncrowded cape-hugging trails, and kelp-strewn waters brimming with marine life. In addition to the usual harbor seals and Steller's sea lions, tufted puffins and porpoises are sometimes visible. Stop at one of the many state parks along this stretch (possibilities include the trail up Humbug Mountain, in the state park of the same name, and the rocky vistas and isolated beaches within Cape Sebastian State Park). The photo ops are endless, and the beachcombing is superb.

The towns, however, are few and far between. In **Gold Beach**, which sits at the mouth of the Rogue River, you can glean local knowledge, or rent fishing gear or clam shovels, at Rogue Outdoor Store (560 N Ellensburg Avenue, Gold Beach; (503)247-7142). Farther south in Brookings, Pelican Bay Seafoods (16403 Lower Harbor Road, Brookings; (503)469-7971) is the place to soak up the Chetco Harbor ambience, rub shoulders with local fisherfolk, and scarf an order of halibut 'n' chips. The Plum Pudding (519 Chetco Avenue, Brookings; (503)469-6961) purveys ambitious breakfasts and lunches—try the Tex-Mex chicken "enchirito." Choice pizza is handcrafted at Mama's Authentic Italian Restaurant (703 Chetco Avenue, Brookings; (503)469-7611).

CHEAP SLEEPS

The See Vue
95590 Highway 101, Yachats, OR 97498 • (503)547-3227

Perched cliffside between Cape Perpetua and Heceta Head, the See Vue lives up to its name. Each of the 11 units in the cedar-shaked lodging is different. The Salish, with its Northwest Indian motif, is an excellent deal, and most rooms are less than $45. Your hosts can fill you in on Yachats or Florence happenings, or you may prefer to meander down to the uncrowded beach a few hundred yards away. Pets are welcome for a small additional charge.

Gull Haven Lodge
94770 Highway 101, Florence, OR 97439 • (503)547-3583

Gull Haven is actually closer to Yachats than Florence, and the setting is perhaps as close to perfect as any lodging on the Oregon Coast. A 360-degree panorama is available from the Shag's Nest, an isolated one-room cabin equipped with a fireplace, kitchenette, and private deck (you'll need to book it well in advance). For the bath, you must scamper across to the lodge 30 yards away. The lodge units aren't as good a deal, except for two cedar-lined sleeping rooms (less than $40), which share a bath and a kitchen. Be sure to ask about minimum-stay requirements, which apply here year-round.

Blackberry Inn
843 Central Avenue, Coos Bay, OR 97420 • (503)267-6951

The Blackberry Inn offers a different twist on the usual B&B arrangement. Guests here have the renovated 1903 Victorian home to themselves; the owners live elsewhere. Breakfast is a continental affair, but a kitchen is available, and eggs and bread are supplied. A night in the small but adequate Rose Room is a genuine bargain ($50 summers; $35 off season), especially in urbanized Coos Bay. Unfortunately, the inn is located on a busy thoroughfare.

Bandon Wayside Motel
1175 SE 2nd Street (on Highway 42 S), Bandon, OR 97411
(503)347-3421

This 10-unit, out-of-the-way motel occupies a parklike setting on the road to Coquille. Rooms (less than $35) are simple and clean, with an outdoor barbecue in the large backyard. The motel's quiet isolation, 2 miles from the beach, occasionally spares the visitor from the summer coastal fog. Housebroken pets are allowed at no extra charge in some units.

Sea Star Guest House and Hostel
370 1st Street, Bandon, OR 97411 • (503)347-9632

If Bandon encapsulates the coast—dramatic seascapes, quaint atmosphere, unspoiled beaches, good eats and sleeps, even a lighthouse and a free daily morning-news sheet—the Sea Star encapsulates Bandon. A four-unit guest house is connected to a hostel by a diminutive courtyard. The guest house is considerably more lavish, so cheapsters should check into the men's and women's dorms. Here guests share bath, kitchen, dining room, laundry facilities, and a laid-back lounge (and help with the chores). Bunks are $15 a night (less for AYH members and young kids); private rooms with shared baths go for about twice as much. The guest house has excellent off-season rates. Breakfast at the Sea Star Bistro is some of the best chow in town.

Sunset Motel
1755 Beach Loop Road, Bandon, OR 97411
(503)347-2453 or (800)842-2407

Everywhere along the coast, the closer you get to the ocean, the more expensive the room. The Sunset is a worthwhile compromise. A clean, comfortable unit with a limited view and a double bed is yours for $50, while an ocean-front unit is more than twice as much. So opt for economy—you're just across Beach Loop Road from the ocean, anyway. All rooms include TV, use of a sizable indoor Jacuzzi, and morning coffee.

Snow Camp Lookout

Chetco Ranger District, 555 5th Street, Brookings, OR 97415
(503)469-2196

This Pacific penthouse is located 21 miles northeast of Brookings. There's no indoor plumbing, electricity, or water. And yet this fire lookout atop the 4,223-foot Snow Camp Mountain in the Siskiyou National Forest is a very special place. Inside, there's a wood-burning stove, a single bed, and a table and chairs; a pit toilet is located outside. You bring the rest. You can drive to within sight of the lookout, but you must hike the final 200 yards to the summit. For $30, five of you can sleep here during the snowfree months of May through October. Reservations for a given year are taken in January—and it's popular. Contact the Forest Service to get an application for this windy, remote getaway.

Battle Rock Motel

136 S 6th Street (PO Box 288), Port Orford, OR 97465 • (503)332-7331

Although this nothin'-fancy, retro-looking motel is on the wrong side of Highway 101, your room ($40 for two) is only a stone's throw from the cliffside trail of Battle Rock Wayside Park (a good whale-watching vista) and a wonderful stretch of uncrowded beach. You're also within walking distance of most of Port Orford.

Chetco Inn

417 Fern Street (PO Box 1386), Brookings, OR 97415 • (503)469-5347

Much has changed since the Chetco Inn became the talk of the town three-quarters of a century ago, when luminaries such as Clark Gable and Carole Lombard made the new hotel their weekend retreat. Although the matronly 44-room edifice is but a shadow of its former self, it has retained its character, making it an island of nostalgia in the sea of Brookings' architectural modernity. And it's being renovated, albeit at a snail's pace. The prices ($30–$40) reflect this progress. The inside parlor can be noisy and smoky; fortunately, the comfortable outside porch isn't.

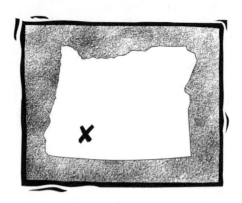

The Rogue River & Crater Lake

The Rogue River has been immortalized in song, literature, and film. Western author Zane Grey lived in a cabin beside its waters; Ginger Rogers had a ranch along its banks. Clark Gable loved the Rogue, and so did John Wayne. The Rogue travels a circuitous 215-mile route across southwestern Oregon, from its headwaters west of Crater Lake National Park to its Pacific Ocean terminus at Gold Beach. Along the way it passes through Douglas fir forests, cattle ranches, pear orchards, vineyards, rugged canyons, and more than one backyard.

The head of the Rogue is Crater Lake, all that remains of the 12,000-foot-high volcano called Mazama that blew its top some 6,000 years ago. The river begins here as a rushing stream, goes underground at one point, becomes a lake behind Lost Creek Dam, and serves as a whitewater playground for rafters and kayakers. It's one long fishing hole too, although some have recently found the lure under par. (Former president Jimmy Carter complained about the lack of bites, and former president George Bush didn't hook anything either.) During its final 30 miles, the Rogue widens and calms as it folds into the Pacific Ocean.

ON THE ROAD

A prospector searching for gold found the treasure now known as **Crater Lake** in 1853. In 1902 it was designated a national park, the only one in Oregon. Millions have admired this jewel, the deepest lake in the United States (1,932 feet), for its dark blue water and rugged rock walls.

Summer is the peak season at Crater Lake, but the park is open all year. Avoid summertime and you'll steer clear of the $5-a-car entry fee as well as the crowds. Fall and spring are good times to visit, and the **cross-country skiing** in winter is spectacular. At 6,000 feet above sea level, the area gets hundreds of inches of snow in an average winter (when only the south entrance is open). Call the park headquarters at (503)594-2211 for information. If you're hungry, Beckie's Cafe, a rustic spot at Union Creek (Highway 62, mile marker 56, Union Creek; (503)560-3563) has been there for decades. The pies aren't bad.

The **Rogue River** heads southwest from Crater Lake. Just past Union Creek, watch for Natural Bridge on the right. If you follow the trail that crosses the river and continues on the other side, you'll come to the spot where the Rogue goes underground for a few hundred feet. It's a dandy; the roar of rushing water makes it sound like a junior Niagara.

Another 10 miles down tree-lined Highway 62, look for the turnoff to **Prospect**. This old road, Mill Creek Drive, parallels the new highway for several miles. Mill Creek Falls is only a quarter-mile walk off the road. Backtrack a bit to another trail that leads to the aptly named **Avenue of Giant Boulders**. Rocks of another kind and purpose await you at Lost Creek Dam, a massive flood-control project completed in the mid-1970s, resulting in the formation of Lost Creek Lake. The power-house is open for tours in summer. Nearby Stewart State Park offers camping as well as day-use areas.

Below the dam, the highway hugs the Rogue as it gently twists and turns through occasional whitewater sections. This is a popular spot for beginning **whitewater rafters**. Rafting companies spring up like mush-rooms in Shady Cove, but two that have been around for a while are Rapid Pleasure, (503)878-2500, and Rogue Rafting, (503)878-2585. Figure on $30–$40 for a three-hour river outing.

Rent a raft or a Rogue Drifter (a big burlap bag filled with Styrofoam balls) from River Trips in Gold Hill; (503)855-7238. The river from Gold Hill to the city of Rogue River is the gentlest part for floating. **Valley of the Rogue**, the other major state park in the area, is a popular and often crowded camping spot.

In the town of Rogue River, look up Suzu-Ya (206 Main Street,

Rogue River; (503)582-1443), a neat little Japanese-American cafe. Dine on katsudon, teriyaki chicken, gyoza, or yakitori. Get there early and during the week; it closes at 7pm and on weekends. For Oklahoma-style barbecue, head to Baizer's in the Rogue River Shopping Center, just east of town on the north side of the river; (503)582-3556.

If you want a more pampered river experience, try a **jet-boat ride**. These noisy boats propel themselves by taking water in the front end and shooting it out the back, and they can operate in just a few inches of river. Arrange a ride with Jet Boat River Excursions at Rogue River, (503)582-0800, or the older, more experienced Hellgate Excursions at Grants Pass, (503)479-7204. Rides, including dinner, run about $35 (knock half off if you skip dinner).

At the mouth of the Rogue, two other companies send jet boats upstream. They are Jerry's Rogue Jets, (503)247-7601 or (800)451-3645, and Mail Boat Hydro-Jets, (503)247-7033 or (800)458-3511. They charge the same prices: about $25 for a round trip to Agness, 32 miles upriver (meal extra); and $65 to Paradise Lodge, 52 miles up (meal included).

Grants Pass, population 17,000, is the largest city on the Rogue. It is the staging area for the fabled three-day rafting trips through the wild and scenic part of the Rogue, a 40-mile stretch. Rafters sleep in the open or stay at wilderness lodges. These trips are not cheap—they cost hundreds of dollars—but if you're interested, try Orange Torpedo Trips; (503)479-5061.

Finally, there's **Gold Beach**, a nice little coastal town with an unusually large number of motels and restaurants for its size. Check out the free Rogue River Museum, next to Jerry's Rogue Jets at the port, which tells all about how this part of the world came to be. For a bite, take the road up the south side of the Rogue to Grant's Pancake and Omelette House (Jerry's Flat Road, Gold Beach; (503)247-7208).

CHEAP SLEEPS

Prospect Historical Hotel
391 Mill Creek Drive, Prospect, OR 97536 • (503)560-3664

In 1990, this century-old hotel was restored and opened as a bed and breakfast, motel, and restaurant complex. B&B-style rooms in the hotel rent for $65, although several of the newer motel units out back are just $45. The restaurant serves Sunday brunch and a four-course dinner for $11–$19. Good food, too.

Acker Lookout

This lookout has only one cot, but you can fit three other people on the floor in sleeping bags. A half-mile hike offers pleasant rewards: views of the Rogue Basin from sheer cliffs dropping from the lookout to the west and south (be careful). As with most lookouts, the Forest Service provides the wood stove, propane refrigerator, stove, and oven, and you provide the rest. For $40 a night (three-night maximum), it's not a bad deal at all. For directions or reservations, call the Tiller Ranger District; (503)825-3201.

Union Creek Resort
56484 Highway 62, Prospect, OR 97536 • (503)560-3339
or (503)560-3565

You and a friend can spend the night in this rather rustic lodge for as little as $38, if you don't mind sharing a bath on the second floor. A "historic" cabin for two, with private bath, starts at $45. Families and other groups may enjoy one of the larger cabins that sleep up to six. You can't beat the scenery—replete with the tall trees of the Rogue River National Forest. The river itself (at this point a rushing stream not far from its headwaters) is a short walk away.

Royal Coachman Motel
21906 Highway 62 (PO Box 509), Shady Cove, OR 97539
(503)878-2481

A number of small motels dot the banks of the upper Rogue from Trail to Shady Cove. This one is about the best. If you don't care about seeing the water, you can get in for as little as $33. Next door is the best restaurant in the territory, Bel Di's, serving three-course dinners (try the Louisiana stuffed prawns); (503)878-2010.

Wolf Creek Tavern
100 Front Street, Wolf Creek, OR 97497 • (503)866-2474

Okay, it's not on the Rogue—not even close. But the 20-mile drive north on I-5 from Grants Pass is worth the side trip for a chance to stay at this charmer (and the journey won't take long). Once a stagecoach stop, the inn was acquired by the state of Oregon and restored in 1979. The building dates back to the 1850s. Of the eight upstairs rooms, seven rent for about $50 (rates increase a fiver in summer). Downstairs is a homey parlor and a good restaurant.

A Farmstay

When was the last time you set foot on a farm? Saw a lamb being born? A sheep shorn? A sheepdog in action? It can happen at Sonka's Sheep Station Inn, a bed and breakfast on a 400-acre working sheep ranch (901 NW Chadwick Lane, Myrtle Creek, OR 97457; (503)863-5168). This is not a dude ranch; there are no poolside drinks or square dances. But farmers do love to eat breakfast, and Louis and Evelyn Sonka are no exception. With rates starting at $50, including the morning feast, Sonka's is a bargain.

Rogue River Inn
6285 Rogue River Highway, Grants Pass, OR 97527 • (503)582-1120

In pre-freeway days, Rogue River Highway was the main road from California to points north, and it was dotted with small motels near the river. This is about the best of the few that remain. It's not right on the river, but it's close enough for a view. Choose from among 16 units ($48–$53), and take a dip in the swimming pool.

Rogue Valley Motel
7799 Rogue River Highway, Grants Pass, OR 97527 • (503)582-3762

This smallish place has only seven units, but there is a pool. You are across the highway from the river but close enough to see the water, and it's only a short walk away. Some units have kitchens. Everything's less than $50.

Cougar Lane Resort
04219 Agness Road, Agness, OR 97406 • (503)247-7233

Nothing fancy here, but you are on the Rogue. Lucas Lodge, across the river, is nicer but more expensive. The motel is open from April to October. Rooms cost about $35; cabins are available too. The deck seating in the restaurant is nice in the summer. Jet boats stop here from May to October so passengers can order meals.

Ireland's Rustic Lodges
1120 Ellensburg Avenue (PO Box 774), Gold Beach, OR 97444
(503)247-7718

This lodging is really two motels. The original eight cottages are rustic and inexpensive. They don't have an ocean view but do have attractive log walls, fireplaces, and lovely gardens. (Cottage 4 is a fave.) Newer units have an ocean view and cost a little more. No phones.

Shortcut to Paradise

You can hike the **Rogue River Trail** to **Paradise Lodge**, but it's a rigorous walk from the Grave Creek trailhead that takes several days with some careful map reading. Here's another way: drive to Marial, which is in the middle of the wilderness area, and hike to the lodge from there. It's an adventurous drive (six hours round trip), although mostly on paved roads. Take I-5 north to the Glendale exit, proceed into Glendale, and turn right at the Shell station onto Cow Creek Road. Continue 14 miles, turning left onto West Fork Road. Follow signs to Marial, 26 miles away. Although the road is narrow, the view makes it worthwhile. The last 11 miles are unpaved; the last 6 miles are on a one-lane road with turnouts. After miles of dust and canyons you come to Rogue River Ranch, an 1880s landmark now operated by the BLM as a mini-museum. Its white-trimmed, bright red buildings and green lawns may seem a bit like a mirage. A half mile farther is Marial Lodge, which is heavily booked by guides and hard to get into, so keep on going. After another quarter mile, the road dead-ends at a trailhead. This is Foster Bar, the "park and walk" spot for those hiking the shortcut to Paradise Lodge (about 4 miles).

Paradise Lodge

PO Box 456, Gold Beach, OR 97444 • (503)247-6022 or (800)525-2161

This is the best wilderness lodge along the wild and scenic part of the Rogue between Grants Pass and Gold Beach. It's accessible by raft, jet boat, hiking trail, or private plane (a small cow pasture doubles as an airstrip), but not by car. Most visitors arrive by jet boat, a three-hour run upriver from Gold Beach, but you can cut costs by hiking in from Foster Bar, 4 miles upriver (see box). You might find yourself walking through a herd of deer to get to your room, and you may have to share the room with a squirrel (so hide those nuts). The electric power here is created by a generator that a hair dryer can blow out, so bring a flashlight. The power is shut off from 10pm to 6am. We suggest hiking in May or thereabouts, before high season begins, when $68 includes three meals and a snack. However, in the middle of the summer you can still get the whole package for $85.

Ashland & Beyond

The entire town of Ashland, which dates back to the Gold Rush years of the 1850s, is a historic landmark. The remarkable success of the Oregon Shakespeare Festival has transformed this sleepy town into the Rogue River Valley's biggest single tourist attraction.

Ashland's population consists of five groups of people: natives, tourists, actors, students, and former owners of the Mark Antony Hotel. The festival now draws an audience of nearly 350,000 through the nine-month season (February through October). Amazingly, the town of 17,000 still retains its soul. For the most part, it seems a happy little college town, set amid lovely ranch country, that just happens to house the fifth-largest theater company in the United States.

Go where the tourists go, and you too can spend and spend. Many inns and restaurants will charge whatever the market will bear. Follow the students (4,000 attend Southern Oregon State College), actors, and locals, and you may find some bargains.

Northwest of Ashland is another Gold Rush-era town, Jacksonville. The 19th-century hotels, shops, and saloons along California Street have become a popular stage set for films, *including* The Great Northfield, Minnesota Raid *and* Inherit the Wind. *Jacksonville is also the home of another top-notch outdoor event, the Britt Music Festival.*

ON THE ROAD

Without question, the **Oregon Shakespeare Festival** has put Ashland on the national map. And yet, as locals know, there's a good deal more to the place. It's the dining capital of Southern Oregon, has more bed-and-breakfast inns (over 50 at last count) than gas stations, and is home to a wealth of art galleries, small theater groups, street markets, and other artistic endeavors.

Still, the center of attention is the Oregon Shakespeare Festival (15 S Pioneer Street, Ashland, OR 97520; (503)482-4331). It produces an average of 11 plays each season, in three theaters. The Angus Bowmer Theatre, named for the festival's founder, is the principal indoor venue. Some of the more offbeat, arty plays open in the smaller Black Swan. Major Shakespearean productions are mounted outdoors on the Elizabethan stage, which was remodeled during the 1991-92 off season to enhance seating and reduce traffic noise. Indoor plays run from February through October, outdoor ones from mid-June to late September. Performances occur daily except Monday.

Tickets for the Shakespeare Festival range from $17.50 to $26.50, but there are ways to cut costs. Attend one of the previews that run for about two weeks prior to the opening of each show, for which tickets cost about 20 percent less. If you plan to attend several plays, or are part of a group, consider buying a membership pass ($50 base price). The pass affords you considerable discounts on preview, rush, and off-season tickets (prior to June and after September). Theater enthusiasts shouldn't miss

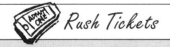 *Rush Tickets*

Shakespeare Festival tickets sold within the last 30 minutes before curtain time are substantially discounted. Still, your chances of obtaining a ticket are slim, unless you try a midweek performance during off season (February through early May, or late September through October) or opt for a performance of a less popular, more obscure play.

Off-Bardway

Off-Bardway is Ashland's pet name for the part of its theater scene that isn't restricted to renditions of Shakespeare. The performances are generally cheaper and of very high quality. Oregon Cabaret Theatre (First and Hargardine streets, Ashland, OR 97520; (503)488-2902) performs in the Old Pink Church (which isn't pink anymore). Actors' Theatre stages productions at the Minshall Theater (101 Talent Avenue, Talent; (503)535-5250). The new kid on the block is Ashland Community Theatre (208 Oak Street, Ashland; (503)482-7532). The Southern Oregon State College Theatre Arts Department puts on several plays a year by theater arts majors at the college; (503)552-6346.

the backstage tour, which offers an intriguing two-hour look behind the scenes ($8, starts at 10am; (503)482-4331).

To explore Ashland, concentrate your efforts on what the locals call the Plaza (Main Street from Water to Pioneer streets), an area with a number of good galleries. The Greenleaf Deli (49 N Main Street, Ashland; (503)482-2808) dishes up good spanakopita. Adjacent to the Plaza is **Lithia Park**, a 99-acre beauty. The band shell in the middle of the park is used for free outdoor concerts and ballet performances during summer months. Call the Chamber of Commerce for a schedule of events; (503)482-3486. Another good place to spend some time is the **Schneider Museum of Art** at Southern Oregon State College (1250 Siskiyou Boulevard near Highway 66, Ashland; (503)552-6245). New as of mid-1994 is the **Pacific Northwest Museum of Natural History** (1500 E Main Street, Ashland; (503)488-1084), noted for interactive exhibits that deliver more questions than answers.

In Ashland, expensive restaurants abound, mostly in the theater district. Avoid them and join those in the know at either Omar's or Geppetto's. Omar's (1380 Siskiyou Boulevard, Ashland; (503)482-1281) has been a fixture at the edge of campus since 1946. Budget-conscious diners return for his toad in a hole (chopped beef served in a baked potato with country gravy and chives). Geppetto's (345 E Main Street, Ashland; (503)482-1138) is noted for its organic veggie burgers, which are popular with actors and students. About 3 miles north of Ashland is **Talent**, a quiet community of around 3,000. If you enjoy Eastern European fare (moussaka, bigos, and chicken paprika), try Chata (1212 S Pacific Highway, Talent; (503)535-2575).

See J'Ville by Trolley

Come summertime, schoolteacher Stan Morkert leases a motorized San Francisco cable-car replica, dons dark glasses and a conductor's hat, and becomes Stan the Trolley Man. He gives hour-long narrated tours of historic Jacksonville just about every day from early June to Labor Day. It's a good way to get a feel for the town and see where everything is, including the spot where gold was discovered in 1851. Look for signs at Third and California streets. Fares are around $3; half price for children.

About halfway between Medford and Phoenix, you'll find the headquarters of **Harry and David** and **Jackson and Perkins**. These two mail-order giants are part of a parent company called Bear Creek Corporation (2836 S Pacific Highway, Medford; (503)776-2770). The firm maintains a country store and restaurant offering everything from fresh produce to myrtlewood pepper shakers. Free tours of the main packing plant are available most weekdays. Ask at the country store.

Medford is the biggest city in this part of the world, and its Rogue Valley Mall, with 80-odd stores, is your proof. Two dandy luncheon spots are Deli Down (406 E Main Street, Medford; (503)772-4520) and Genessee Place (203 Genessee Street, Medford; (503)772-5581). Both ladle out delicious soups and dish up salads and health-conscious sandwiches. Ali's Thai Kitchen (2392 N Pacific Highway, Medford; (503)770-3104) has little atmosphere but lots of punch.

And finally, there's **Jacksonville**, the historic 1850s Gold Rush town. Most visitors come for the **Britt Music Festival**, held from mid-June through early September. Unlike Ashland's festival, the Britt Music Festival has no rush-ticket policy, and we've yet to find any way to get around the high ticket prices. The general-admission tickets are, of course, the better bargain. Occasionally there are discounted Sunday morning tickets. Write to Britt Music Festival, PO Box 1124, Medford, OR 97501; (503)779-0847.

Crater Lake

From Medford, travel northeast on Oregon Highway 62 for approximately 75 miles to Crater Lake National Park for spectacular scenery and the deepest lake in the United States.

CHEAP SLEEPS

Ashland Hostel

150 N Main Street, Ashland, OR 97520 • (503)482-9217

The Ashland Hostel's dormitory-style rooms are open to all ages. If you're lucky, you and a friend can get a private room for $28 off season, $32 during the summer. Hours are strict (as are rules prohibiting smoking and alcohol). Guests share a common kitchen and living space. The two-story building is well maintained and pleasant. Best of all, the Shakespeare Festival theaters are only a few blocks away.

Green Springs Inn

11470 Highway 66, Ashland, OR 97520 • (503)482-0614

If you don't mind driving 17 miles up a winding mountain highway, this rustic lodge is one of the Ashland area's best values. The eight-room motel complex out back (rooms $40–$50) is only a few years old. It sits behind a popular rural restaurant (of the same name) that offers great fresh pasta. The forest setting is beautiful. Rogue Valley temperatures can top 100 degrees on some summer days, but it's almost always 10 to 15 degrees cooler up here.

Manor Motel

476 N Main Street, Ashland, OR 97520 • (503)482-2246

A 12-unit, single-story structure near downtown Ashland, the Manor Motel has its drawbacks: older place, smallish rooms, right on a busy main street. But it is reasonably well maintained, and you can walk to the theaters, about a half mile away. Besides, the rates are hard to beat.

Ashland Clearinghouse

(503)488-0338

This reservation service for lodging (from Ashland to Jacksonville and beyond) offers mainly the more pricey bed and breakfasts. The service is worth a call anyway, for two reasons: 1) these folks know the area and can make suggestions, and 2) they also represent a number of house rentals, available by the night or week. You might be able to get a good deal on a place for a party of six or eight with a several-day discount. If you plan a visit during off season, the clearinghouse can find you some bargains at the better motels or even B&Bs.

Palm Motel and Houses

1065 Siskiyou Boulevard, Ashland, OR 97520 • (503)482-2636

Located across the boulevard from Southern Oregon State College, the Palm's 13 single-story, cabinlike units are on the cutesy side, with white walls and green trim. Out back are several two- and three-bedroom houses for rent in the summer (they're rented to college students during the rest of the year). There's a small swimming pool too.

Phoenix Motel

510 N Main Street, Phoenix, OR 97535 • (503)535-1555

This older motel lies on the old highway in Phoenix, about 6 miles north of Ashland. It has been remodeled and has a tidy look. There are 22 rooms and a swimming pool. Pets are allowed but cost a little extra.

Timbers Motel

1450 Ashland Street, Ashland, OR 97520 • (503)482-4242

Jim and Ginger Travis manage what may be Ashland's best older motel. It sits on the edge of a pie-shaped shopping center, bounded by Highways 99 and 66, across the street from Southern Oregon State College. The two-story structure has 28 clean, comfortable units. There's a small swimming pool on the premises. You can walk to stores and restaurants (Omar's is just across Siskiyou Boulevard), but the theater district is more than a mile away.

Royal Crest Motel

411 E Barnett Road, Medford, OR 97501 • (503)772-6144

Jacksonville, 5 miles to the west, has five B&Bs and just one motel, all of them well over $50 a night. Instead, stay in Medford at the two-story Royal Crest. It was built in the early 1960s but is about the best the town has to offer in this price range. Figure on $34 for a party of two. Access to both Ashland and Jacksonville is easy from here.

Columbia River Gorge & Mount Hood

Mount Hood, Oregon's highest peak—known as Wy'East to early dwellers in the area—rises to 11,285 feet, a striking center-piece for a region blessed in geographical abundance. To the north, the Columbia River follows the path it cut through the basaltic Cascades millions of years ago, forming cliffs up to 400 feet high. In some places, the river rushes by in a flurry of swells and white-caps; at others, federal dams have turned it into a series of lakes. Lush lands north and east of Mount Hood, on the climatic cusp between the arid desert and the moist Oregon Coast, give rise to fertile orchards and farms; the southern slopes draw skiers, climbers, and sight-seekers all year round.

ON THE ROAD

As you drive east from Portland on Interstate 84, the city's outskirts persist right up to the beginning of the Columbia River Gorge Scenic Area, which begins after Troutdale. If you want some sustenance before making the drive, stop by McMenamins Edgefield for a hearty breakfast or burger—and, of course, a brew (2126 SW Halsey Street, Troutdale; (503)669-8610). Or join other bargain diners at Tad's Chicken 'n' Dumplings (1 mile east of Troutdale on Highway 30; (503)666-5337).

Almost immediately, the scenery progresses from merely interesting to most spectacular.

Exit I-84 and take the Columbia River Scenic Highway for 22 miles between Troutdale and Ainsworth State Park. Along the way you'll pass a series of elegant, slender waterfalls cascading down steep precipices: Latourell, Shepperds Dell, Bridal Veil, Coopney, Mist, Wahkeena, Oneonta, Horsetail, and the 620-foot Multnomah Falls (second highest in the country). From **Multnomah Falls**, hike up Larch Mountain to one of the best views of the gorge (especially at sunset). The trail runs right by the top of the falls. For more information, call the Multnomah Falls Lodge; (503)695-2376.

You can also drive up **Larch Mountain**, starting from Crown Point (with an English Tudor vista house 725 feet above the Columbia) off the Old Scenic Highway. Oneonta Gorge, a couple of miles past Multnomah Falls, is a narrow, dramatic cleft through which a slippery half-mile trail winds to secluded **Oneonta Falls** (call the Columbia River Gorge National Scenic Area; (503)386-2333). Back on the main highway (I-84 and the scenic highway join forces until Mosier), you're deep into the dramatic beauty of the gorge.

At Cascade Locks, you can still see the locks built to help boats across the Columbia's rapids (before dams calmed the waters). Tour the **Bonneville Dam**, the oldest of the 10 dams on the river, and watch the salmon in the fish ladders during the seasonal runs. Stop for a bite at CharBurger Restaurant (714 SW Wa-Na-Pa Street, Cascade Locks; (503)374-8477). A two-hour trip on the M.V. *Columbia Gorge*, an old-fashioned sternwheeler, costs $11.95 (three trips daily June through September; times vary in winter) and evokes something of the river's past; (503)223-3928.

Salmon are not the only creatures flying through the surf of the Columbia; **board sailors** skim across the waves like brightly colored water bugs. Here's where the wind blows east against the west-flowing current in the spring and summer months, careening down the narrow canyon formed by the Columbia Gorge's basalt cliffs—ideal windsurfing conditions. Lured to the town of Hood River (a mecca for wind surfers), the board sailors try to harness the gorge's endless winds. "Bingen" Bart Vervloet delivers morning wind reports every day (during peak season) on KMCQ 104. Swell City and Doug's Beach (on the Washington side) and the Hood River Marina Sailpark, Hood River Waterfront Events Area, and Rowena Park (on the Oregon side) are some of the boarders' choice launching spots (although you can take off virtually anywhere land meets water). Spectators gather on the West Jetty, at Port Marina Park, and at the Waterfront Events Area.

Hood River has something for everyone—not just those obsessed with wind. Hikers explore the network of trails on the Columbia's cliffs; mountain bikers migrate to the Forest Service roads around Mount Hood. Oenophiles sip the valley's vintages at various wineries, including Three Rivers Winery (275 Country Club Road, Hood River; (503)386-5453) and Hood River Vineyards (4693 Westwood Drive, Hood River; (503)386-3772). The farms around Hood River are blessed with the right combination of moisture and sun. A plenitude of orchards and farms sell U-pick and ready-picked fruits and vegetables. Call the Hood River County Extension, (503)386-3343, for locations. Or drop by the Fruit Tree (4140 West Cliff Drive, Hood River; (503)386-6688) or the River Bend Country Store (2363 Tucker Road, Hood River; (503)386-8766) for fresh produce and local specialty foods. The Mount Hood Railroad (Hood River Depot; (503)386-3556) makes round trips from the quaint Hood River Depot into the heart of orchard country, April through October. The four-hour trip to Parkdale is $19.95 ($11.95 for kids).

Boarders know the best breakfast is at Purple Rocks Art Bar and Cafe (606 Oak Street, Hood River; (503)386-6061). Locals enjoy Yaya's (207 Oak Street, Hood River; (503)386-1996) for Greek, El Sombrero (1945 12th Street, Hood River; (503)386-7300) for Mexican, and Hood River Restaurant (108 2nd Street, Hood River; (503)386-3966) for Chinese. Pick up sandwiches and espresso at the Coffee Spot (12 Oak Street, Hood River; (503)386-1772) or sip a microbrew at the Full Sail Brewpub (506 Columbia Street, Hood River; (503)386-2247), home of Full Sail ales and light meals.

The Dalles was once the largest Indian trading center in North America and the end of the overland portion of the Oregon Trail. The town vies with Astoria for the title of the oldest white settlement in the Northwest, and is the historic stop along this stretch. Take a quick walking

---

✈ Salmon Feast

A little-known tribal festival takes place every year around Easter in the little town of Celilo, 15 miles east of The Dalles. Roughly coinciding with the spring salmon run, this festival of thanksgiving includes dancing, ceremonies, and a traditional feast (roots, meats, and—of course—salmon) for local tribal groups. Visitors are welcome and the feast is free, but we should point out that this is a religious ceremony, not a tourist attraction, so please go with consideration and respect, and perhaps a small donation. For dates, call The Dalles Chamber of Commerce; (503)296-2231.

tour of the town and examine the hybrid architecture (including Gothic Revival, Italianate, and American Renaissance) that lines the town's hybrid streets. Visit the **Fort Dalles Museum**, housed in an 1856 surgeon's quarters. Crate's Point, 3 miles west of The Dalles, is the future site of the Gorge Discovery Center (scheduled to open in 1997), where exhibits and educational programs will document the geologic, natural, and anthropological history of the area. Picnic in **Celilo Park**, where Native Americans used to net and spear fish from platforms on the former Celilo Falls. (The falls once lined the river but were slowed and eventually stayed by the Bonneville Dam.)

The Dobre Deli (308 E 4th Street, The Dalles; (503)298-8239) serves up sweets, sandwiches, and espresso. The unassuming House of Chin (310 E 2nd Street, The Dalles; (503)296-6500) is the spot for huge, cheap portions and great seaweed soup. Locals also like Johnny's (408 E 2nd Street, The Dalles; (503)296-4565) for big, inexpensive steaks in a small-town atmosphere.

Take Highway 35 south from Hood River, where apple and pear trees line the roads near Parkdale and lava fields appear among the orchards. Lolo Pass Road is a scenic bypass drive from Hood River around the north and west sides of Mount Hood to Zig Zag (the road is closed in winter); an easy and rewarding hike from this road leads to the cascading **Ramona Falls**.

Five ski areas grace the flanks of Mount Hood. The first one you reach when driving south on Highway 35 is also the oldest and the smallest (500 vertical feet). But **Cooper Spur** (11000 Cloud Cap Road, Mount Hood; (503)352-7803) can be a bargain if the conditions are right. This family-owned and -run area has a good learning hill with one T-bar and one rope tow ($5), and $15 buys a lift ticket good all day and all night. The area also has a large network of cross-country ski trails. After working up an appetite, have dinner at the Cooper Spur Restaurant (10755 Cooper Spur Road, Mount Hood; (503)352-6037), where the prime rib is so big that the potato comes on a separate plate. Or visit

Ski Tip

From Portland, Timberline's $24 bus-and-ski package is a deal. You'll be picked up from one of three cities (Portland, Beaverton, or Gresham) and returned at the end of the day. Call G.I. Joe's Ticketmaster for reservations; (503)224-4400.

the town of Mount Hood (north of Cooper Spur on Highway 35) and stop in at the Mount Hood Country Store (6545 Cooper Spur Road, Mount Hood; (503)352-6024), a general market with a deli, for good pizza by the slice and housemade soups and sandwiches.

Timberline will give you the most skiing for your dollar if you plan correctly; (503)272-3311. Weekday tickets are $22; weekend lift tickets are $28. In summer (Timberline offers the only lift-serviced, all-summer skiing in America), tickets are $28 every day, good for the two chair lifts that carry skiers to the top of the Palmer Snowfield. The mountain is accessible to nonskiers as well in summer; take the Mile chair lift up as a foot passenger for the stunning view (around $8 round trip).

Mount Hood Meadows has some of the best and most varied terrain in the area, accessible by nine chair lifts. Lift tickets are $32 ($5 more if you want to ski day and night). Occasionally, cheaper promotional deals may be offered; call (503)227-SNOW for information. If it's a lousy ski day, return your lift ticket within 45 minutes and you'll get a voucher for another day's ticket; (503)337-2222.

Two other lift areas are **Mount Hood Skibowl** (8700 E Highway 26, Government Camp; (503)222-2695), where lift tickets run $22, and **Summit** (Government Camp; (503)272-0256), where one lift on two hills costs $10.

The Snow Bunny area in Government Camp is best for sledding and tubing, even though officially it's a ski area. The nearby Mount Hood Brewpub (Highway 26, Government Camp; (503)272-3724) pours a good pint of Timberline Ale (from the original pre-Prohibition recipe) and serves some casual eats.

From a distance, Hood looks like the archetypal mountain—two diagonal brush strokes creating a tippy, pointed peak. Close up, the dramatic ridges and cliffs are a subtle reminder of the mountain's power. Summertime at Mount Hood finds crowds of climbers, hikers, and wilderness fans enjoying the glaciers and flowers. The lower parts of the mountain are ablaze with rhododendrons (peaking in June) and wildflowers (peaking in July); all are easily reached from trails that spread out

Permit to Ski

All Mount Hood ski areas require a Sno-Park permit from
November to April. If you have a Washington Sno-Park permit,
they'll honor it in Oregon (and Idaho). Don't skip the permit; the
areas fine rebels. All the ski areas and most ski shops sell the permit.

from Timberline Lodge. One of the best trails leads 4½ miles west from
Timberline to flower-studded **Paradise Park**.

What you need to **climb Mount Hood** is either experience or a
guide. The best time to ascend is from May to early July. Most climbers
take one of the southside routes, up the Palmer and White River glaciers. It's a technical climb, so if you're unsure of your skills, arrange for a
guide from the Northwest School of Survival (PO Box 1465, Sandy, OR
97055; (503)668-8264) or The Mazamas (909 NW 19th Avenue,
Portland; (503)227-2345), a Portland-based climbing club that organizes
climbs from May to mid-June. Climbing fees are $5 for members and
$10 for nonmembers, although the club doesn't provide any equipment.
You can spend the night before your climb in the club's cabin.

Hardy hikers circumnavigate the peak on the **Timberline Trail**, a 40-
mile path leading through forest and over snowfield. Call the ranger station
at Zig Zag or Parkdale for information; (503)666-0704 or (503)666-0701.

Above Government Camp, the main attraction is the Depression-era
Timberline Lodge, a WPA project dedicated by Franklin Delano

Fire Lookouts

Flag Point (5,650 feet) and Fivemile (4,627 feet) lookouts are both
still used by fire watchers in the summer. In the winter, these
crow's nests in the Mount Hood National Forest are available to
the public at roughly $25 a night. You'll need to bring the usual
amount of gear (sleeping bags, food, water, and dishes). The Forest
Service provides the stove, the firewood, and the view. You can ski
up to the lookouts. The length of the trek is determined by where
the road becomes inaccessible; you may end up with an 11-mile
hike, or you may be able to drive right up to the gate for an easy
jaunt to the lookout. For detailed directions and information on the
permit process, call the Barlow Ranger District; (503)467-2291.

Mount Hood Festival of Jazz (PO Box 2001, Gresham, OR 97030; (503)666-3810). This premier jazz fest has featured such acclaimed performers as David Sanborn and Al Jarreau. The festival is held in the Gresham Community College football stadium, with tickets running around $25 a day; order them through Ticketmaster.

Roosevelt in 1937. Every part of the lodge—from the rough-hewn columns to the huge stone fireplace—was crafted by hand, and the lodge is filled with art—mosaics, wood-carvings, paintings, and hand-loomed textiles. Even if you don't ski, drive up to the lodge (which you may recognize from Stanley Kubrick's film *The Shining*) and sit by the fire, or sip a drink in the Blue Ox Bar.

Stop in **Zig Zag** for fried chicken at the Barlow Trail Inn (69580 E Highway 26, Zig Zag; (503)622-3112). The little town of Wemme, also known as Welches (because so many Welches settled here), offers Michael's Bread and Breakfast (24525 E Welches Road, Wemme; (503)622-5333), where one aficionado likes the oatmeal-raisin and spice cookies and baked apple fritters.

Sandy is the first town you encounter as you head west out of the Mount Hood area (and the best place to stop for gas when you're going the other way; prices go up exponentially as you approach the mountain). Visit **Oral Hull Park**, designed for the blind, with fragrant plants and splashing water (43233 Oral Hull Road, Sandy; (503)668-6195). Sandy is also home to 30 different hamburgers at Calamity Jane's (42015 SE Highway 26, Sandy; (503)668-7817). Microbrews, burgers, and great atmosphere await you at the Elusive Trout Pub (39333 Proctor Avenue, Sandy; (503)668-7884).

CHEAP SLEEPS

McMenamins Edgefield
2126 SW Halsey Street, Troutdale, OR 97060 • (503)669-8610

The latest venture of McMenamins is by far their most extravagant. The former Multnomah County Poor Farm, established in 1911, was purchased by McMenamins in 1990 and turned into a 91-room inn (complete with restaurant, sitting porches, library, brew pub, movie theater, gardens, and outdoor amphitheater where big-name bands play to crowds that can number up to 4,000). You'll pay $35–$45 for a single twin room (bathroom down the hall, robe provided, breakfast included); a night in the men's or women's hostel—one large room with bunk beds and a bath down the hall—sets you back a mere $18 (private locker included, but no breakfast).

Scandian Motor Lodge
25 Oneonta Street (PO Box 217), Cascade Locks, OR 97014
(503)374-8417

The Scandian has large, woodsy rooms with bright Scandinavian colors and tiled baths (one with a sauna). A very clean upstairs room with a river view comes with a reasonable price tag ($46 in the summer). Reservations are a good idea for the summer; bring your small pet if you like.

Gorge View Bed and Breakfast
1009 Columbia Street, Hood River, OR 97031 • (503)386-5770

Want to touch base with Hood River's predominant windsurfing culture? Here's where the surfers like to stay. There are regular rooms in Pat and Ann Frodel's B&B, but the "bunk room" in a renovated sun porch attracts a loyal and eclectic following, from cheapsters to windsurfing pros. For about $29 per boardhead (May through September), you get all the interesting conversation that evolves when four strangers end up in one room. The new hot tub helps, too. Breakfast may be a carbo-loading Mexican fiesta. Talk shop with Pat, a windsurfing accessories manufacturer.

Prater's Motel
1306 Oak Street, Hood River, OR 97031 • (503)386-3566

A short strip of seven rooms on the main drag, Prater's boasts an unhindered view of the Columbia and proximity to all things Hood River. The rooms are small, but they're also clean, quaint, and very reasonable.

Vagabond Lodge
4070 Westcliff Drive, Hood River, OR 97031 • (503)386-2992

The Vagabond is so close to the Columbia Gorge Hotel that it could almost be another wing. It's got the identical view, and the rooms are twice the size at a fraction of the price. The front building is nothing but a nondescript highway-facing unit. The surprise is in back—three newer buildings house riverfront rooms available for just under and over $50. Pets are allowed.

The Colonial House
904 E 16th Place, The Dalles, OR 97058 • (503)296-3032

The two rooms with private bath in this homespun B&B are $45 each, and come with a full country breakfast. Bob and Wilma Peterson have filled

When All Else Fails

Thunderhead Lodge (PO Box 129, Government Camp, OR 97028; (503)272-3368) rents out privately owned condominiums, complete with fully furnished kitchens. For larger groups, they can be a great deal: $80 for 4 people, $250 for 10. Trudie England, of England's Lodging (PO Box 9, Government Camp, OR 97028; (503)272-3350), has a number of three- and five-bedroom chalets and duplexes—great for families—which range $75–$500, depending on the number of people and the type of accommodation. On winter weekends there's a two-night minimum.

their home with antiques; guests relax in front of the fireplace or eat their morning meal in the garden, depending on the whims of the weather.

Timberline Lodge
Timberline Ski Area, OR 97028 • (503)272-3311 or (800)547-1406

For cheapskates who have a hankering to spend a night in a 1937 National Historic Monument, here's your chance. Timberline Lodge's "chalet rooms" run about $59 for two (bunk beds, mind you), plus $8 for each additional guest. So, using a little math, in a four-person room you spend less than $20 apiece to stay in this grand WPA project, with its rock and timber decor, fire-warmed lobby with resident Saint Bernard, and proximity to year-round skiing. Late sleepers: beware of clomping ski boots at dawn.

Huckleberry Inn
PO Box 249, Government Camp, OR 97028 • (503)272-3325

Here's a newer accommodation among the '50s-style motor lodges along the loop. The rooms here start under $50 and zoom up pretty quickly from there, but a bunk in the dorm costs just $16. Relax in one of the common rooms, or grab a bite in the 24-hour restaurant.

Snowline Motel
Highway 26 (PO Box 175), Rhododendron, OR 97049 • (503)622-3137

Eight miles from Government Camp, the Snowline Motel offers eight wood-paneled rooms (some with fireplaces) and five cabins at excellent prices. The rustic cabins (built in 1923) bear the Steiner wishbone mark, indicating that the craftsman of the famous hand-hewn columns in the Timberline Lodge had his hand in here somewhere as well. Not bad for $40–$60 for two (and if an extra someone—or pet—wants to unroll a sleeping bag by the large fireplace, that's okay).

Bend & Three Sisters Wilderness

Central Oregon is dominated by 10,000-foot Cascade peaks such as Mount Jefferson and the Three Sisters. Ancient glaciers creep downward from the summits of these dormant volcanoes until they meet vegetation at about the 7,000-foot level. Below, forested slopes hiding hundreds of high mountain lakes and unsullied alpine meadows contrast dramatically with ancient lava flows hardened to a gray-black pumice. Finally, the eastern edge of the Cascades gives way to an undulating high-desert landscape.

It's here that the central Oregon cities of Madras, Redmond, Bend, and La Pine are situated. The geography is marked by rugged rimrock canyons carved by the Deschutes and Crooked rivers, and by the many human-made lakes where these and other rivers have been dammed. The Cascade summits block most of the precipitation prevalent on the west side of Oregon, so the climate is dry and sunny—300 days a year.

As recently as 30 years ago, Bend was a smallish cowboy town located on a big curve in the Deschutes River, and residents were a mix of farmers, ranchers, a smattering of small-town folk, and a sizable Native American population centered on the

Warm Springs area. How things change: these days, a loaded ski rack (carrying a mountain bike, a sailboard, and a pair of skis) is more common than a gun rack. Even in an Old West city such as Redmond, you're as likely to meet an accountant as a cowboy (or the person you see may well be both).

The bend in the Deschutes is still there, but Bend itself and its almost urban environs have changed dramatically with the influx of folks from Portland, Salem, Seattle, Southern California, and elsewhere. Today, Bend draws outdoor fanatics from all over: not just skiers but whitewater devotees, hikers, rock climbers, backpackers, boaters, board sailors, and road and mountain cyclists. In addition to the rank-and-file participants, many world-class competitors come here to play; that may well have been Bill Koch you saw skating on Bachelor's groomed Nordic trails, or snow boarder Chris Karol shredding the mountain's lower slopes. Lynn Hill has put up some new climbing routes at Smith Rocks, a few miles north. And come July, the country's best bicyclists take part in the Cascade Cycling Classic.

ON THE ROAD

The focal point of Bend, **Drake Park**, is the logical locale for a picnic. Kids (and adults) on bikes, skateboards, and roller blades will pass by as you attempt to keep your lunch away from the hundreds of birds (mostly drakes) that inhabit the park. There are footpaths along the Deschutes River, which slices through the park and forms its center-piece, Mirror Pond.

Foodwise, you'll find a couple of good spots to start your day. Right on the edge of Drake Park, Cafe Santé (718 NW Franklin Street, Bend; (503)383-3530) purveys breakfasts (multigrain pancakes, huevos rancheros, and rice patties) and lunches (fruit smoothies, pastas, soups, and sandwiches) prepared with mostly organic ingredients. A little farther out, the West Side Bakery and Cafe (1005½ NW Galveston Avenue, Bend; (503)382-3426) is a crowded breakfast stop for the folks on their way up to Bachelor. Pancakes, egg dishes, sandwiches built with home-baked bread, or a simple bowl of fruit and yogurt are good bets here. You can also find Bend's best bagels and some pretty good breads, but for a more extensive baked-goods selection, check out Pastries by Hans (915 NW Wall Street, Bend; (503)389-9700), a sit-down bakery popular with the downtown set.

There are some inexpensive dinner choices nearby, too. The Deschutes Brewery (1044 NW Bond Street, Bend; (503)382-9242) offers four different handcrafted ales, ginger ale, and yummy root beer alongside nightly specials, such as pasta and veggies, chicken, and fish. This non-smoking pub serves barnburner burgers, chili, and huge baskets of world-class french fries after most other places have closed for the evening. Just across Bond Street, Cafe Paradiso (945 NW Bond Street, Bend; (503)385-5931) is a comfy evening hangout with tables and chairs, couches, and live music. The pizza's tasty at the ever-popular Papandrea's (1854 NE Division Street, Bend; (503)388-4645), also in Sisters (corner of Highway 20 and Cascade Street, Sisters; (503)549-6081) and Madras (543 SW 4th Street, Madras; (503)475-6545); and at Stuft Pizza (125 Oregon Avenue, Bend; (503)382-4022), a nonsmoking pizza joint with live comedy.

Neither man nor woman lives by food alone. A foray up **Century Drive** (which turns into Cascade Lakes Highway) on your road or mountain bike, on roller blades, or in your car is a worthwhile endeavor any time of the year. In winter, the road is plowed only to the base of Mount Bachelor, at the 6,000-foot level. Folks have been known to cross-country ski to Elk Lake (mostly downhill) and get picked up for the drive back to Bend the long way. (Century Drive/Cascade Lakes Highway is a 100-mile loop. The section between the base of Mount Bachelor and Elk Lake remains unplowed until Memorial Day weekend.)

A dormant volcano, **Mount Bachelor** sits on the east slope—the dry side—of the Cascades, rising gracefully to an elevation of 9,065 feet. The base elevation is almost 6,000 feet, and therein lies one key to Bachelor's abundance of powder. The skiing possibilities are so numerous at Bachelor, and the mountain so huge, that you can ski in good snow

 *Free Ski Bus*

The very convenient Mount Bachelor Super Shuttle is a free ski bus that leaves Century Drive in Bend, adjacent to the Mount Bachelor corporate offices, three times daily. The shuttle returns to Bend from the mountain four times a day.

The Bend Outback

Bend has some of the Northwest's best cross-country conditions. You probably already know about the 56 kilometers of groomed trails, suitable for skating or traditional skiing. But there are also miles of backcountry opportunities, with trailheads located just off Century Drive. Not to be missed:

• The Meissner area, 12 miles west of Bend, designed for beginners and intermediates (a warming shelter provides a welcome refuge 1 mile in from the parking area).

• Swampy Lakes, 3 miles farther up Century Drive, which offers a variety of marked trails, 2 to 10 miles in length, and five shelters that are usually stocked with wood (there are snowmobile trails on the other side of the highway).

• The Dutchman Flat area, farther still up Century Drive adjacent to the Mount Bachelor entrance, with trails leading into the nearby Three Sisters Wilderness. Dutchman Flat is wide open, with few obstructions, because the pumicey soil cannot sustain much plant life.

In the off season, these same cross-country skiing trails make for awesome mountain biking or trail running. The areas require Sno-Park permits in the winter. For permit information and trail maps, phone the Deschutes National Forest office in Bend; (503)388-2715.

throughout the winter—which lasts for seven months of the year; (503)382-2607.

Additional vital stats about Bachelor: 300 inches of annual snowfall, a vertical drop of 3,100 feet, and 10 chair lifts, as well as five lodges serving 60 different downhill runs. The **Nordic area** has its own lodge and 56 kilometers (35 miles) of groomed trails. There's even a day-care facility. Lift tickets cost $33 for adults. Three- and five-day discounts are available, as well as "flextime point" tickets, good for a three-year period and geared to infrequent skiers. An adult one-day cross-country ticket goes for $9.50 ($4.50 for youth). Children age 6 and under ski free anywhere on the mountain. Call the Ski Report, (503)382-7888, for up-to-date conditions. Off season (June through early September), the chair lift runs to the summit, providing for an impressive three-state view and unlimited hiking, trail-running, and mountain-biking ventures. Call (800)829-2442 for additional information. Equipment rentals are available on the mountain, but you can find better prices and a superior selection in Bend.

The best places to **rent skis** in Bend include Skjersaa's Ski Shop (130 SW Century Drive, Bend; (503)382-2154), where downhill-ski packages are $11 a day and Nordic packages are $7; Sunnyside Sports (930 NW Newport Avenue, Bend; (503)382-8018), which rents cross-country skis and boots for $8 a day; and Tri-Mountain Sports (815 NW Wall Street, Bend; (503)382-8330), which offers a $9 Nordic package and is a useful source for climbing equipment and info. Winter Wave (225 SW Century Drive, Bend; (503)383-2833) offers a big selection of rental snow boards.

In June, the Cascade Lakes Highway reopens and winds into the prettiest lake region in the Northwest, the gateway to the 200,000-acre **Three Sisters Wilderness**. A number of trailheads begin from parking areas just off the road. (If you park in any of them, secure your vehicle and take valuables with you, or lock them in the trunk.) The Deschutes River recreation sites, the Swampy Lakes area, the back side of Bachelor, and Todd Lake—all on national forestland—are good mountain-biking areas. Maps are available at the Deschutes National Forest headquarters (1645 Highway 20 E, Bend; (503)388-2715).

Bend's best bike shop, Century Cycles (1135 NW Galveston Avenue, Bend; (503)389-4224) dispenses free information on riding areas and rents snow boards in the winter. You can rent good-quality mountain bikes at Skjersaa's (see aforementioned address) for $15 a day or $4 an hour, including a helmet and lock. Any of the larger lakes in this area are excellent for board sailing as well as fishing. If you're hiking into the Three Sisters Wilderness (no mountain bikes or mechanized vehicles are allowed), avoid the congested Green Lakes, Elk Lake, and Sisters Mirror Lake trailheads. Instead, choose the Six Lake trailhead or, if you intend to scale the 10,358-foot South Sister (Oregon's third-highest peak and a nontechnical climb), head for the Devil's Lake parking area and the Sisters' Climbing Trail.

Six miles south of Bend on Highway 97, the **High Desert Museum** (59800 S Highway 97, Bend; (503)382-4754) offers interesting art and natural history exhibits, as well as entertaining outdoor wildlife demonstrations involving river otters, porcupines, and birds of prey. Two miles farther south, you can view an extinct volcanic cone and learn about the area's geology at **Lava Lands** (58201 S Highway 97, Bend; (503)593-2421), which is free and open mid-March through October. While there, ask about lava caves to explore in the area.

Turn west at the Sunriver Resort exit to visit the free **Sunriver Nature Center**, with its raptor rehabilitation area; (503)593-1221. Eight miles south is Newberry Crater, Oregon's largest Ice Age volcano and the site of Paulina and East lakes, which are hot spots for windsurfing, fishing, swimming, boating, and cross-country skiing. In the winter, the road is plowed for only the first 10 miles.

Twenty-five miles east of Bend on Highway 20 is the University of Oregon's Pine Mountain Observatory (9 miles south of Millican; (503)382-8331), the astronomy research center of the Northwest. Visiting hours are limited, so call first. A small donation is requested. But even if you don't venture inside the observatory, the view from Pine Mountain is worth the drive.

One of the most popular multisport events in the country is Bend's annual **Pole, Pedal, and Paddle Race** in mid-May. This six-leg relay begins on a three-quarter-mile alpine skiing run on Mount Bachelor, followed by 8 kilometers of cross-country skiing (classic or skate technique allowed); a 22-mile, mostly downhill bike ride to Bend's Colorado Avenue; a 2-mile paddle on Deschutes River; and, finally, a 400-meter footrace across the grass in Drake Park. The event is open to teams, pairs, and individuals; (503)382-3282.

The route west from Bend to Sisters via Highway 20 is a pleasant sojourn through pastoral grazing fields with wonderful views of Bachelor, the Three Sisters, Black Butte, and Mount Washington, Mount Jefferson, and Three-Fingered Jack. At the west end of Sisters, turn on Highway 242 for a drive (or bike ride) past the nation's largest llama ranch; then continue on to the Dee Wright Memorial (a castlelike, covered viewing area) and the high point of McKenzie Pass. The spectacular road at the 5,324-foot summit (closed to vehicles during the winter) separates the Three Sisters and Mount Washington wilderness areas. The **Pacific Crest Trail**, along with climbing trails for scaling Washington and the North and Middle Sister, are located nearby.

For yet another breathtaking scene, follow Highway 20 west past Sisters to the Metolius River headwaters via the paved Forest Road 14 (followed by a half-mile walk on a blacktop trail). Here the crystal-clear Metolius emerges from an unknown underground source, and is an excellent photo opportunity with 10,497-foot Mount Jefferson as a backdrop. The surrounding area offers unlimited outdoor adventures. Visit Eurosports in Sisters (115 SW Hood Street, Sisters; (503)549-2471) for inspiration, maps, and rentals. Farther west, on the Santiam Pass summit, Hoodoo Ski Bowl (Highway 20, 42 miles west of Bend; (503)822-3799) offers free skiing from 9am to 10am every day, so you can test the conditions before buying a lift ticket.

Smith Rocks State Park, a half hour north of Bend on Highway 97, is an internationally known rock-climbing area centered on the

The Museum at Warm Springs

Warm Springs is just a small bend in the road at the bottom of a rimrock canyon on Highway 26, but the Museum at Warm Springs, (503)553-3331, is a sight to behold. Built in 1993 by three Native American tribes (Wasco, Paiute, and Warm Springs), it houses a permanent collection that includes prized heirlooms, protected by tribal families for generations, now on view to the public for the first time. The best feature of the architecturally magnificent museum is a representation of a ceremonial Wasco wedding: tule-mat lodge, wickiup and plankhouse, song chamber, and drums accompanying rhythmic hoop dancing.

majestic rock spires of the Crooked River Canyon. This day-use-only area, adjacent to the town of Terrebonne, plays host to climbing "stars" from the United States, Europe, and Japan. Stop at Redpoint Climbing and Mountaineering Supply (975 NE Smith Rock Way, Terrebonne; (503)923-6207) for more information. The area's best chow is available at La Siesta Cafe (8320 N Highway 97, Terrebonne; (503)548-4848), where Lycra-clad climbers rub shoulders with local ranch hands over platters of Tex-Mex grub.

CHEAP SLEEPS

Kah-Ne-Tah
100 Main Street (PO Box K), Warm Springs, OR 97761
(503)553-1112 or (800)831-0100

Located in the middle of the high desert, halfway between Mount Hood and Bend, this posh resort isn't for everyone traveling on a budget. Nevertheless, a large family or group of friends can stay in one of the tepees for a modest sum ($50 for three, then $12 per additional person). You're right near the big attraction, the hot mineral springs pool, as well as the golf course—and you're in a tepee, for goodness' sake. (We don't advise visits in the sweltering summer.)

Breitenbush Hot Springs
PO Box 578, Detroit, OR 97342 • (503)854-3314

Slightly New Age, this old mountain spa is a favorite of counterculture Portlanders and those just looking for a quiet, cleansing time in the woods and perhaps a dip in one of the natural springs. Individuals and couples are welcome, but the place is best for families or spiritual groups. Two crystalline meeting rooms are the setting for enlightening activities such as yoga, meditation, and relationship seminars; cross–country ski weekends and ancient-forest walks are equally inspiring (Breitenbush is located on the edge of the Mount Jefferson Wilderness). You sleep in tiny, electrically heated cabins, eat family-style vegetarian (mostly organic) food, and find peace in a steam room (heated by the hot springs) where clothing is optional. Bring bedding and towels, and be prepared for a half-mile walk from your vehicle to the main lodge. Also, even if you're just popping in for a daytime soak, make certain you call ahead to check on space availability.

Metolius River Lodges
County Road 700 (PO Box 110), Camp Sherman, OR 97730
(503)595-6290 or (800)595-6290

This collection of 12 rustic cabins is about 30 miles from Bend (10 miles from Sisters) and a world away from urban hassles. Nestled under a canopy of old-growth ponderosa pine, the lodges are just a cast away from the swiftly flowing Metolius River. The best deals are two duplexes, which sleep up to four. Units 2, 3, and 4 (not available in the winter) feature kitchens and fireplaces with sweet-smelling wood logs. All guests are served beverages and muffins at their door each morning. If you're looking for meticulously clean, well-appointed lodgings with a decidedly outdoorsy feel, it doesn't get any better than this.

The Country Inn the City Bed and Breakfast
1776 NE 8th Street, Bend, OR 97701 • (503)385-7639

This two-story home, built in 1920, occupies a large corner lot in a quiet northeast neighborhood. The house is chock full of knickknacks, and the library is stocked with books, videos, and board games. Outdoor enthusiasts can enjoy croquet, horseshoes, and the basketball court, and then relax in the hammock underneath the ponderosa pines. There are but two guest rooms ($40 and $45). Breakfast is nutritious (and the evening fudge fest is, thankfully, not).

Cultus Lake Resort
Highway 46 (PO Box 262), Bend, OR 97709
Winter phone: (503)389-3230
Summer phone: (503)389-5125, wait for beep, then 037244

You're well into the mountains here in the Deschutes National Forest, 50 miles southwest of Bend, alongside a large lake popular with anglers, boaters, board sailors, and swimmers (yes, it's warm enough in late

Vacation Rentals

Want to rent a house? In Bend, rental arrangements are made through private owners or property management firms. Vacation rental management companies include Central Oregon Leasing and Management (1250 NE 3rd Street, Suite B110, Bend, OR 97701; (503)385-6830) and Mirror Pond Management (961 NW Brooks Street, Bend, OR 97701; (503)382-6766). Coldwell Banker/First Resort Realty (PO Box 4306, Sunriver, OR 97707; (800)452-6870 in Oregon or (800)544-0300 outside of Oregon) handles Sunriver Resort rentals, and Black Butte Ranch Corporation (Black Butte Ranch, Highway 20, approximately 5 miles west of Sisters; (800)452-7455) handles rentals at Black Butte Ranch.

summer). You're also adjacent to the Three Sisters Wilderness and in the midst of an expansive trail system custom-tailored to hiking, running, or cross-country skiing. Unfortunately, this resort is open only from mid-May through mid-October. Nevertheless, catch it while you can, because the 23 cabins are reasonably priced at $45 and up. A serviceable restaurant and a small grocery store are in the handsome main lodge, and boat rentals (including canoes, kayaks, a Hobiecat, and a wind surfer) are easily managed.

Mill Inn Bed and Breakfast
642 NW Colorado Street, Bend, OR 97701 • (503)389-9198

Formerly a hotel and boardinghouse, the Mill Inn is now a nine-unit B&B, with the added attraction of the super-deal, four-bunk Locker Room ($15 a person). Couples should opt for the Duffers Room or the Timber Room. The High Desert Room has twin beds, a shared bath, and fetches $40. Group rates are available (small ski teams stay here and have been known to fill the spa on the outdoor deck). Even bunk rates include a full breakfast, and there's a washer, dryer, and refrigerator for guest use.

Westward Ho Motel
904 SE 3rd Street, Bend, OR 97701 • (503)382-2111 or (800)999-8143

Highway 97, the main north-south thoroughfare in central Oregon, cuts an unattractive swath of motels, fast-food joints, and car dealerships right through Bend. Of the numerous lodging choices, the Westward Ho is

Three Sisters Wilderness Cabin

In rare instances, the U.S. Forest Service has let stand small, unobtrusive, hand-built structures in wilderness areas where no signs of humanity—save hikers—are supposed to be seen. Head into the lake-splashed area of the Three Sisters Wilderness and you'll stumble upon a picture-perfect cabin located on the Muskrat Lake shoreline. It's a 5½-mile hike or horseback ride from the trailhead in the Cultus Lake North Unit, so you'll most likely have it to yourself. Built by a trapper earlier in this century, it includes a potbelly stove, a bunk bed, and cupboards sometimes stocked with nonperishable food. There are no rules (though you're expected to leave it clean and replace firewood and food used), no fees, and no disturbances. Be prepared for snow nine months of the year, lots of bugs (including pesky mosquitoes) in July and early August, and perfect conditions in September; (503)549-2111.

the best value of the traditional-motel bunch ($35 and up). Most of the well-heated rooms are far enough off the highway that traffic noise isn't a problem. There's a small indoor pool and Jacuzzi for après-ski warm-ups, and enough TV channels to satisfy the addicted.

Wallowas & the Blue Mountains

The high desert of northeastern Oregon ends east of the round-'em-up town of Pendleton. From here, ascend into either the piney Blue Mountains or the alpine terrain of the Wallowas. These are two very different mountain ranges settled into the same blue-sky corner of the state.

The high and dry Blues, once rich in gold and timber, are now littered with ghost towns, dilapidated hot-springs resorts, and lots of wide-open valleys where hunters, hikers, fishermen, horseback riders, snowmobilers, and a slowly increasing number of cross-country skiers like to set up camp and lasso a good time.

The peaks of the Wallowas reach even higher than the Blues and are topped by the Eagle Cap Wilderness, where the mountain timber terrain turns rocky and alpine. Natural features such as glistening Wallowa Lake, at the base of the Wallowa Whitman National Forest, and awesome Hells Canyon, the continent's deepest gorge, on the east side of the range, have kept the looming ghosts at bay. Indeed, it is quiet here. Even in the height of summer, you may hear locals lamenting that there are never enough people around.

ON THE ROAD

Pendleton, equidistant from Portland, Seattle, and Boise, is the hub of northeastern Oregon. The home of the Pendleton Roundup has become almost synonymous with saddles and wool. Hamley's Saddlery (30 SE Court Street, Pendleton; (503)276-2321) is practically a local shrine—kind of an L.L. Bean of the West. They've been selling Western clothing, boots, hats, tack items, and custom-made saddles since 1883. Pendleton Woolen Mills (1307 SE Court Place, Pendleton; (503)276-6911), makers of the nationally known Pendleton Wools, gives tours Monday through Friday and sells woolen yardage and imperfect (but still warm) blankets at reduced prices. The town of Pendleton is also a key point on the historic **Oregon Trail**, which recently celebrated its 150th anniversary.

Midway between Pendleton and Baker City is **La Grande**, the gateway to the Wallowas. One of the liveliest eateries in town is Mamacita's (110 Depot Street, La Grande; (503)963-6223), which serves Mexican fare. Linger over a book and a cup of java at the Sunflower Cafe and Bookstore (1114 Washington Avenue, La Grande; (503)963-5242).

From here, you'll want to drive east on Route 82 into the magical **Wallowas**. At the end of the road is the town of Joseph, the ancestral home of the Nez Percé leader Chief Joseph. Wallowa Lake State Park, on the edge of the Wallowa Whitman National Forest and the Eagle Cap Wilderness, has ample room for all who wish to explore it—even in midsummer, when the pristine lake and its shores are buzzing with go-carts, sailboats, and wind surfers. The majestic mountains, just an arm's length away, remain essentially unpeopled.

A dinner at Vali's Alpine Deli (59811 Wallowa Lake Highway, Joseph; (503)432-5691) usually requires reservations and always requires a big appetite. The food is Hungarian and German (the wiener schnitzels are exceptional). At breakfast, Maggie Vali's housemade sweet doughnuts are a local legend.

Ride the Wallowa Lake Tramway up a steep ascent to the top of 8,200-foot Mount Howard, which has spectacular overlooks and a couple of miles of hiking trails; (503)432-5331. One of the best ways to explore the lake-laden Eagle Cap Wilderness is on foot, letting smiling llamas lug your gear (it's a long way into the wilderness area). Reserve a space with Hurricane Creek Llama; (503)432-4455 or (800)528-9609.

When snow falls in the Wallowas, it's light, dry, and plentiful. There are miles and miles of quiet cross-country trails throughout the lovely highlands. Backcountry **skiers** seeking the best of the Wallowa winterland might want to check out the powder-bound tours with Wallowa Alpine Huts (you stay in spartan tents and dine in a yurt); (208)882-1955.

The continent's deepest gorge, **Hells Canyon**, is 35 miles east of Joseph. It's an awesome trench cut through sheer lava walls by the Snake River. The best view is from Hat Point near Imnaha, although you'll find McGraw Lookout more accessible than Hat Point if you don't have four-wheel drive. In summer, you can drive the dirt-road shortcut from Joseph to Oxbow (Highway 82 to Forest Road 39). Maps of the region's roads and trails, as well as information on conditions, are available at the Wallowa Valley Ranger District in Joseph, (503)426-4978, or at the Forest Service office just outside Halfway, (503)742-7511.

Between the steep cliffs of Hells Canyon and the southern slopes of the Wallowas is **Halfway**. It's a quiet town, the centerpiece of Pine Valley, with a few good restaurants and a couple of bed and breakfasts.

For those who would rather experience the river up close, river trips down Hells Canyon begin at Oxbow Dam, 16 miles east of Halfway. Hells Canyon Adventures in Oxbow arranges jet-boat tours or float-and-horseback combination excursions leaving from the Hells Canyon Dam; (503)785-3352.

Between the Wallowas and the Elkhorns, **Baker City** makes a good base camp for forays into the **Blue Mountains**. The 100-mile scenic Elkhorn Loop, west of Baker, winds by numerous ghost towns, which once boomed with people reaping the area's timber and gold. There's not much left of either these days, and most of the towns are skeletal

Pendleton Roundup

Each September the Pendleton Roundup rolls into town. It's a big event that features a dandy rodeo; call (800)524-2984 for tickets and information. Unfortunately, the roundup has become so popular that the expensive lodgings jack up their prices for the second week in September. Your best bet (if you neglected to make reservations a year in advance) is to look for a motel on the outskirts of town. Try the motels on the east side (the farthest from the Portland and Seattle traffic), and check with the Pioneer Motel (1807 SE Court Street, Pendleton; (503)276-4521). If you're coming from the west and spy a vacancy at the 7 Inn (Exit 202 off I-84; (503)276-4711), book it. You're not far from Pendleton. You want cheap? The *cheapest* is the Let'er Buck Motel (205 SE Dorion Avenue, Pendleton; (503)276-3293), near the rodeo grounds.

remains, having been ravaged by fire or abandoned in despair once the natural resources were depleted.

The most accessible (and the most active) ghost town is **Sumpter**, destroyed by a fire and subsequently abandoned in 1917. The valley, dredged for gold three times, remains scarred with piles of very clean rocks. The last dredge machine (which cost $300,000 and mined $4.5 million worth of gold) still stands on the west side of town. The town has begun to perk up a bit lately; there are now a couple of places to eat. We favor One-Eyed Charlie's (175 Mill Street, Sumpter; (503)894-2245), where you can chow down on home-style fixings.

Pick your way around the loop. Stop by Granite (population 8), which has a general store that doubles as the local tavern, eatery, and post stop. Fall elk-hunting season is big around here. Even less populated (zero) is Whitney, where 150 people once lived in the wide-open Whitney Valley until the train stopped coming in 1947.

Although the gold may have dwindled, the abundance of snow in these mountains now attracts a whole new kind of prospector. Snowmobilers charge in to explore the 500 miles of groomed snow-mo trails. Cross-country skiers are gaining status here too, with a few skier-only trails sprouting up. Tucked away in the middle of the Blues is a one-lift ski area that has a surprisingly glittering reputation among powder hounds. You're deceptively high here. The base at **Anthony Lakes Ski Area** is above the 7,000-foot level. That translates into powder—and lots of lightness. There's been talk about opening up more ski terrain. Trouble is, it's 300 miles from Portland and even farther from Seattle. (No problem, say Pendletonites.) It's a long way to the closest accommodations, but with some prearranging, ski groups can camp out in the day lodge (for a small charge); (503)963-4599 or (503)856-3277.

A number of natural hot springs bubble up in this part of Oregon. Many, such as Hot Lake, Ritter, and Medical Springs, were originally developed for medicinal purposes but have long since been forgotten and are now dilapidated. **Lehman Hot Springs** (PO Box 263, Ukiah, OR 97880; (503)427-3015), just east of Ukiah, is the only one officially open to the public. Basic A-frames are available for overnight stays in this remote territory.

John Day is in the middle of dry cattle country. The **Kah Wah Chung and Company Museum** (adjacent to the city park; no phone), open May through October, is a good stop if you're in the area. The museum includes an 1887 opium den (John Day served as a center for the Chinese community in Eastern Oregon until the early 1940s). The only other thing to do in town is to visit the **John Day Fossil Beds**; (503)575-0721. The beds lie in three distinct groupings: the banded

Painted Hills, extremely ancient fossils, and fascinating geological layers. They're a good half hour west of John Day. Drop by 420 W Main Street for maps and brochures.

CHEAP SLEEPS

Hells Canyon Bed and Breakfast
PO Box 159, Oxbow, OR 97840 • (503)785-3352 or (800)422-3568

Now owned by Doris and Brett Armacost (previously the B&B was known as Dixie's and was owned by Dixie Taylor and Gary Armacost, Brett's brother), this place offers the best location for those wishing to launch a trip down Hells Canyon. There are five rooms ($45 for two), and jet-boat and raft trips are available for river adventurers.

Clear Creek Farm
Route 1, Box 138, Halfway, OR 97834 • (503)742-2238

Owners Matt and Denise Phillips stayed here as guests in 1989 and fell in love with the place. Four years later, they bought it. Open during the warmer months (May through September), Clear Creek is quirky but paradisiacal, with four homey bedrooms in the farmhouse and two board-and-batten cabins—perfect for small groups. There are several ponds for swimming, a field of lavender, a fragrant herb and vegetable garden, and an orchard filled with fruit trees. Bring your friends; group rates are even cheaper—and they've got a new hot tub that'll soak 10.

Chandler's—Bed, Bread, and Trail Inn
700 S Main Street (PO Box 639), Joseph, OR 97846
(503)432-9765 or (800)452-3781

Ethel and Jim Chandler's comfy bed and breakfast resembles an alpine ski lodge—cedar shingles, multiangled roof lines, and plush wall-to-wall carpets. A log staircase climbs from the comfortable living rooms to a loft where five simple bedrooms share three baths, a sitting room, and a kitchenette. The substantial breakfast and knowledgeable hosts make this a wonderful stopover for area explorers. Closed in November.

Best Western Sunridge Inn
1 Sunridge Lane, Baker, OR 97814 • (503)523-6444

A sprawling Best Western, this is the best of the lodgings in town, with 124 comfortable, spacious, air-conditioned rooms and an attractive pine finish. In the hot summer, you'll appreciate the grassy courtyard and pool area. Come winter, move indoors to the 18-foot whirlpool.

Powder River Bed and Breakfast
HCR 87, Box 500, Baker, OR 97814 • (503)523-7143

Part tackle company, part bass-fishing guide service, part color analysis, part bed and breakfast. You gotta hand it to anyone who can make a living out in these parts. Campers and trailers (but no hookups) pull in here during the summer to accompany Phil Simonski on his fishing trips. When the snow falls, the Simonskis' two extra rooms are the closest accommodations to Anthony Lakes Ski Area (still 40 minutes away).

Sumpter Bed and Breakfast
344 NE Columbia Street, Sumpter, OR 97877 • (503)894-2229

The town's former hospital is now taking good care of travelers. Though it may look a bit rickety from the outside, inside it's a comfortable put-your-feet-up kind of place. In the living room, heated by a big barrel-like wood stove, you'll find plenty of reading material on local gold lore. The rooms upstairs are charmingly simple; the shower is shared. Owners Joy and Gerry Myers recently fixed up the back part of the building, adding two more rooms and a second bath.

Fireside Lodge
PO Box 712, Prairie City, OR 97869 • (503)820-4677

At the Western bar adjacent to these lodgings, big Western belt buckles and pointy cowboy boots swing on the huge dance floor. (You could probably fit the whole town of Prairie City in the place.) Owner George Stevenson reopens the bar for meals (wake up to breakfast at 5am?), and lodgers stay in one of six tiny campers' cabins out back.

Dreamer's Lodge
144 N Canyon Boulevard, John Day, OR 97845 • (503)575-0526

Although this is not the stuff dreams are made of, you'll sleep just fine here knowing that you paid about $40 for your room. Lava rocks decorate the roof, and '50s-style furnishings fill each of the 24 rooms. The two-story motel is located half a block north of the only stoplight in the county.

Malheur Bird Refuge & Steens Mountain

The lovely thing about southeastern Oregon is that there's a lot to look at and not much to buy, except gas (and you should buy it in Burns). Yes, this is sage land—dry, desolate cattle country—branded on the American consciousness by hundreds of Western movies.

But suddenly, just south of Burns, the geography changes dramatically. The tumbleweed terrain is transformed into verdant marshlands that surround Harney and Malheur lakes, marshes that are a vital stop for migrating birds. Beyond the lakes, massive Steens Mountain rises abruptly to almost 10,000 feet. East of this formidable escarpment, nothing remains of the former Alvord Lake except a vast wasteland of sun-bleached borax.

ON THE ROAD

Malheur National Wildlife Refuge, 37 miles south of Burns, is one of the major bird refuges in the United States—184,000 acres of marshland and lakes. It is an important stop for migrating waterfowl in spring and fall, and is the breeding ground for magnificent sandhill cranes (with wingspans approaching 100 inches), trumpeter swans, and many other water birds, shorebirds, and songbirds. We recommend visiting in April, when you can experience the sandhill's courtship dance. A migratory festival in early April provides tours, entertainment, and informational exhibits. Call the ranger station in Hines for information; (503)573-7292.

You can drive through the refuge, although it's more rewarding to see it on foot or by mountain bike. Make your first stop Malheur's free museum, just inside the refuge. The museum is open year-round and provides an excellent primer on the birds that frequent the refuge; (503)493-2612. Bring your binoculars.

On the south end of the refuge is the beautiful little town of **Frenchglen** (population 10). The Frenchglen Hotel is the only place to eat for miles and, even so, it's closed three months of the year (see listing under "Cheap Sleeps"). Frenchglen's biggest attraction is **Steens Mountain**, the world's largest block fault, created by volcanic lava flows and glacial action. The massive mountain rises gently from the west to an elevation of 9,670 feet, and then drops sharply to the white borax expanses of the **Alvord Desert** in the east.

During the summer and early fall, a dirt road climbs almost all the way to the summit. The road stops a half mile short of the top, but the short hike is worth the small effort. The road completes a 67-mile loop that starts and ends at Frenchglen. It's a slow drive, so pack a picnic (or stop at the Frenchglen Hotel and ask them to pack one for you), and plan for an all-day excursion. Four-wheel-drive vehicles are recommended but not vital.

En route around Steens Mountain, look for **Alvord Hot Springs**, located about 100 yards east of the road in the Alvord Desert. The springs are on the private property of the Alvord Ranch, but they're open to the respectful public. At the northeastern side of Steens, Mann Lake is reportedly loaded with Lahottan cutthroat trout. For more information on Steens, contact the Bureau of Land Management (HC 74-12533, Highway 20, Hines, OR 97738; (503)573-5241).

CHEAP SLEEPS

Best Western Ponderosa
Highway 20, 577 W Monroe Street, Burns, OR 97720 • (503)573-2047

Blessed with a swimming pool to cool you off after a hot day's drive, the Ponderosa might be the best motel in this part of the state (it's virtually the only one, too). Burns is the closest sizable town to the Malheur

Wildlife Refuge. Pets are welcome; prices for two start at $40 (and peak at $50, for an executive suite with its own living room).

Malheur Field Station
HC-72, Box 260, Princeton, OR 97721 • (503)493-2629

Call ahead for a reservation at the field station in the Malheur National Wildlife Refuge, since schools and conferences sometimes fill the place. Bunks in the dorm rooms are for rent ($13 per person), although the nine two- and three-bedroom trailers ($26 for two) are more accommodating. The trailers provide comfortable living spaces with fully equipped kitchens (bring your own bedding). The dining room's a great bargain: two bits more than five bucks buys a breakfast that's not for the birds, a little less buys a sack lunch, and a little more fills you at dinner. The dining room is closed October through March, but the station is open to overnighters all year.

Diamond Hotel
PO Box 10, Diamond, OR 97722 • (503)493-1898

Twelve miles east of Highway 207, Diamond's handful of residents keeps the ghosts at bay. In 1991, Judy and Jerry Santillie, formerly of the Frenchglen Hotel, remodeled this building and opened it to those exploring Malheur territory. It now quintuples as hotel, general store, deli, post office, and—late in the afternoon—local watering hole. The five small bedrooms upstairs ($45) share two baths and two sitting areas. Dinners could satisfy any ranch hand (but they're available only to hotel guests). Come early and have a family-style meal that may include potatoes, green vegetables, salad, bread, and all the tenderloin you can possibly eat. If you miss the 6:30pm seating, you can always get a nibble (and save some money) at 7:30pm, when the Santillies serve a smaller dinner of salad and soup or maybe a stew. Open March through October.

Frenchglen Hotel
General Delivery, Frenchglen, OR 97736 • (503)493-2825

This small, white-framed building that dates back to 1916 is owned by the Oregon Parks Department State Wayside System. The historic inn has eight small, plain bedrooms upstairs with shared baths, renting for just over $40 a night; room 2 is the largest ($48), with a full and twin bed. Nothing's very square or level here, and that's part of the charm. Downstairs you'll find a large, screened verandah and the dining room. Manager John Ross prepares good, simple meals for guests and drop-by visitors. The ranch-style dinner ($10–$15) has only one seating (6:30pm sharp), and reservations are a must. Closed mid-November through February.

WASHINGTON

Seattle

Puget Sound

San Juan Islands

Olympic Peninsula & the Pacific Coast

Long Beach Peninsula & Willapa Bay

The North Cascades

The South Cascades

Columbia River Gorge & Mount Adams

Lake Chelan

The Methow Valley

Yakima Valley & Beyond

Spokane & the Palouse

Seattle

Here's a city that is both proud of and a little smug about the attention it continues to receive. The boom in the past decade belies what both natives and transplants try to keep as quiet as possible: Seattle's quality of life remains very good.

Here's a city that prides itself on cultural richness and ethnic diversity, comfortable neighborhoods and open, green spaces. A city whose theater, dance, opera, sports, and music enjoy increasing national attention, and whose inhabitants—a friendly and hardy set—exhibit a spirit not readily dampened by the fine Northwest mist. Here's a city whose major tourist attraction—the Pike Place Market—is less for tourists than it is for locals, and where a diverse nightclub scene, offering everything from grunge to R&B to country-and-western, has grown considerably over the past few years (though you'd still never mistake it for New York).

Most of all, here's a city enhanced by its proximity to all things wild and wonderful—mountains on two sides and glimmering Puget Sound in between. Bask in a late summer evening's view—the sky turquoise and glowing orange, the Olympic Mountains casting a stark, sapphire shadow against the horizon, and a night-lit ferry heading west. You'll understand what attracts people here for vacations—and for good.

ON THE ROAD

Downtown Seattle is a good place to begin your exploration of the city. The downtown core is bookended by two of the city's favorite attractions, Pioneer Square and Pike Place Market. In the retail core, between Third and Sixth avenues from Stewart Street to University Street, you'll find plenty of department stores and boutiques for window shopping. At the glossy, centrally located mall known as Westlake Center (Pine Street between Fourth and Fifth avenues), upscale shops share space with a food court chock full of cheap eats.

Pioneer Square, to the south, has some of Seattle's oldest architecture, built after the fire of 1889 leveled the city. Six bucks buys you an underground tour complete with corny humor and historical insights. When downtown Seattle began to move northward, Pioneer Square acquired an artsy bent, housing galleries, artist studios, and the famous Elliott Bay Book Company (101 S Main Street, Seattle; (206)624-6600), where free readings are held nearly every day (call the bookstore for a schedule). On the first Thursday of each month, art galleries stay open late to preview new exhibits in a free see-and-be-seen scene known (appropriately enough) as First Thursday.

A small but genuine slice of Asian culture, the **International District** is home to a number of Chinese, Japanese, Thai, Vietnamese, Philippine, and Cambodian businesses and restaurants, a good number of them reasonably priced. For a history of Asian immigration to the United States, including photographs and a reconstructed vintage Chinese pharmacy, visit the Wing Luke Museum (407 7th Avenue S, Seattle; (206)623-5124); admission is $2.50 (free on Thursdays). The International District is also a gold mine for all manner of cheap, excellent Asian food. Locals prefer Huong Binh (1207 S Jackson Street, Seattle; (206)720-4907) for lovely, fresh Vietnamese food and King Cafe (723 S King Street, Seattle; (206)622-6373) for great dim sum (though it's short on atmosphere). The squat gray Kingdome watches over the International District and south Seattle (known optimistically as SoDo, or South of the Dome) like a giant clam. The Kingdome is the venue for the popular Seahawks and the Mariners; tours ($3) take you up to the highest seating level, the scoreboard, the VIP lounge, the press area, and the Royal Brougham Sports Museum; (206)296-3126.

At the north end of the downtown area, **Pike Place Market** attracts throngs of visitors in the summer and a steady stream of local devotees throughout the year. Seattleites shop the produce stands and specialty food stores as one would shop in Europe, buying meat from the

Ferry to Bainbridge Island

Riding a ferry is the best way to appreciate the sea breeze, Seattle's skyline, and the grandeur of Puget Sound and its surrounding mountain ranges. Ferries leave regularly from Pier 52 (Alaskan Way and Marion Street) to Bainbridge Island (Washington State Ferries; (206)464-6400). The island's only town, Winslow, is an easy walk from the ferry dock. Depending on the time of day, you can linger over coffee at the estimable home branch of Pegasus Espresso (131 Parfitt Way SW, Bainbridge Island; (206)842-3113); brunch on waffles or salsa omelets at the steamy little Streamliner Diner (397 Winslow Way E, Bainbridge Island; (206)842-8595); sample the wines from Bainbridge Island Winery (682 Highway 305, Bainbridge Island; (206)842-WINE); or imbibe a microbrew at the island's favorite pub, The Harbour Public House (231 Parfitt Way, Bainbridge Island; (206)842-0969).

With a little more time, take your bike (or car) and explore a bit more thoroughly. Look for **Fay Bainbridge State Park** on the island's northeast corner, with a vast view of Seattle from the beach (there are about 25 tent sites here too); **Fort Ward**, a prime spot for hikes and picnics; and **Bloedel Reserve**, a 150-acre parklike estate (reservations essential; (206)842-7631).

butcher shop, fruit and vegetables from the produce stands, and bread from the bakery. Craftspeople—from jewelers and quilters to T-shirt and souvenir-photo vendors—fill the other stalls, attracting the most tourists and causing the greatest traffic problems in the summer (real Seattleites don't drive through the market). Pick up a self-guided tour pamphlet at the information booth at First Avenue and Pike Street; (206)682-7453.

Ethnic and other culinary traditions converge at the market, from the popular Mexican take-out window, Burrito Express (First Avenue and Pike Street, Seattle; (206)467-8267), to the fresh bivalves at Emmett Watson's Oyster Bar (Pike Place Market, Seattle; (206)448-7721), or the funky, modern vegetarian fare at the nearby Gravity Bar (113 Virginia Street, Seattle; (206)448-8826). New enterprises that have taken hold in the market and quickly become favorites include Piroshky Piroshky (Pike Place Market, Seattle; (206)441-6068) and the Incredible Link (1511 Pike Place Market, Seattle; (206)622-8002). But half the fun of the eats in the market area is discovering them yourself, so go with a growling stomach and follow your nose.

Just north and slightly east of the market is the neighborhood-in-progress known as Belltown. The streets are in various stages of development, promising slick new residences and upscale stores, but you can still find little pockets of **vintage Belltown**, the haunt of artists, musicians, and actors. There are lots of used-clothing stores (where the real "Seattle look" comes from) and great little cafes that come and go too fast to keep up with them all, though you should try the exceptional Macrina Bakery and Cafe, at 2408 1st Avenue, Seattle; (206)448-4032.

Despite Seattle's relentless gentrification, Belltown retains a natural mix of real people, many of whom converge at the Two Bells Tavern (2313 4th Avenue, Seattle; (206)441-3050) for some of the city's best burgers, good beer, and often excellent music. The ruthlessly hip crowd gathers at the Crocodile Cafe (2200 2nd Avenue, Seattle; (206)448-2114) for some of the music that has turned the country's ears toward Seattle, as well as food and drinks in the atmospheric bar. On weekends, the Croc is packed with scene-makers and hangers-on. Finally, the cafe/art space/laundromat Sit & Spin (2219 4th Avenue, Seattle; (206)441-9484) has garnered far-ranging media attention; it may be the hippest spot to do your laundry in the known universe. A load there isn't particularly cheap (a buck a wash), but you can nibble on a snack or play a game while you wait.

Lake Union, the body of fresh water connected to Puget Sound at the Hiram M. Chittenden Locks (where errant sea lions are known to feast during the salmon runs), is *the* spot for water recreation, drawing kayakers, sailors, canoeists, and others who rent traditional wooden vessels from the Center for Wooden Boats (1010 Valley Street, Seattle; (206)382-2628). This museum harbors an eclectic collection of boats; wandering is free, and rentals don't cost much. From the water you'll find the best views of the houseboats along Fairview Avenue E (on the east side of the lake) and on the south side of the Fremont Bridge.

Visit the locks, at the west arm of Lake Union (there's a pretty park and a garden that flowers all year long), or paddle over to the east arm, through Portage Bay and the Montlake Cut, and enter the **Washington**

Tower of Visual Power

Instead of forking out six bucks to ride to the top of the Space Needle, take in the excellent 360-degree view from the top of the water tower in Volunteer Park (15th Avenue E and E Prospect Street). All it costs you is a (long) walk up the stairs.

Summer Festivals

Summer begins and ends in Seattle with two of the area's best festivals, both held at Seattle Center. The free **Northwest Folklife Festival**, held on Memorial Day weekend, brings diverse folk-art traditions (dance, music, crafts, and food) to Seattle. It's the largest folk festival in the nation; (206)684-7300. **Bumbershoot**, held on Labor Day weekend, includes many of the same street performers you'll see at Folklife. This multiarts festival has a considerably more frenzied feel, however, perhaps because of the plethora of local and national musicians who perform simultaneously during the four-day event (Joan Baez, Bonnie Raitt, and Jackson Browne were some recent headliners). Bumbershoot is free on Friday; tickets are $9 per day ($1 for kids and seniors) throughout the rest of the weekend. Call (206)682-4FUN for information.

Park Arboretum. Foster Island is a great place for a picnic and bird watching (but beware the hungry, uninhibited ducks and geese). If you're starting at the Arboretum, rent a canoe from the University of Washington Waterfront Activities Center, behind Husky Stadium, for $3.50 per hour; (206)543-9433.

Try to time your visit to the Arboretum's 200-acre preserve to coincide with the blooming of the azaleas in the spring. Meet at the Arboretum Visitor Center (these folks know their plants!) for free tours on Sundays and for other information about the park (2300 Arboretum Drive E, Seattle; (206)543-8800). The quiet **Japanese Garden** ($2) has a pagoda, a carp pond, and a teahouse; (206)684-4725. Spring cherry blossoms explode on the nearby campus of the University of Washington (UW, pronounced "U-Dub"). The parklike, accessible campus makes for a lovely stroll. On clear days, look for Mount Rainier at the end of Rainier Vista.

North of the University District, a series of parks winds from Ravenna to Greenwood. Ravenna Park extends to **Green Lake** along a grassy boulevard popular with joggers and dogs. The paths around Green Lake, though overpopulated with runners, bikers, roller bladers, and strollers, are still a fine place to exercise your right to exercise. Roller blades and bikes are available at Gregg's Greenlake Cycle (7007 Woodlawn Avenue NE, Seattle; (206)523-1822)—you can't beat it for convenience. Green Lake is also appropriate for simply sitting under a tree and watching the world skate by. To refresh after your run/walk/skate/bike, stop in at Ed's Juice and Java (7907 Wallingford Avenue N,

---

Cinema City

Seattleites have acquired a reputation as serious film buffs. It's no wonder, then, that the city's film festivals garner considerable national attention as well as enthusiastic local support. The Seattle International Film Festival (various locations; (206)324-9996) has been bringing an impressively wide range of movies to town since 1976. The International Festival of Films by Women Directors (various locations; (206)621-2231), despite its growing popularity, is still an intimate event, featuring thought-provoking films and talks by nationally and internationally acclaimed directors.

Seattle; (206)524-7570), one of the best of the many juice bars springing up all over the city. Ed's a personality, and his juice concoctions are very good.

The **Woodland Park Zoo**, next to Green Lake, is for the most part wonderfully open, providing animals enough room to dispel the caged-cat atmosphere. Elephants wander a replica of a Thai logging camp, while lions (not always visible) roam a modified African savannah (the antelopes and giraffes, thankfully, have their own area). Don't miss the gorillas; (206)684-4800.

Cyclists are as common as rain in Seattle. On the third Sunday and first Saturday of the month from May to September, the winding Lake Washington Boulevard is closed to traffic, and cyclists truly own the road. Take the Lake Washington Boulevard-Lakeside Avenue connection south to Seward Park; you'll definitely feel as if you're far away from the city. Two-wheel fans also enjoy the Burke-Gilman Trail (more so than crowded Green Lake) for a long ride from the Fremont neighborhood, along the top of Lake Union, through the University District, and up and over the north end of Lake Washington. The newly connected Sammamish River Trail takes you to one of Western Washington's favorite wineries, Chateau Ste. Michelle (14111 NE 145th Street, Woodinville; (206)488-4633).

Other **favorite parks** in the city include Golden Gardens and the Shilshole Marina, just north of Ballard, with its beach, marina view, and easy access to good, greasy fish 'n' chips at Gordo's (6226 Seaview Avenue NW, Seattle; (206)784-7333), which serves good milkshakes too. To the south, Discovery Park in the Magnolia neighborhood offers a bit of wildlife in the city, providing a home for a couple of bald eagles as well as goldfinches, red-tailed hawks, and various falcons. Take one

Cheap Tix

Discounted theater tickets for all but the most popular Seattle shows are pretty easy to come by. Ticket/Ticket, in Pike Place Market (near the brass pig) and the Broadway Market (401 Broadway E, Seattle; (206)324-2744), offers same-day tickets for half price (both outlets are open Tuesday through Sunday). Many local theaters offer discounted preview tickets, decent matinee prices, and "rush" (day of show) tickets; some have special pay-what-you-will performances (Bathhouse Theatre, Empty Space Theatre, and New City Theater come to mind).

Theatresports, the brand of improvisational theater practiced at the Market Theater (1429 Post Alley, Seattle; (206)781-9273), makes for one of the funniest—and certainly one of the most unpredictable—productions in town; Friday and Saturday at 10:30pm ($7) and Sunday at 7pm ($5). Another good bet in the summer is the Brown Bag Theatre, (206)343-7328, which offers free lunchtime performances at various outdoor locations throughout Seattle (mostly downtown).

of the trails winding through the park, go on an interpretive nature walk, or explore the remnants of Fort Lawton (a barracks house and training field), Discovery Park's former incarnation. On Lake Washington, Magnuson Park, neighbor to the National Oceanic and Atmospheric Administration (NOAA), has a beach walk lined with sculptures that interact with the environment in different ways—for example, the *Sound Garden* is composed of fluted chimes that use the wind as an artistic medium.

Art and culture lovers won't feel deprived in Seattle. The downtown Seattle Art Museum (100 University Street, Seattle; (206)654-3100) is free the first Tuesday of every month. Stop by to see its highly original architecture and the fantastic African mask exhibit. The newly opened Seattle Asian Art Museum, in Volunteer Park (14th Avenue E and E Prospect Street), has one of the most extraordinary collections of Asian art in the country. (If used within two days, your admission ticket from either of the two Seattle art museums is good for free admission at the other.)

Visit the Burke Museum (NE 45th Street and 17th Avenue NE, Seattle; (206)543-5590) on the UW campus for natural history and archaeology exhibits; admission varies, topping out at $3. The Museum of History and Industry (2700 24th Avenue E, Seattle; (206)324-1125) chronicles the growth of the Northwest through artifacts and memorabilia; it's free on Tuesdays. At the Museum of Flight (9404 E Marginal Way, Seattle; (206)764-5720), you can follow the area's airborne history and contrast a replica of the Wright brothers' original glider with the planes taking off and landing in Boeing Field, on either side of the museum's glass-walled exhibit hall. Admission is $6.

Movies are just two bucks at the Crest (16505 5th Avenue NE, Seattle; (206)363-6338) and the United Artists Cinema 150 (6th Avenue and Blanchard Street, Seattle; (206)443-9591).

As for **cheap eats**, try a bounteous breakfast at the Hi-Spot (1410 34th Avenue, Seattle; (206)325-7905), the Western Coffee Shop (911½ Western Avenue, Seattle; (206)682-5001), or Benny Lyle's (1801 N 34th Street, Seattle; (206)633-4595), where the breakfast tacos are an absolute steal. Seattle's diverse ethnic population has given birth to such moderately priced gems as Kabul (2301 N 45th Street, Seattle; (206)545-9000) for Afghan eats, Phnom Penh (414 Maynard Avenue S, Seattle; (206)682-5690) for Cambodian noodles, and Axum (4142 Brooklyn Avenue NE, Seattle; (206)547-6848) for an Ethiopian feast—to name some of the most exotic. But this is just the tip of the culinary iceberg. And, of course, there's always Dick's (various locations), Seattle's classic cheap burger joint; a full dinner here won't run you much more than a fiver.

Fans of **brews and microbrews** will find plenty of the hoppy stuff around. The area's commercial baby, Rainier Beer (the place you can smell if you approach the city from the south), offers free brewery tours Monday through Saturday, which include taste testing in the taproom (3100 Airport Way S, Seattle; (206)622-2600). Red Hook (3400 Phinney Avenue N, Seattle; (206)548-8000), a local favorite, opens its brewery to the public every day for tours. Younger and older folks peacefully coexist at the brewery's appealing, smokefree Trolleyman Pub next door. Seattle has a number of independent brew pubs, including the Big Time Brewery and Ale House in the University District (4133 University Way NE, Seattle; (206)545-4509), which offers fun sandwiches as an accompaniment, and the Pacific Northwest Brewing Company in Pioneer Square (322 Occidental Avenue S, Seattle; (206)621-7002).

For a thorough guide to what's going on around town, pick up a copy of *The Stranger*, a free alternative paper focusing on the arts and music scene and geared toward the twentysomething crowd, or *Seattle Weekly*, a more mainstream paper covering the arts and local politics, available for 75 cents.

CHEAP SLEEPS

The College Inn Guest House

4000 University Way NE, Seattle, WA 98105 • (206)633-4441

Wood trim, window seats, antiques, and pastel comforters create a cozy if somewhat spartan atmosphere in this hospitable inn designed along the lines of a European pension. Housed in a renovated 1909 Tudor building, it's in the heart of the lively University District, with a cafe and rathskeller (be warned: late-night noise travels quite readily into rooms on the west side). Each room has a sink but no toilet, TV, radio, or phone. For the musically inclined, there's an upright piano in room 305. Bathrooms reminiscent of a college dorm, with rows of showers and plenty of cold tiles (but clean at that), are found at the end of each hall. A living room is tucked away on the fourth floor, where a generous continental breakfast is served.

Green Tortoise Backpackers Guest House

715 2nd Avenue N, Seattle, WA 98109 • (206)322-1222

This Queen Anne neighborhood hostel, located in a 100-year-old Victorian just three blocks north of the Space Needle (and the rest of Seattle Center) offers a variety of accommodations. Dorm-style rooms are $11 ($12 for a room with a bath in it); a "shared double," perfect for couples, is $18; and a "private double," available with advance reservations, sets you back a mere $30 (for the bath-down-the-hall version) or $35 (for one with private bath). The Tortoise has no curfew, and it does have kitchen and laundry facilities, a yard and garden, and an affiliation with the laid-back travel-adventure company of the same name that squires budget travelers around the nation by bus.

Inn at Queen Anne

505 1st Avenue N, Seattle, WA 98109 • (206)282-7357 or (206)282-7619

This reasonable find is tucked conveniently between Seattle Center and bustling lower Queen Anne. Formerly an apartment building, the Inn at Queen Anne is still home to some permanent residents, but it manages to avoid the usual pitfalls of such arrangements (loud music from permanent stereos and loud noise from the permanent friends of permanent residents). It's run by friendly, competent folks, and the rooms, though small, are equipped with nice kitchenettes and walk-in (well, a short walk) closets. A room for two is $65; stay a week and you're down to $60 a night. Stay a month, and the price plummets to $37 a night.

Seattle International Youth Hostel
84 Union Street, Seattle, WA 98101 • (206)622-5443

Seattle's no-nonsense, nonsmoking hostel offers the comforts of hostels the world over: a cheap bed ($14) and a communal kitchen. Off season, the dormitories (male/female) are available to non-AYH members for an additional $3; $5 more gains a private room. The rooms are closed from 11am to 4pm.

Vincent's Guest House
527 Malden Avenue E, Seattle, WA 98112 • (206)323-7849

At best, Vincent's looks like postcollegiate group housing—postered walls, bodies lounging everywhere (on the steps, in front of the TV). It's an AYH, but cheapies have lauded it for its unstructured atmosphere— less rigid than most hostels, with no required chores and no off hours (that is, hours you're required not to be there). Of course, hostels aren't for everyone. While one guest sighs nostalgically, "It reminds me of the hostels in Europe," another says simply, "It's livable." Dorm beds are $12; some private rooms available.

ACCESS

Metro, the city's bus line, goes almost anywhere. Call (206)553-3000 for rider information. The bus is free until 7pm in downtown's commercial core, which is bordered by the waterfront, Interstate 5, Jackson Street to the south, and Battery Street to the north. Otherwise the fare is 85 cents within the city ($1.10 during peak hours) and $1.10 if you cross the city lines ($1.60 peak).

Seattle-Tacoma International Airport is located 13 miles south of Seattle, barely a half-hour freeway ride from downtown. Several Metro buses go to Sea-Tac Airport: the #174 goes from Second Avenue in downtown Seattle to the airport every half hour (a 45-minute trip), and the #194 makes a half-hour trip to Sea-Tac from the downtown bus tunnel (also every half hour). The Gray Line Airport Express is also reasonable ($12 round trip, $7 one way) if you don't mind leaving from or being dropped off downtown; the shuttle stops every half hour at 10 downtown hotels. Shuttle Express picks you up or drops you off at your door for $16 in Seattle, $21 on the Eastside. Reservations are a must for departures and are a good idea for arrivals, too; (206)622-1424 or (800)942-0711. Capital Aeroporter provides service to and from both Tacoma and Olympia; (206)754-7113.

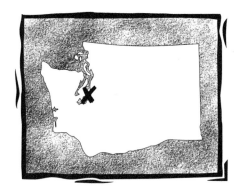

Puget Sound

P uget Sound, which cuts a 100-mile-long swath between the Olympic and Cascade mountain ranges, is dotted with hundreds of fir-covered islands, etched by a multitude of inlets, and trimmed with long stretches of sandy beaches and wind-twisted madrona trees. On clear days, the jagged blue outlines of the Cascades and Olympics, topped by the summits of Mount Baker and Mount Rainier, frame the Sound's shimmering waters. From a handful of places, you can see the whole panorama in one graceful, stirring, 360-degree turn.

Two hundred years after Captain George Vancouver poked around the waters of Puget Sound, the area has been transformed (some would say ravaged) by the industry of those who followed. No fewer than nine major cities thrive off the riches of these waters. With I-5 tracing the Sound from the Canadian border to Olympia, too many travelers speed from city to city, missing the area's many delights. Seattle, the centerpiece city on Puget Sound, is beginning to touch the outer boundaries of Everett to the north and tickle the fringes of Tacoma to the south. But a number of cities around the Sound still march to a small-town drum.

ON THE ROAD

State Highway 9 ambles from the Canadian border at Sumas to Snohomish, as nice a country two-lane jaunt as you'll ever find (and a perfect alternative to the interstate). The route skirts six pretty little lakes, meanders the country wilds, and forges into the heart of timber country—with plenty of spots along the way for a picnic.

Three miles south of the Canadian border, off Highway 13, is **Lynden**, a picture-perfect, neat and tidy community sporting immaculate yards and colorful gardens lining the shady avenue into downtown. The town has adopted a Dutch theme (slightly overdone) in tribute to a community of early inhabitants. Visit the Lynden Pioneer Museum (217 W Front Street, Lynden; (360)354-3675) to see one of the best collections of antique vehicles and farm machinery anywhere. The museum also contains representations of historic rooms and businesses, a print shop, a barbershop, and a department store circa 1920. The curator can arrange to open the collections of privately donated Haida Indian artifacts. Two miles south of town is a direct ticket back to, say, 1962—the Lunchbucket (880 East Pole Road, Lynden; (360)354-3360), with an $8 sirloin steak dinner and 13 kinds of housemade pie.

Situated near Blaine, the charming **Semiahmoo Public Park** is approached (somewhat awkwardly) through the Semiahmoo Resort. From its 1½ miles of sandspit beach (with picnic tables, fire pits, and good clam digging), you can practically reach out and touch Point Roberts and view the Canadian Gulf Islands farther west. The former cannery bunkhouses stand as an interpretive center that chronicles the history of the Northwest salmon fishery.

Fine architectural gems abound in Bellingham and at **Western Washington University** (WWU). An outdoor public art collection dots the campus of WWU. With the unique audio-phone tour, you can listen to artists talk about their own works (Western Gallery, Western Washington University, Bellingham; (360)650-3963 or (360)650-3000).

The **Whatcom Museum of History and Art** (121 Prospect Street, Bellingham; (360)676-6981), in the massive Romanesque Bellingham City Hall building, has an excellent Northwest Native American and Eskimo art exhibit, and pioneer photographs. The museum has expanded to the neighboring antique firehouse and the Arco Gallery (across the street), which features traveling exhibits. There's no admission, but donations are accepted.

The **Old Town** around W Holly and Commercial streets hosts antique and junk shops and some decent eateries, such as the ethnic hippie Old Town Cafe (316 W Holly Street, Bellingham; (360)671-4431), serving breakfast and lunch every day. Other inexpensive favorites include the Bagelry (1319 Railroad Avenue, Bellingham; (360)676-5288), with dense New York-style bagels; the jazzy Bluewater Bistro (1215½ Cornwall Avenue, Bellingham; (360)733-6762), with a delicious garlic burger; the tiny and popular Cafe Toulouse (114 W Magnolia Street, Bellingham; (360)733-8996), known for its inventive sandwiches on housemade bread; the soul-satisfying Vietnamese fare at La Patisserie (3098 Northwest Avenue, Bellingham; (360)671-3671); and the Colophon Cafe (1208 11th Street, Bellingham; (360)647-0092), in the best bookstore in town, with an incredible African peanut soup.

Bellingham's **Fairhaven**, the product of a short-lived railroad boom (1889–1893), has experienced a resurgence of life in its red-brick buildings and is worth exploring. The Marketplace, the grand dame and central figure among the attractive old buildings, was restored in 1988 and houses a number of interesting shops and dining options. The district is richly diverse, with craft galleries, coffeehouses, bookstores, a charming garden emporium, and a lively evening scene unique for Bellingham. The **Lake Whatcom Railway** (left over from the railway boom), near Wickersham on Highway 9, makes scenic summer runs using a working steam locomotive; (360)595-2218. An old electric railway is now a beautiful 5-mile-long **Interurban Trail** connecting Fairhaven, Arroyo, and Larrabee state parks at the north end of Chuckanut Drive. The trail is well used by runners, walkers, and mountain bikers.

The spectacular 20-mile **Chuckanut Drive**, from the rocky shoreline at the base of Bellingham's Chuckanut Mountain to the fertile Skagit flats (just north of Burlington), is one of the prettiest drives in the state. A narrow, winding road, it curves along the mountainside, with cliff-hanging views over the water and the San Juans. Aside from a couple of good restaurants, almost no commercial development spoils the route; however, there are a number of places to stop and admire. **Teddy Bear Cove**, a nudist beach and a pretty one at that, is just south of Bellingham. No signs—watch for the crowd of cars. **Larrabee State Park**, Washington's first state park, has beautiful sandstone sculptures along the beaches and cliffs. It also has good picnic areas and camping. A wonderful day hike leads you up to Lost Lake near the top of Chuckanut Mountain.

At the hairpin curve halfway down Chuckanut near Oyster Creek Inn, a white wooden gate opens onto a dirt road that leads steeply down to the creek. Once locked and forbidden, the **Chuckanut Drive Samish Bay Shellfish Farm** (188 Chuckanut Drive, Bow; (360)766-6002) now welcomes visitors. Park your car at the top and walk (an easy three-quarters of a mile) through the forest to the shellfish farm. Oysters

Ferry Rides

Getting around the Puget Sound area often involves riding a Washington State Ferry, and no activity better captures the spirit of the Sound than a ferry ride—both for commuters, who rely on them for transportation, and for sightseers, who ride them to enjoy the views. The Washington State Ferries system is the largest in the country (eight routes serve 20 terminals in Puget Sound). Your fare will be much cheaper, and you can be sure you'll catch the ferry you want, if you leave your car behind and walk on. Summer congestion means those with cars should arrive a few hours before the scheduled sailing. For schedule and route information, call (206)464-6400 or (800)843-3779.

(smoked, shucked, or in the shell), Dungeness crab, steamer clams, and sometimes scallops are for sale in the icy processing shed.

Whidbey Island now qualifies as the longest island in the United States, since New York's Long Island was declared a peninsula. Boasting pretty villages, viewpoint parks, sandy beaches, and some scenic, rolling farmland, Whidbey makes for a particularly nice family outing. The treacherous but beautiful **Deception Pass** at the north end of the island has a lovely, if often crowded, state park with 2,300 acres of prime camping land, forests, and beach. Strom's Shrimp Fountain and Grill (1480 Highway 20, just north of Deception Pass; (360)293-2531) sells fresh seafood and shrimp for your cookout. They also grill up a mean oyster burger to go. Or check out Kyoto Japanese Restaurant (9041 90th Street NW, Oak Harbor; (360)679-1433), where it's hard to spend more than $10 a person for simple Japanese fare. At Lucy's Mi Casita (1380 W Pioneer Way, Oak Harbor; (360)675-4800) savor housemade Mexican food in a hodgepodge atmosphere of cardboard flamenco dancers and beer-bottle-cap curtains.

Whidbey's flat, relatively untrafficked roads make for great **biking**. All Island Bicycles (302 N Maine Street, Coupeville; (360)678-3351) is a good place for bike rentals. A bike lane follows Engle Road 3 miles south of Coupeville to Fort Casey, a decommissioned fort with splendid gun mounts, beaches, and commanding bluffs. The magnificent bluff and beach at Ebey's Landing and Fort Ebey State Park are good spots to explore, with ancient wild-rose hedgerows (in bloom May and June), 100-year-old barns, and scraggly orchards that still mark the course of a pioneer settlement.

The Whidbey Fish and Market Cafe (3080 S Highway 525, Greenbank; (360)678-3474) hosts an all-you-can-eat fish feed, a local fave, on Mondays and Saturdays. The fish-market-cum-cafe has become something of a communal dining experience, serving some of the best seafood on the island (at the most reasonable prices). Stop by Whidbey's Greenbank Loganberry Farm (on Highway 525, 5 miles south of the Highway 20 junction; (360)678-7788) for a short tour and a sample of **Whidbeys Loganberry Liqueur**. Don't pass up the pretty picnicking spots. Golfers won't find a clubhouse at the alternative Island Greens (3890 East French Road, Clinton; (360)321-6042), built on former farmland and maintained with minimal pesticides. But this par-three, nine-hole course is challenging, the location scenic, and fees delightfully low ($5 per person).

Langley evinces small-town virtues. The tidy downtown strip along First Street provides all a visitor could want: espresso, ice cream, and benches overlooking Saratoga Passage. The residents like to attend first-run movies at the Clyde Theatre, (360)221-5525, drink pitchers of ale at the Dog House Backdoor Restaurant (230 1st Street, Langley; (360)221-9996), and swap stories with Josh Hauser at Moonraker Books (209 1st Street, Langley; (360)321-6962).

Once not much more than a trading post for the farming and fishing communities in the fertile **Skagit Valley**, La Conner in this century became a literary haven for nonconformists (Wobblies, beatniks, and bikers), always with a fair smattering of artists and writers, including Mark Tobey, Morris Graves, Guy Anderson, and Tom Robbins. Most of the town's intelligentsia now congregate in Cafe Pojante (610 1st Street, La Conner; (360)466-4818). La Conner has a few other good places to eat, such as Calico Cupboard (720 S 1st Street, La Conner; (360)466-4451) for carrot muffins or currant scones. But you'll find

🌷 Skagit Valley in Bloom

The fertile farmlands of the Skagit Valley (between Mount Vernon and La Conner) are painted with fields of flowers in the spring: daffodils (March 15 to April 15), tulips (April 1 to May 10), and irises (May 15 to June 15). The pastoral countryside is flat and ideal for bicyclists, except for the gridlock that occurs on the small farm lanes during the Tulip Festival, usually held in early April; call (800)4-TULIPS for information and a map of farms. Vegetable stands dot Skagit Valley roadsides late in summer and fall.

Boeing

For a glimpse at the region's industrial strengths, zoom up I-5 to Everett's Paine Field for a free tour of Boeing's assembly line for 747s and 767s. You'll behold the largest building, by volume, in the world and learn how the planes are assembled. No reservations but space for the tours is limited, so arrive early. Tickets must be picked up at the tour center the same day; (206)342-4801 or (206)544-1260 (in Seattle).

better, reasonably priced eateries in nearby Mount Vernon, a rare working-class town where good restaurants and bookstores outnumber taverns and churches.

Pacione's Pizzeria (606 S 1st Street, Mount Vernon; (360)336-3314) bakes all its pizza pies to order. The Deli Next Door (202 S 1st Street, Mount Vernon; (360)336-3886), located in the Skagit Valley Food Co-op, offers a super-healthy, super-tasty afternoon nosh. On the other end of the spectrum, the Chuck Wagon Drive Inn (800 N 4th Street, Mount Vernon; (360)336-2732) has 50 different kinds of burgers, as well as electric trains and the largest collection of whiskey-bottle cowboys in the free world. **Little Mountain Park**, at the southeast end of town, sports a terrific picnic spot with a knockout vista of the valley (look for migratory trumpeter swans in February).

The **Pilchuck Glass School**, in Stanwood, is an internationally renowned glass-art school. An open house each summer gives folks a chance to see craftspeople at work; call (360)517-1351 or (360)621-8422.

There's a Pilchuck School connection in south Puget Sound as well. Glass artist Dale Chihuly, one of the school's famous founders, is a native son of Tacoma. You'll find a mesmerizing collection of Chihuly glass sculptures in the **Tacoma Art Museum** (1123 Pacific Avenue, Tacoma; (206)272-4258), displayed against muslin-screened windows and lit from behind by the sun. Admission is free on Tuesdays. For a more traditional use of glass, check out the free **W. W. Seymour Botanical Conservatory** in Wright Park (316 S "G" Street, Tacoma). An elegant, old-fashioned hothouse dating from 1907, it contains an exotic collection of cacti, orchids, and ferns.

The **Washington State Historical Museum** is scheduled to move to its expansive new building downtown, behind the grandly restored Union Station, in 1996. Until then you can still enjoy imaginative regional-history displays at the old building, perched on a bluff above

Puget Sound in the Stadium Historic District (315 N Stadium Way, Tacoma; (206)593-2830). Admission is $2.50.

In the industrial docklands near the Lincoln Avenue Bridge sprawls the **Gog-le-hi-te Wetland** (the name means "where the land and waters meet"). More than 100 species of birds inhabit this human-made estuary, which the Port of Tacoma constructed to compensate the Puyallup Indians for wild marshes the port destroyed.

Tacomans dine out without breaking the bank at Lessie's Southern Kitchen (1716 6th Avenue, Tacoma; (206)627-4282), where they feast on corn cakes, fried chicken, and ribs. If you're looking for a waterfront view with your meals, skip the upscale restaurants on Ruston Way and head instead for the Spar (2121 N 30th Street, Tacoma; (206)627-8215), a classic Northwest tavern in gentrified Old Town. Frisko Freeze (1201 Division Street, Tacoma; (206)272-6843) is a true '50s burger hangout, still as popular as ever. Java Jive (2102 S Tacoma Way, Tacoma; (206)475-9843) is notable more for its ambience than its menu. Built in 1927 and shaped like an oversized teapot—despite its coffee-inspired name—it was once a dance hall and speakeasy. Worth a look as a piece of history; make your own call on the food.

In 700-acre **Point Defiance Park** (5400 N Pearl Street, Tacoma) you'll find woodland trails, formal gardens, and reconstructed Fort Nisqually—a former Hudson's Bay outpost—all free of charge. Also in the park is the Point Defiance Zoo and Aquarium (206)591-5335, which bills itself as "the Pacific Rim zoo," with specialized habitats ranging from tundra to tropical reefs. One-time admission is $6.50, but the zoo honors membership passes from many other Northwest zoos. A few blocks outside the park gates is the Antique Sandwich Company (5102 N Pearl Street, Tacoma; (206)752-4069), with such child pleasers as peanut butter, jelly, and banana sandwiches and toys on the carpeted stage, which doubles as a set for folk musicians later in the day.

North, off Point Defiance, lies pastoral **Vashon Island** (served by car ferries from Point Defiance and Fauntleroy, and by foot-passenger ferry from downtown Seattle). This lazy, rural island is great for biking, and the squat Point Robinson lighthouse makes a good destination (the lighthouse is open for tours on weekends only, but the grounds are open daily). The best views are from the causeway linking Vashon with Maury Island. A number of Vashon Island companies are open for tours, including SBC Coffee, (206)463-3932; Maury Island Farms, (206)463-9659; Vashon Island Winery, (206)463-2990; and Island Spring, Inc., (206)463-5670. Call ahead for details. Or stop by the Country Store and Garden (Valley Center, Vashon; (206)463-3655), where most island products are for sale.

Do What?

People don't go to Puyallup, they "do the Puyallup." The granddaddy blowout of the year is September's 17-day Puyallup Fair (officially the Western Washington State Fair, but nobody calls it that). It's one of the nation's largest state fairs. Puyallup may not be the farm town it once was, but you'll still see plenty of pigs and lambs. A big country star usually headlines the entertainment. Go on a weekday if possible; weekends are crowded. Commercial sponsors sometimes offer midweek reductions on ticket prices. Call (206)845-1771 for exact dates and ticket information.

Gig Harbor, bent like a horseshoe around its namesake bay, is home to a working fishing fleet and a spate of tourist shops. New construction nibbles away at the edges of the town, rapidly transforming it into a Tacoma suburb, at the west end of the Narrows Bridge. Still, the town remains a pleasant, well-known gateway to lesser-known places beyond. On the Key Peninsula, for example, quiet coves and forgotten towns seem dreamily lost in time. The back roads are good for biking, and Penrose State Park, (206)884-2514, is a favorite with clam diggers.

Steilacoom, platted by a Maine sea captain in the late 19th century, has a distinctly New England air. On weekends long lines of visitors spill out of Bair Drug and Hardware (1617 Lafayette Street, Steilacoom; (206)588-9668), a false-fronted general store now run as a small cafe. Nostalgia is clearly as big a draw as the food. But it's cheap and fun, especially the antique soda fountain, which still serves sarsaparilla and gooey black-and-white sundaes.

The towering landmark of **Olympia**, seat of state government, is its neoclassical capitol building, spectacularly set on a bluff at the foot of Puget Sound. It was built to impress, and it does. Rumor has it that you could squeeze a Volkswagen Beetle inside the rotunda's 5-ton Tiffany chandelier. Admission and daily tours are free. You can get a free tour of the governor's mansion next door, by appointment, on Wednesday afternoons; (360)586-8687.

Directly behind the capitol grounds lies the historic **South Capitol Neighborhood**, one of the largest historic districts in the state on the National Register of Historic Places. Pick up a free, self-guided tour brochure at the State Capitol Visitors Center (14th Avenue and S Capitol Way, Olympia; (360)586-3460).

Downtown Olympia remains wonderfully human in scale. Sylvester

Park is a town square straight out of *The Music Man*, complete with a bandstand where free Friday lunchtime concerts are held in summer. For a cheap night out, Olympians head for the State Tri-Cinemas (204 4th Avenue E, Olympia; (360)357-4010) to catch recent films for $1.

At the **open-air Olympia Farmers Market**, the vendors who sell you produce are the people who actually grew it. Stalls overflow with vegetables, berries, baked goods, handicrafts, fresh herbs, and flowers. (Currently located at N Capitol Way and Thurston Avenue, the market expects to move a few blocks in 1996. Call (360)352-9096 to check location and hours.) You can lunch here cheaply and reasonably well: choose from Bavarian wurst, Oriental noodles, salmon burgers, and more. Other good-value eateries include Saigon Rendezvous (117 5th Avenue W, Olympia; (360)352-1989), a Vietnamese restaurant with a good vegetarian selection, and Olympia's favorite downtown gathering place, The Spar (114 E 4th Avenue, Olympia; (360)357-6444; no relation to the tavern in Tacoma). For Turkish coffee and inexpensive Middle Eastern meals, try Sweet Oasis Mediterranean Cafe (507-A Capitol Way S; Olympia; (360)956-0470).

Every day in May, Art Zabel opens his backyard to the public, free. Zabel's passion is **rhododendrons**, and more than 1,200 of them bloom in his four-acre Olympia garden (2432 Bethel Street NE, Olympia). He doesn't sell them; he just lets you roam around.

Ten miles north of Olympia, where the glacier-fed Nisqually River flows into Puget Sound, lies the **Nisqually Wildlife Refuge** (I-5 exit 114, Olympia; (360)753-9467). Woodlands, grasslands, and marshes provide a rich habitat for wildlife, especially for migrating birds. Easy trails range from a half-mile walk to a 5-mile loop with photo blinds and observation decks. There's a daily fee of $2 per family.

Equally intriguing is the **Mima Mounds Natural Area Preserve**, 12 miles south of Olympia near the village of Littlerock. Thousands of inexplicable mounds, roughly 10 feet high, cover the Mima prairie. Nobody knows for sure whether they were formed by glaciers or by gophers, but they're lovely when wildflowers bloom in late spring, thick with blossoms and butterflies.

Wolfhaven International, near Tenino, is a private sanctuary for wolves that cannot be returned to the wild. Volunteer guides give tours and explain the workings of wolf society. Admission is $5.00 for adults, $2.50 for kids. "Howl-Ins" on summer Friday nights, when visitors howl with the wolves, cost a little bit more (3111 Offut Lake Road, Olympia; (360)264-HOWL).

The heyday of sandstone has come and gone, but **Tenino** remembers it well. You'd never expect such a tiny town to have so many shops and houses built out of hand-hewn stone. An abandoned sandstone quarry is now a public park, where an old stone railway depot serves as a small museum. And what better way to spend a hot afternoon than down at the old swimming hole? The craggy quarry pit itself has been transformed into a free swimming pool (open Wednesdays through Sundays in summer).

CHEAP SLEEPS

Silver Lake Park Cabins
9006 Silver Lake Road, Sumas, WA 98295 • (360)599-2776

Few counties in the Northwest can match Whatcom County's well-run parks program. On the shores of Silver Lake are six rustic mountain cabins; "rustic" here means no bathrooms, no hot water, no bedding. But there are kitchens with a gas stove and refrigerator and outbuildings with baths. Still with us? Believe it or not, the cabins themselves are comfortable. In addition, the 400-acre park has 100 campsites, a maze of hiking trails, and cutthroat ready to bite.

Wilkins Farm B&B
4165 South Pass Road, Everson, WA 98247 • (360)966-7616

In the cool shadow of Sumas Mountain, wedged between Breckenridge and Swift creeks, is the ultimate family bed and breakfast. The atmosphere is low-key and friendly, and so is the price ($35). Carmela Wilkins's warm Italian heart and Italian breakfasts add to the charm of this old farmhouse (circa 1887).

Coupeville Inn
200 NW Coveland Street (PO Box 370), Coupeville, WA 98239
(360)678-6668 or (800)247-6162

This attractive blue-and-gray inn is a 24-unit motel. What makes it an inn? The eccentric innkeeper, Alan Dutcher. Fourteen rooms slide in at just under $50 in the winter, and just over $50 as the season warms up. They're all large, and everyone gets a continental-style nibble in the morning.

Mutiny Bay Resort
5856 S Mutiny Bay Road (PO Box 249), Freeland, WA 98249
(360)321-4500

Here is one of the last of the old-time fishing resorts on Whidbey Island. Years ago, this was the place for wild parties. It's now quieter, with family atmosphere. The beach chalets are nice but pricey, unless you come with a few extra friends. Instead, request one of the old fishermen's cabins. They have kitchens, although showers are in the central bathhouse. Cabin #3 is a budget honeymooner with private shower, airtight wood stove, and nicer furnishings.

Drake's Landing

203 Wharf Street (PO Box 613), Langley, WA 98260 • (360)221-3999

Diminutive Pat Drake's little blue house at the working end of the Langley waterfront is a modern-day version of the respectable overnight boardinghouse. Her four rooms are small, but each has its own private bath. Guests relax and mingle in the parlor or the upstairs sun room and deck. Coffee and juice get you started in the morning. This might not be the Inn at Langley, but it's a good night's sleep in the same quaint town.

The Tulip Valley Inn

2200 Freeway Drive, Mount Vernon, WA 98273 • (360)428-5969

There are times in life when a good motel room at a reasonable rate is all you are going to find and maybe all you really want. Comfortable beds in a new no-frills 40-room motel (no pool or hot tub) mean a good night's sleep in the fast-growing hub of the Skagit Valley. Some units are fully handicapped-accessible; some have kitchens.

Hart's Tayberry House

7406 80th Street E, Puyallup, WA 98371 • (206)848-4594

The house is a fake—a copy of the Victorian home that Puyallup pioneer Ezra Meeker built as a gift for his daughter—but it's a nice imitation. Set on the rural outskirts of Puyallup, it's also a blessedly quiet place. In summer, breakfast is served on a porch that overlooks farms in the valley below. Two guest rooms (one with a balcony) share a bath; a third has a bath of its own. Tayberry House is only 7 miles from downtown Tacoma. You won't find better any closer (certainly not at this price).

Deep Lake Resort

12405 Tilley Road S, Olympia, WA 98512 • (360)352-7388

Back in the 1920s and '30s, the small lakes around Olympia were peppered with this kind of resort. Most have disappeared, but Deep Lake Resort—adjacent to Millersylvania State Park—still thrives. Sunny in the center and woodsy around the edges, it has tidy green lawns and masses of summer flowers. The resort is unabashedly aimed at families, with swimming, horseshoes, volleyball, and basketball at no charge, and boats and bikes for rent. Six simple cabins line up along the lakefront, each with its own picnic table and fire pit. All have kitchens and toilets; four even have showers. Guests must bring their own linens, dishes, and cooking utensils. Public showers and a laundry room are located nearby, as are RV and tent sites. Open late April through September. In July and August, cabins are rented only by the week.

Golden Gavel Motor Hotel
909 Capitol Way, Olympia, WA 98501 • (360)352-8533

The folks are friendly, the rooms are well maintained, and the price is good for the location—3 blocks north of the capitol and 4 blocks south of downtown. You can walk to practically everything from here (including the bus station). Wander over to Wagner's European Bakery, just up the street, for morning espresso and good pastries.

AYH Ranch/Hostel
12119 SW Cove Road, Vashon, WA 98070 • (206)463-2592

This 10-acre spread on Vashon Island has a wonderfully hokey Old West theme, and it's also wonderfully cheap. Buckaroos of all ages can sleep in a covered wagon or a Sioux-style dorm tepee, equipped with beds and a fire circle, for $12 per person. Couples and families can reserve a tepee all to themselves. Or the whole passel can bunk in hostel dorm rooms. All guests have access to firewood, bicycles, and do-it-yourself pancake breakfasts at no extra charge. A private bed-and-breakfast room (with bath) is available for $55.

No Cabbages
7712 Goodman Drive NW, Gig Harbor, WA 98335 • (206)858-7797

"Not for the terminally uptight," reads the sign near the door of this charmingly funky beachfront cottage in the woods. From your rustic four-poster bed with patchwork quilts—the Grateful Dead meets *Victoria* magazine—you can look through old-fashioned casement windows at Gig Harbor below. The two knotty pine guest rooms, tucked underneath the main house, share a bath and their own outside entrance. The hostess is mellow, friendly, and a good cook to boot. Breakfast might be popovers with whipped cream, or maybe a spinach, garlic and feta-cheese omelet. A great escape from the real world for only $50.

Still Waters Bed & Breakfast

13202 Olympic Road SE, Olalla, WA 98359 • (360)876-8608

A country retreat to restore the soul. This split-level plantation-style home sits on 5 peaceful acres midway between Port Orchard and Gig Harbor, with 100-year-old fruit trees in front and a view of the Olympics in back. Three guest rooms are done up with wicker furniture and braided rag rugs. The huge cottage garden has lawn chairs for reading and a big outdoor Jacuzzi open to the stars. Stay for two nights and get a price reduction. Or *pay* for two nights, stay one, and receive a 90-minute massage.

Twin River Ranch

E 5730 Highway 3, Shelton, WA 98584 • (360)426-1023

The driveway winds through a grove of dark conifers and over a wooden bridge to a 140-acre cattle ranch. Puget Sound shimmers seductively beyond the edge of the clearing, and salmon spawn in the stream that runs under your bedroom window. This Craftsman-style farmhouse, with its stone fireplace and beamed ceilings, was built in 1918 as a duck-hunting lodge. The guest rooms (one has twin beds) share a half-bath; slippers, robes, and towels are provided for the trip to the full bath downstairs. Expect a ranch hand's breakfast in the morning.

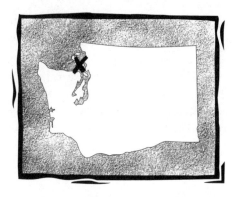

San Juan Islands

Clustered between the Strait of Juan de Fuca and Georgia Strait
are 457 islands set against a backdrop of forbidding mountain
peaks to the east and west. Many of the islands are no more than
a seagull perch; others support small communities accessible only
by private boat or seaplane. Four of them—Lopez, Shaw, Orcas,
and San Juan—are serviced by the Washington State Ferries
system and are home to 10,000 full-time residents.

Condé Nast Traveler calls the San Juan Islands one of the
best-kept secrets in the United States. Travel and Leisure
suggests avoiding the San Juans altogether in June, July, and
August. We say neither is telling the entire truth. True, in the
summer you can feel overwhelmed by a Coney Island atmosphere
and too many T-shirt shops. But secluded hideaways can still be
found. And in the winter, tourists are scarce, while the locals settle
in for a long, cold, private season. (In fact, Orcas Islanders have
two nicknames for their island: Orcapulco in the summer,
Orcatraz in the winter.) But the magic of the islands makes them
worth braving summer tourists or winter chill. Don't go seeking
nirvana, but don't be surprised if you find it after all.

In the San Juans, gnarled madrona trees cling to rock
outcroppings above tide pools, and giant firs stretch from the

crystalline waters of Cascade Lake to the summit of Mount Constitution on Orcas. Plenty of protected coves shelter gleaming sailboats in the summer months. A wealth of wildlife inhabits the islands and surrounding waters, from the famous killer whales to bald eagles. And despite the commercialization, you need only meander a piece down the road or travel in the autumn to discover the true pace of this Northwest archipelago.

ON THE ROAD

The ferry to the San Juan Islands leaves from the shipbuilding and oil-refinery town of **Anacortes**, about 1½ hours north of Seattle. Swing by Gere-a-Deli (502 Commercial Avenue, Anacortes; (360)293-7383) for reasonably priced sandwiches, salads, pastas, and soups. Or try El Jinete, an authentic Mexican restaurant (509 Commercial Avenue, Anacortes; (360)293-2631). Then move on to the islands.

Getting to the San Juans on the Washington State Ferries in the summer is a big (though not insurmountable) problem—especially if you have a car. Bring a good book—you can expect to wait in line for hours, and there are few diversions at the terminal. Unfortunately, we don't (yet) know of any way to sneak your car onto the ferry at the last minute—and if we did, it would be one secret we'd have to keep to ourselves.

Basically, if you don't like lines and refuse to get to the Anacortes ferry terminal four hours ahead of time, then by all means leave your car and bike or walk on. (With prearrangements, a number of lodge owners will pick you up. Island taxis can get expensive.) If you need your car,

Traveler's Tip

On Washington State Ferries to the San Juan Islands, you pay only going westbound. So try to make your first stop Friday Harbor; then backtrack island to island for free. Expect to pay about $20 round trip (car and driver) plus $5 for each passenger. Once aboard, you'll find the trip undeniably scenic and enjoyable. Bring a picnic (the ferry food is costly and unappetizing) and snag a window table for a view.

try to schedule your trip to the islands between October and May. For general ferry information, call (206)464-6400.

The first ferry stop is **Lopez**—the bucolic island, the quiet island, the friendly island. Bicyclists like Lopez for its gentle inclines and for the drivers who actually wave. The island is laced with country lanes and picturesque farms with weathered barns; on the west side is the not-so-thriving center of Lopez Village. The village is small, with just a few craft shops and good restaurants such as the Bay Cafe, (360)468-3700, and Gail's, (360)468-2150. The former is popular and offers good value for the buck, with an interesting, slightly ethnic menu. Reservations are a must in summer. For lunch, try Gail's, which offers a deck and lookout toward Fisherman Bay. Better yet, head to the shore with a loaf of toasted-walnut French bread (and some cappuccino bars) from Holly B's Bakery (Village Center, Lopez; (360)458-2133). If you're really hungry, add some deli meats from the Village Market and then venture to the beach at **Spencer Spit State Park**, 5 miles east.

At the southwest corner of the island is **Shark Reef**, a day park reachable by surefooted hikers. A forested trail ends suddenly at granite cliffs high above the tide pools of the San Juan Channel. Colonies of seals and otters often reside on a small, rocky island just offshore.

The second ferry stop is **Shaw**, the smallest of the ferry-accessible islands. It's fun to watch the Franciscan nuns operate the ferry dock, but other than a campground and a grocery store run by the order, Shaw has no tourist facilities. The island is home to little more than a retreat center for nuns, a three-cow dairy, and a private enclave of residential properties whose owners want to keep it that way.

Across from Shaw is the largest island in the San Juans, **Orcas**. Explore the villages of Eastsound, Olga, and Deer Harbor. Eastsound is the most commercial, with a number of somewhat trendy restaurants. A few places serve up big bites for little bucks. The popular Bilbo's (North Beach Road, Eastsound; (360)376-4728) has great Mexican fixings and an outside terrace. Islanders opt for a round of appetizers and a couple of margaritas. The Bungalow (Horseshoe Highway, Eastsound; (360)376-4338) has switched to a buffet-style dinner ($9.95 for adults, $6.00 for children) with good soups and salads, so-so entrées, a great view, and crayons.

Islanders, however, hang out at what they call the "upper" and "lower" taverns. The former is Eby's (Horseshoe Highway, Eastsound; (360)376-4900); locals pack the place on Prime Rib Night (posted on the sign) and Liver and Onions Night. The waterfront Lower Tavern (Horseshoe Highway, Eastsound; (360)376-4848) serves burgers and soups with a great view (plus darts and pool). Mornings start at Rose's

Winter Warmth

Doe Bay Resort, Star Route Box 86, Olga (Orcas Island), WA 98279 • (360)376-2291
The location of this age-old hippie resort is great, with plenty of trails, two small beaches, a campground, a small store, a good vegetarian restaurant, and an outdoor mineral-spring hot tub (bathing suits optional); however, the minimalist cabins are a bit rickety, have no screens, and are not exactly sanitary. We suggest you stay elsewhere but enjoy the use of the hot tub during a slow winter week (for a small extra fee). On a full moon, book a kayak trip ($25), which departs from Doe Bay's beach, through Island Kayak Guides; (360)376-4755.

(Northbeach Road, Eastsound; (360)376-2009), in Eastsound Square, with a latte or regular coffee. The Orcas Homegrown Market has an interesting selection of salads-to-go, which you might consider before heading off to the remote **Obstruction Pass State Park**, at the southwest tip of the island. A half-mile hike leads to a pretty beach.

Moran State Park offers a spectacular setting of 5,000 wooded acres with 30 miles of trails surrounding several lakes and Mount Constitution. It's like summer camp (and just about as crowded). You can rent sailboards and small boats at Cascade Lake, swim at a supervised beach, or stay in one of the numerous campsites. If it's too cool to swim and you need to wear off your third bagel, hike (or drive) the 6½ miles up Mount Constitution. You will be well rewarded by the panorama (and maybe even a bald eagle) below you.

Beyond Moran, the sleepy hamlet of **Olga** seduces the puckish with the unforgettable cinnamon rolls and blackberry pie at the Olga Cafe; (360)376-5098. The cafe, built by a cooperative of local artists, displays a variety of arts and crafts. It's open from 10am to 6pm every day.

On the other side of the island is the **gold coast**, which features numerous estates of old Seattle families, though few of the homes are visible from the road. Westsound Deli (Crow Valley Road and Deer Harbor Road, Eastsound; (360)376-4440) makes good tortilla pies, Indonesian rice, and meat loaf to eat in or take out.

To get out on the water, reserve space on one of the many kayak trips offered by Island Kayak Guides, (360)376-4755, the most unusual being the moonlight trip for $25 and a kids' trip open to three-year-olds and up (with a parent) for $20. Bigger boats mean bigger bucks, but if a

Musical Note

For Dixieland jazz fans, Friday Harbor is the place to be on the last weekend in July. The whole town swings with well-known jazz artists performing in various locales. Suggestion: Reserve lodging far in advance (or stay on Orcas and walk over on the ferry for the events), as this has become a very popular event. For details on bands and ticket prices, call (360)378-5509.

33-foot sloop will float your boat, call Skippered Sail Tours, (360)376-4231; sailing trips cost $25 per person. For fishing expeditions, try Moby Max Charters, (360)376-2970, or Bounty Charters, (360)376-2165. But listening to the waves roll onto the beach, watching the seagulls hunt for dinner, or discovering hermit crabs in tide pools might be a better (and cheaper) alternative.

The last ferry stop before British Columbia is **San Juan Island**, the county seat and definitely the most bustling of the islands. The landing is smack in the middle of Friday Harbor and is crammed with shops, galleries, grocery stores, and a large marina. The most notable attraction is the **Whale Museum** (62 1st Street, Friday Harbor; (360)378-4710), which has become the base of operation for the study of the 90 or so orcas that reside in the San Juan vicinity. The museum offers exhibits as well as a short film about the individual killer whales that have been tracked over the years (admission $3).

If you're an early riser, head up to the Donut Shop (209 Spring Street, Friday Harbor; (360)378-2271), which opens at 5am. Later in the day, it's a great spot for a good burger ($2 and up) and a pastry to go. Split one of the giant steamed sandwiches (around $5) at the Cannery House (174 1st Street, Friday Harbor; (360)378-2500).

The best way to see San Juan Island is to head out on bike (rent one from Island Bicycles, 380 Argyle Avenue, Friday Harbor; (360)387-4941; $2–$5 per hour, $15–$25 per day) or by car on Roche Harbor Road, which winds its way past large farms and ranches. All roads heading northwest seem to lead to **Roche Harbor**, the site of a Hudson's Bay Company trading post in the 1800s, then the largest lime quarry in the West, and now a very charming resort, especially popular with boaters. Dally among the exquisite gardens and walk the dock as though your cruiser is tied up at slip 55. Also on this end of the island is English Camp, the site of the 12-year British occupation during the not-so-famous Pig War. An interesting museum explains this conflict.

American Camp (on the opposite side of the island) is much more interesting. Allow a couple of hours there to enjoy the windswept South Beach, the longest public beach in the islands. There are picnic tables, and it's a perfect setting for beachcombing. On Saturdays and Sundays from June through August, there are historical reenactments and guided hikes through the camp. Just beyond San Juan County Park on Mitchell Bay Road (off West Valley Road) is the first whale-watching park established in the nation. **Lime Kiln Point** has been a whale research station since 1983, and has installed underwater microphones to allow eavesdropping on unsuspecting orcas. The killer whales pass by regularly, especially in the summer months. The grassy slopes, with their wild orange poppies, and the westerly views toward Vancouver Island are enough of a diversion when the whales are not.

For San Juan Island eats, try to get a seat on the deck at the lively Mexican restaurant Amigo's (40 Spring Street, Friday Harbor; (360)378-5908), open June through September. If you want to rub shoulders with locals, stop in at Herb's Tavern, an institution that's been doling out beers (and chili and burgers) for over 50 years under one name or another. To grab dinner to go, for the ferry or your campsite, try the take-out smoked chicken cooked daily at Madelyn's Yogurt and Espresso Bar (225 A Street, Friday Harbor; (360)378-4545). Psst: Locals say she has the best lattes in town.

CHEAP SLEEPS

Unfortunately, summertime forces last-minute planners to forget price concerns and just find a room—any room. Peak-season lodging is so tight on these islands that even the tiniest room with one twin bed might go for $69 a night. Add another person and the price increases by $10. So, if you're really looking for a deal, go in the off season, when price and availability are much better. Below, we've listed the best deals on the island, even if some of their prices are a little beyond our budgetery expectations.

Those who insist on visiting in the summer may wish to try the lodging hotlines for San Juan Island, (360)378-3030, and Orcas Island, (360)376-8888. For other island information, call the islands' Chamber of Commerce, (360)378-5240.

The Island Farmhouse
Hummel Lake Road (PO Box 3114), Lopez Island, WA 98261
(360)468-2864

Aside from campsites, this 12-acre working farm is the only resting spot that's much of a deal on Lopez. The owners, Ted and Susan Sanchez,

Vacation Rentals

Orcas Island, (360)376-2204
San Juan Island, (360)378-5171 or (800)992-1904
Cherie Lindholm Real Estate is the only real estate company on
Orcas to handle vacation rentals. The list is not huge, mind you,
but a waterfront cabin on Orcas isn't a bad way to spend a week or
two. Dockside Property Company handles most of the rental
properties on San Juan Island, but they are considerably more
pricey than those on Orcas.

have added a large room off the back of their home with its own deck
and private entry. It is generous in size and decorated à la Laura Ashley.
The private bath is quite large, and there's a kitchen nook. Sit on your
deck in the morning and watch the sheepdog at work on the herd of
Suffolks in this pastoral setting.

Beach Haven Resort

Route 1, Box 12, Eastsound (Orcas Island), WA 98245 • (360)376-2288

"Leaving the world, entering Beach Haven," reads the sign at the top of
a winding wooded road that leads down to a secluded pebble beach lined
with 50-year-old log cabins. This is old Northwest tradition modernized
with plumbing and kitchens. The best bet for your money is one of the
two beach apartments. They share a deck on the top floor of a larger
building at the water's edge, and provide you with a living room,
kitchen, bedroom, and bath.

West Beach Resort

Route 1, Box 510, Eastsound (Orcas Island), WA 98245 • (360)376-2240

The West Beach Resort is a throwback to the kind of place your parents
took you as a kid. The entrance signage looks as if the signmaker went
loco, so head straight for the cabins, just feet from a gravel beach. There
is a small marina and boat rental (human-powered $7 an hour, motor
powered $40 an hour), and the general store stocks everything from bait
to s'mores fixings, with a few rubber sharks thrown in for good mea-
sure. The pine-and-burl wood-heated cabins include kitchen and bath.
Two-person cabins are available, but the two- and three-bedroom ones
are much nicer (and a better deal). Great fire pits dot the beach.
Covered porches with tables and chairs are the spot for morning coffee
and heron watching.

 *Consider Camping*

For real cheap sleeps in the San Juans, try camping. Rangers suggest June or September; the weather's still good, and your chances of landing a campsite are much better than in midsummer. State parks accept written reservations after January 1 and phone reservations from Memorial Day through Labor Day.

• **San Juan Island**: This island's best campsites are just beyond the whale-watching park at **San Juan County Park**. This pretty cove has only 18 campsites, so be sure to call for reservations in summer; (360)378-2992. **Lakedale Campground** (2627 Roche Harbor Road, Friday Harbor, WA 98250; (360)378-2350) is a privately owned property of 50 acres with two lakes, fishing, swimming, boating, and 125 campsites. You can rent canoes and rowboats.

• **Orcas**: The mammoth **Moran State Park**, offering swimming, sailboarding, and canoeing, is like summer camp (and just about as crowded). The 148 campsites fill up way before most people are even thinking of summer. Reserve early by writing to Moran State Park anytime after January 1 (Star Route Box 22, Eastsound, WA 98245; (360)376-2326). **Obstruction Pass State Park** is at the south tip of the island. This remote campground has only nine sites and no running water, and it's a half-mile hike to the beach. We like it for these reasons.

• **Shaw**: The best bet for a campsite is, oddly enough, at one of the smallest campgrounds in the islands. **Shaw Island State Park**, at the south end of the island, has only 12 sites. No reservations.

• **Lopez**: **Spencer Spit State Park** is a fir-covered slope that leads down to a sandy spit almost touching the shore of Frost Island. Of the 40 campsites, the nicest are the eight walk-ins on the beach, which have barbecues and picnic tables. No advance reservations; (360)468-2251. **Odlin State Park**, only 1¾ miles from the ferry landing, has 30 sites ($10) scattered along a small beach and facing Shaw Island; (360)468-2496.

Olympic Peninsula & the Pacific Coast

Geographically and historically, the Olympic Peninsula might as well be an island, encircled as it is by Puget Sound, Hood Canal, the Strait of Juan de Fuca, and the Pacific. Olympic National Park, a jumble of rugged peaks crowned by the 7,965-foot, glaciated Mount Olympus, occupies nearly a million acres in the middle of the peninsula. Alpine meadows aglow with wildflowers, temperate rain forests, rivers to raft or paddle, and 589 miles of hiking trails pattern the rest of the peninsula.

Around the perimeter of the park are small towns inhabited by friendly people. Some are descendants of the hardy settlers who carved homesteads out of the forest during the last century. Some are transplants from crowded cities, seeking a nice place to retire or a quiet place to work. And some are descendants of the Native Americans who occupied these lands for centuries before Captain George Vancouver laid eyes on these shores 200 years ago. Nine main tribes lived here, including the Quinault, Hoh, Queets, Quileute, and Makah; many of their descendants now live on reservations. The Makah tribe has built a world-famous museum at Neah Bay, at the northwestern corner of the peninsula, to display artifacts unearthed from a long-buried village of their ancestors. Ancient petroglyphs along the Pacific shore also attest to life here long before the existence of Highway 101.

Highway 101 is the loop road around the peninsula. You can drive it in a day, but a more leisurely approach allows time to explore side roads, walk the beach, shop at country stores, dig clams, hike a rain-forest trail, or hole up in an oceanside cabin and watch the storm-tossed sea attack the shore. Weather on the peninsula is unpredictable at best; rainfall averages between 200 inches per year on the west slopes of the mountains and 17 inches in the Dungeness Valley on the northeast corner of the peninsula—the rain shadow of the Olympics.

ON THE ROAD

Port Townsend is a microcosm of Victorian-era elegance, with its handsome mansions on the bluff and its highly decorated brick and stone buildings along the waterfront. A stroll down Water Street is, in part, a trip through the counterculture of the '60s: historic buildings occupied by boutiques selling handmade jewelry, pottery, and new-to-you *objets*, as well as a connoisseur's selection of galleries, fine shops, and bookstores.

The Historical Museum (210 Madison Street, Port Townsend; (360)385-1003) in City Hall offers a gallimaufry of old photos, Native American artifacts, and mementos of the Chinese colony, as well as a view of the gloomy dungeon room where Jack London reputedly spent a night on his way to the Klondike. The Rothschild House (Jefferson and Taylor streets, Port Townsend; (360)385-4730) is an 1868 home now maintained by the Washington State Parks Commission; it's open for tours daily in summer, weekends in winter.

Reach uptown by a steep stairway at Taylor and Washington streets, heralded by the voluptuous Galatea fountain. Nineteenth-century merchants and magnates built their fine homes on the bluff, far above the hurly-burly of the waterfront. Many homes are now bed and breakfasts, open to the public during the annual spring and fall historic-home tours. The oldest church in the Episcopal Diocese of Olympia—a white, steepled little structure—perches on the bluff, as does an old bell tower once used to summon firemen from near and far. If it's food you're after, try Aldrich's (940 Lawrence Street, Port Townsend; (360)385-0500), a grocery-cum-specialty shop with excellent deli foods. Stock up here for a picnic at **Chetzemoka Park**, with its playground, beach, and rose arbor.

Two miles from town is **Fort Worden State Park**, a former military base that's now a recreation and cultural center. Centrum Foundation is headquartered here, with its rich selection of seminars, plays, concerts, writers conferences, poetry readings, and dance performances; (360)385-3102. Many events take place in the former balloon hangar, now a performing arts center. Plenty of trails wind through Fort Worden's forests and meadows, including a self-guided history walk. Wander through old gun emplacements, camp on the beach, surf at North Beach, or touch a three-spine stickleback in the small aquarium at the Marine Science Center.

Port Townsend's annual **Wooden Boat Festival** (Wooden Boat Foundation; (360)385-3628), on the first weekend after Labor Day, is a dandy time to see what fun a small-town wingding can be—and you don't even have to be a boater. It's centered at Point Hudson, although events take place all over town and include jazz concerts, crafts shows, and strolling entertainers.

For breakfast or lunch there's Salal Cafe (634 Water Street, Port Townsend; (360)385-6532), a relaxed, hospitable hangout. Try the housemade oatmeal, cooked to order, with sliced bananas on top. The relaxed Landfall (412 Water Street, Port Townsend; (360)385-5814)

Dungeness Spit

Dungeness Spit juts 5½ miles into the Strait of Juan de Fuca and has a lighthouse at its tip. Walking is easiest at low tide; otherwise you have to scramble over driftwood. Bird watching is best from September through May; eagle sightings are common in winter. In summer the spit is very popular, but people spread out, so it still isn't hard to find an uncrowded spot for a picnic or clam digging. For swimming, stay on the bay side—it's safer, if chilly. The entire spit is a National Wildlife Refuge, so behave yourself: no beach fires, no vehicles, no pets (horses okay at certain times of the year), and no jogging. The fee is $2 per family (free with Golden Age pass or duck stamp pass). Contact the Port Angeles Fish and Wildlife Office; (360)457-8451. Summer camping only in the adjacent county park (no reservations, $8 fee; (360)683-5847).

overlooks the marina and offers highly respectable seafood, sandwiches and salads at surprisingly low prices. Probably the best and almost the only Thai food on the peninsula is at Khu Larb Thai (225 Adams Street, Port Townsend; (360)385-5023), where service is quick and gracious. The gold-plate and wood-handled flatware has authority, and so does the food. South of town, the Chimacum Cafe (4900 Rhody Drive, Chimacum; (360)732-4631) does wondrous things with basics like fish 'n' chips, steaks, and oysters—at rock-bottom prices—and serves breakfast, lunch, and dinner.

Along Hood Canal, **oysters** reign; oyster gathering is permitted at several public beaches, including Potlatch State Park, Lilliwaup, Twanoh State Park, Seal Rock, and Bywater Bay. Check in advance with the state hotline about the possibility of red tide; (800)562-5632. Several oyster farms will shuck the oysters, if you prefer, and sell you the bivalves at excellent prices: Coast Oyster Company (1570 Linger Longer Road, Quilcene; (360)765-3474), Hama Hama Oyster Company (N 35846 Highway 101, Lilliwaup; (360)877-5811), Triton Cove Oyster Farms (39521 Highway 101, Brinnon; (360)796-4360), and Dungeness Oyster House (Dungeness Boat Ramp, Sequim; (360)683-1028).

Near Quilcene, a 5-mile dirt road snakes up and around flat-topped **Mount Walker**, providing one of the best Olympic-to-Sound views on the peninsula. Drive it in June, when the rhodies are flowering exuberantly. Hoodsport Winery (N 23501 Highway 101, Hoodsport; (360)877-9894) invites visitors to try its fruit wines.

Sequim is famous for being on the sunny side of the notoriously wet Olympic Peninsula. Mmm Chicago Cafe (126 E Washington Street, Sequim; (360)683-2736) offers genuine Midwestern fare: hearty sandwiches (beef from Chicago, bratwurst from Milwaukee), malted waffles, and terrific Chicago hot dogs. Another place for a bargain lunch, dinner, or take-out is Son's (206 N Sequim Avenue, Sequim; (360)683-2121), a Szechuan-Vietnamese-American restaurant. Meals are heftier at the Oak Table (292 W Bell Street, Sequim; (360)683-2179), where locals gather for monstrous, puffy apple pancakes; some days the place bakes too many and gives them away.

Two **wineries** are nestled in the foothills of the Olympics. Neuharth Winery (148 Still Road, Sequim; (360)683-9652) is known for its Dungeness reds, whites, and rosés. Lost Mountain Winery (3174 Lost Mountain Road, Sequim; (360)683-5229) produces mostly reds, including the Poesia series: each year the label features a work by a regional poet. Tour Sequim's **Olympic Game Farm** to see 56 species of animals, from bison to bears—many have starred in Disney movies and other nature films (1423 Ward Road, Sequim; (360)683-4295).

From Port Angeles, an 18-mile road splits off Highway 101 and leads you to **Hurricane Ridge**. The Olympic National Park Pioneer Memorial Museum and Visitor Center (about 2 miles up; (360)452-0330 or (360)452-0329) provides the latest weather conditions. There's a $5 entrance fee to the national park in the summer, although it's free in winter. On a clear day you can see into Canada from the top of the ridge. Easy trails lead to spectacular viewpoints. Meander along the nature trail, up the flowery hillside, to Hurricane Hill (3 miles round trip). The lodge offers ranger talks, food, ski rentals, and naturalist-guided snowshoe walks on winter weekends (snowshoes provided free).

Hurricane Ridge is the peninsula's only **downhill skiing** area, with two rope tows and one poma lift ($15, with discounts to members of the Hurricane Ridge Winter Sports Club of Port Angeles; (360)457-5559). The visitors center provides maps of cross-country ski trails. Clallam Transit runs buses between downtown Port Angeles, the visitors center, and Hurricane Ridge on winter weekends (by reservation, $8 round trip; (360)452-4511 or (800)858-3747).

Railroad Avenue, along the **Port Angeles** waterfront, is a tourist-friendly walk. Or take the two-hour city tour by trolley ($6). The nearby municipal pier has an observation tower, a sandy beach with picnic area, and the Arthur D. Feiro Marine Laboratory, with hands-on exhibits of sea life. Dare to touch the sea cucumber.

From the pier, or from Ediz Hook to the west, there are great views of all the harbor activity, including the comings and goings of the **ferry to Victoria**, the *Coho*. Drivers should arrive early for the ferry in the summer. In fact, it's better to leave the car in Port Angeles and walk on, because Victoria is a pedestrian's dream. For ferry schedules, call Black Ball Transport at either the Port Angeles terminal, (360)457-4491, or the administrative offices in Bellevue, (206)622-2222. There are no reservations. A summer alternative for walk-ons is the faster (but a bit more expensive) *Victoria Express* (reservations advised; (800)633-1589).

In downtown Port Angeles, the Coffee House Restaurant & Gallery (118 E 1st Street, Port Angeles; (360)452-1459) serves breakfast, lunch, and dinner, with original soups, salads, crépes, vegetarian dishes, espresso drinks, and beer and wine. Sandwiches are ample—half would do for most folks. Desserts are luscious. A chance to view the gallery's art show by local artists comes with the meal.

There are several public and wilderness **beaches** along the Strait of Juan de Fuca between Port Angeles and the Pacific. Freshwater Bay, 10 miles west of Port Angeles off Highway 112, is a small park where tide pools teem with starfish, sea anemones, and sculpin. Just before Joyce (where there's a funny little free local museum) is Tongue Point/Salt

Creek Recreation Area, with camping, a playground, a kitchen, and a generous stretch of beach.

Take a hike in the woods and learn about modern forestry at Pysht on Highway 112, where Merril & Ring offers guided tours of its tree farm; reservations advised, (800)998-2382. The first good view of the Pacific Ocean is at **Cape Flattery**, just beyond Neah Bay (66 miles from Port Angeles via 112). A half-mile trail leads through the forest to a view of ocean-carved cliffs, storm-wracked Tatoosh Island, and its gleaming lighthouse. See artifacts from a 500-year-old Indian village in the **Makah Cultural and Research Center** in Neah Bay (Front Street, Neah Bay; (360)645-2711).

Lake Crescent, 20 miles west of Port Angeles, has many roadside pullouts for a picnic or a photo. From Barnes Point, just before Lake

Whale Watching

Gray whales migrate along the Pacific coast of the Olympic Peninsula on a predictable schedule: south from Alaska, late October to mid-December; north from Baja California, March to May. Better weather and better chances of sighting whales close to shore occur during the mammals' early spring travels. Westport is the capital of whale watching by boat. About a dozen charters operate three-hour trips ($20–$25). Contact the Chamber of Commerce (2985 S Montesano, Westport, WA 98595; (360)268-9422) for a list of the numerous charter companies. Or bring your binoculars and spy them from shore. Here are some good viewpoints (north to south):

• Cape Flattery: Take the half-mile trail from the Makah Indian Reservation.

• Cape Alava: Take the 3-mile trail from Lake Ozette.

• La Push: Drive through the village and park close to the road on the south side of the Quillayute River.

• Take the trails off Highway 101 to Ruby Beach and Beaches 1 through 7 in the Kalaloch area; stop at the Destruction Island overlook; walk the beach at Kalaloch Lodge; or view from the upstairs lounge of the lodge.

• Point Grenville: Take Highway 109 on the Quinault Indian Reservation (get permission).

• Westport: Head for the whale-watching tower near the marina. Whales sometimes swim right into the harbor.

Crescent Lodge, walk up a shady trail to the 90-foot Marymere Falls. Or take a 75-minute cruise on the *M.V. Storm King*, a 64-foot simulated paddle wheeler, with narration by an Olympic Park ranger; (360)452-4520. The nearby, historic Rosemary Inn is the headquarters of the Olympic Park Institute, which offers field seminars on the peninsula and beyond; it's worth a visit just to see the quaint 75-year-old cabins (111 Barnes Point Road, Port Angeles, WA 98362; (360)928-3720).

Sol Duc Hot Springs Resort (Sol Duc Road, Port Angeles; (360)327-3583), up a 12-mile road from Highway 101 just west of Lake Crescent, has three outdoor soaking pools, one heated swimming pool, a poolside deli, a restaurant, and a variety of cabins. It's perfect for a restorative soak and swim ($5.50). Open mid-May through September. Olympic Hot Springs no longer has cabins or any facilities, but the springs still flow, free to all. Drive to Elwha River Road south from Highway 101, and then follow Boulder Creek Road until it stops. Hike the last 2 miles to the springs and campground.

Lake Ozette, the state's largest natural lake, has free year-round camping and picnicking near the road's end. Hike the 3 miles from lake to ocean by puncheon trail (cedar slabs), pioneer-style. Permits required; (360)452-0300. At the beach, you're near the Makah Indian village archaeological dig; check out the small, informative display. Explore the marshy, wooded shores of Lake Ozette by canoe, or paddle across to a campground on the western shore. (Be careful: the winds whip up quickly.)

West of Forks, via the La Push road, there's access to four wide **wild beaches**. Farthest north is Rialto, which offers picnicking and smelting in season, as well as ranger-guided naturalist walks from nearby Mora Campground. You can approach broad, sandy First Beach to the south through the Quileute village of La Push. Take the trails from the highway to reach Second and Third beaches, which feature astonishing sea stacks, tide pools, and occasional whale sightings.

Since La Push has no restaurants, the best food and best bargains are in **Forks**, among them the South North Garden (140 Sol Duc Way, Forks; (360)374-9779), a bit of Canton in timber country. At the Forks Timber Museum (Highway 101, Forks; (360)374-9663), you can see a veteran steam-donkey engine.

Eight short trails to **wilderness beaches** (a quarter mile each at most) leave Highway 101 in the Kalaloch area. Ruby Beach and Beaches 6 and 7 are to the north of Kalaloch Lodge, and Beaches 1 to 5 are to the south. Beach 4 has good razor clamming in season, surf fishing, and smelting. Smelt nets are for sale at the Kalaloch store; (360)962-2271. Just south of Beach 6, a side road to the east wanders for about a quarter mile through a grove of huge Western red cedars, climaxing with the world's largest—61 feet around.

Roads poke eastward from 101 up four **rain-forest valleys**: Queets, Bogachiel, Hoh, and Quinault. The 19-mile Hoh road leads to an interpretive center, the Hall of Mosses Trail, and other trails through groves of ancient, moss-laden giants. The campground is open all year (free in winter, $6 in summer). The rain forest borders both the north and south shores of Lake Quinault. Near Lake Quinault Lodge on the south shore, visit the interpretive center and take a short loop trail to see more giants of the forest.

At the south end of the **Ocean Shores** peninsula, the passenger ferry *Matador* makes several trips daily, back and forth to Westport, May to September. The ferry is convenient for bikers, day trippers, and travelers overnighting in either location. A trolley shuttles passengers between central Ocean Shores and the docks; Westport, (360)268-0047; Ocean Shores, (360)289-3386.

CHEAP SLEEPS

Fort Flagler Hostel
Fort Flagler State Park, Marrowstone Island, Nordland, WA 98358
(206)385-1288

You needn't be a confirmed hosteler to fall in love with this one, way up at the north tip of Marrowstone Island. The park, once a military outpost, has sensational three-way water views, camping, picnicking, miles of hiking trails, fishing, and a nature conservancy. The hostel is a long, unprepossessing frame building, short on charm but long on utility. It contains dorm rooms with 14 bunk beds, a living room with a wood stove, a big kitchen, and two baths. One room is set aside for families. Bring food and sleeping bags. If you arrive on a bike, you pay only $10. Open April through September.

Point Hudson Motel, Marina and RV Park
Point Hudson, Port Townsend, WA 98368 • (360)385-2828 or
(206)622-5033 (local from Seattle) or (800)826-3854

This derelict Coast Guard station on the north end of town was transformed into a resort in 1970 and has continued to evolve ever since. Tall masts, wheeling gulls, and the smell of diesel and bilge water fill the well-protected marina as pleasure boaters and purse seiners rub decks at the docks. The sprawl of government-built, peak-roofed, clapboard buildings includes a dive shop, boatbuilder, sailmaker, canvasmaker, performing arts center, Chinese restaurant, bait shop, laundry, and a plain 26-room motel. The mood is engagingly informal.

Waterstreet Hotel

635 Water Street, Port Townsend, WA 98368 • (360)385-5467 or
(800)735-9810

Up a tall flight of wooden steps from the mythic Town Tavern, a lobby housing a native art gallery incongruously welcomes guests to this 1889 hotel. The spare, clean rooms are the kind in which Thomases Merton, Wolfe, and Pynchon might have holed up in contemplation. Some rooms have private baths, some don't. Highly recommended for the introspective traveler on a budget.

Granny Sandy's Orchard

405 W Spruce Street, Sequim, WA 98382 • (360)683-5748 or
(800)841-3347

Yes, it's really run by a granny (Sandy Kucera), and it really has an "orchard" (seven apple trees, three cherry, one peach). Not only that, it's very handy to sunny downtown Sequim. Two bedrooms downstairs have private baths; four upstairs share a bath. Starring on the breakfast menu are orange pancakes, whole-wheat waffles, and housemade fruit sauces. The prints and original artwork on display, from Renoir to Jasper Johns to Alden Mason, come from the Seattle gallery owned by Ms. Kucera's son Greg.

Indian Valley Motel and Granny's Cafe

235-471 Highway 101 W, Port Angeles, WA 98362 • (360)928-3266

For 32 years this motel has been a favorite stop for tourists looking for a good Olympic Peninsula value. The nine units are innocent of frilly curtains, TV, or sample toiletries. Out back are an RV park, campsites, and a forest trail. Granny's Cafe, next door, is a blast. A catch-all kind of old-time museum adjoins an alfresco dining space to the rear. There's even an aviary. Granny presides, exchanging banter with the clientele and making sure the chili is hot.

Pond Motel

1425 W Highway 101, Port Angeles, WA 98362 • (360)452-8422

The environmentally correct Pond is an anachronism on busy Highway 101, where the logging trucks roll on, spotted owl or no spotted owl. The acre-sized pond (complete with ducks and fish) is visible from the highway, but it takes a sharp eye to spy the unobtrusive motel units overlooking it. The landscaping is lovely: a wee bridge leads to a wee island in the pond, and perennials bloom along the border. Six of the ten units have kitchens.

Van Riper's Resort

Front and Rice Streets (PO Box 246), Sekiu, WA 98381 • (360)963-2334

Van Riper's is a friendly, family-run hotel, popular with fisherfolk, scuba divers, and beach buffs. Half of the 11 rooms have views of the Strait of Juan de Fuca and Sekiu's busy harbor. The best quarters are the separate house, which sleeps six to eight, and the Penthouse in the main building, which sleeps six. Downstairs rooms are smaller, and some have thin walls. Closed mid-October through January. No pets.

Cape Flattery Resort

*Two miles west of Neah Bay (PO Box 117), Neah Bay, WA 98357
(360)645-2251*

Once an Air Force station, this sprawling complex has been converted by the Makah tribe into a year-round resort and conference center, with cafe, gym, bowling alley, barbecue area, and classrooms. Lodgings are in the former enlisted men's quarters, and each pair of rooms shares a bath. There are also dorm bunks, with the bath down the hall. Furnishings are a serviceable but hilarious hodgepodge gleaned from nationwide government surplus. Convenient to the Makah tribe's museum, hiking to Cape Flattery, ocean beach walks, and fishing.

La Push Ocean Park and Shoreline Resort

*Front Street (PO Box 67), La Push, WA 98350 • (360)374-5267 or
(800)487-1267*

You have many choices here, but choose early; reservations must be made far in advance at this ocean-front resort, a Quileute tribal enterprise. Most of the 26 cabins and all the motel units have ocean views and electric heat. The eight nonview "campers' cabins" cost the least, have wood-burning stoves, and don't include bedding—but even they are only a few yards from the beach. Cabins and motel units sleep two to six. Some have fireplaces. Bring your own drinking and cooking water because the tap water is sulfurous, though harmless. There are no non-smoking rooms, the furnishings are so-so, and the lighting is a bit dim. But who cares, with that ocean so close?

Fossil Creek Ranch Lodging

9772 Oil City Road (Box 712), Forks, WA 98331 • (360)374-2553

Travel almost 10 miles of gravel road from Highway 101 and check in with the Dicksons at the big white house on the right. Your nearby lodging, the last house on the road, has two bedrooms, two baths, a complete kitchen, no TV, no phone, and no traffic roar. It's a just a mile away from the mouth of the Hoh and the mighty Pacific. Surf fishing, river fishing (salmon, steelhead), and beachcombing are only some of the outdoor inducements. This is the southern terminus of the strenuous 15-mile beach hike to La Push.

Hoh Humm Ranch

171763 Highway 101 (Box 780), Forks, WA 98331 • (360)374-5337

Bob Huelsdonk, descended from the Iron Man of the Hoh, has made this old farmhouse into a bed and breakfast where five rooms share 1½ baths. A hearty, farmhand-style breakfast is served at the family dining table in the big, busy all-purpose room, where you can watch sheep, goats, antelopes, and llamas grazing picturesquely in the fields. Meanwhile, the work of the farm, together with Bob's sideline computer-consultant business, goes on all around you. The atmosphere may be chaotic, but the rooms are clean and comfortable—and, who knows, you might get a good price on a llama.

Miller Tree Inn

654 E Division Street (PO Box 953), Forks, WA 98331 • (360)374-6806

Seventy-five years ago, a dairy farm stood on this site. These days it's not contented cows but elk you may see grazing in the nearby meadows. Two of the bedrooms have private half-baths, three more share, and all are comfortable. Breakfasts are part do-it-yourself from the breakfast bar, part cooked-to-order omelets. For fishermen, the Millers serve an early breakfast, suggest a guide, pack a sack lunch, and, at a lucky day's end, package and freeze the catch.

Rain Forest Hostel

169312 Highway 101 (Box 870), Forks, WA 98331 • (360)374-2270

Houseparents Jim Conomos and Kay Ritchie believe firmly in the hostel concept: sharing accommodations, pitching in to clean up, and enjoying the fellowship of like-minded travelers. They go one step further and invite guests into their living room, often the venue for long, deep after-dinner gabfests. Two rooms lined with bunk beds sleep 10 and share two baths. A spacious cedar-walled annex houses 8 to 12 more. A small trailer outside is suitable for families or couples and is allergen-free. Blankets and pillows are provided, but BYO sheets (or rent them for $1). Jim and Kay point guests toward the best mushroom- and berry-picking spots (or fishing, if that's your pleasure), and have even been known to help hostelers make jam.

Three Rivers Resort

7764 La Push Road (Box 280), Forks, WA 98331 • (360)374-5300

Steelhead and salmon leap in the nearby Bogachiel, Soleduck, and Quillayute rivers. Appropriately, the resort store offers guided fishing trips. If fish don't land in your creel, there's always the world-famous

River Burger, 12 flavors of shakes, and espresso to console you back at the resort. The five cabins are modest; two apartments have been added in the main lodge. La Push and ocean beaches are only 10 minutes away.

Lochaerie Resort
638 Northshore Road, Amanda Park, WA 98526 • (360)288-2215

Scattered down a steepish slope on the north shore of Lake Quinault, these five endearing cabins have weathered with considerable grace. The oldest cabins, Ellinor and Olympus (all are named for Olympic peaks), date from 1926. Colonel Bob, the largest (sleeps six), is a recent arrival. The one-bedroom Christie (sleeps three) is closest to the lake, down the most steps, and most in demand. Storm King, with one bed nook that hangs right over the lake, sleeps five with ease. Linens, utensils, and firewood are provided.

Moonstone Beach Motel
4849 Pacific Street, Moclips, WA 98562 • (360)276-4346

You can't miss it: a row of eight little motel units the color of orange sherbet, a few yards north of the bridge into Moclips. Between you and the ocean, there's nothing but a verandah with seen-better-days lounge chairs and picnic tables. Second-floor visitors see a little more sea. All units have kitchens (though not necessarily ovens), and there's a separate six-person cabin. Moclips, the most northern resort town of North Beach, has good razor clamming and driftwood browsing. Plan ahead, as this place fills up fast for the summer.

Iron Springs Resort
Highway 109 (PO Box 207), Copalis Beach, WA 98535 • (360)276-4230

This four-decades-old resort is on one of the most satisfying beaches on the peninsula. Twenty-eight cabins dot the slope from blufftop to creekside, cleverly sited so everybody has an ocean view. Most have fireplaces. Spruce trees and fences form a screen between neighbors. The largest cabin sleeps 10; the others sleep 2 to 4. The two studio apartments in the reception building are the least expensive, and even they have a view of the river mouth and ocean. Take a swim in the covered, heated pool. Buy some of longtime owner Olive Little's tasty clam chowder and cinnamon rolls to supplement your meal. Take the nature walk with the ocean overlook, or the woodsy one along the creek.

West Winds Resort Motel
2537 State Route 109, Ocean City, WA 98569 • (360)289-3448

Five little log-veneer cabins, plus a larger two-unit one, look out at lawn and trees; up above, two motel-style units view dunes and ocean. There's a mini-playground for the kids, and a Clam Galley where you may clean your dig. The management eases access to the beach by providing a raft to cross the creek that meanders through the dunes. All cabins have TV and kitchens and are spotless. The tiniest looks about the right size for Red Riding Hood's grandmother but, reportedly, accommodates four. One cabin has a fireplace and plenty of wood outside the door.

Harbor Resort
871 Neddie Rose Drive, Westport, WA 98595 • (360)268-0169

Way out at the end of the jetty, Mark Dodson runs a fishing and whale-watching charter and a general store with lodgings upstairs. It's as funky as it is authentic. Crabs are the thing: he rents crab traps, educates fledgling crabbers, and even cooks and cleans your catch. No luck? He usually has a supply of fresh-caught crabs for sale. Whales sometimes come right into Westport Harbor and can be spied from the resort's ocean-facing rooms. The cleverest lodgers rent two adjoining rooms, one with kitchen and one without: presto! a suite for four. A spanking-new waterfront cottage next to the main building sleeps four adults and one child, and has a kitchen, TV, deck, and plenty of privacy.

Tokeland Hotel
100 Hotel Road, Tokeland, WA 98590 • (360)267-7006

This landmark hotel has taken on new life and hope under current owners Scott and Catherine White, who are diligently restoring rooms and keeping things up to snuff. Guests find plenty of comfortable spots to relax, whether sunning in the meadow or reading in the fireplace room off the lobby. The bedrooms aren't too gussied up, and the baths down the hall have modern fixtures. The restaurant does a creditable job, with down-home cooking and due deference to fresh local specialties like oysters, crab, and cranberries (e.g., cranberry sausage for breakfast). The best bargains are during the week. Full breakfast, included with the room, is attentively served.

Mike's Beach Resort
*N 38470 Highway 101, Lilliwaup, WA 98555-9734 • (360)877-5324
or (800)231-5324*

The unassuming resort, curving along a cove and only partly visible from Hood Canal's Highway 101, offers an almost bewildering range of activities: kayaking, going out in the resident sailboat, diving to examine sunken vessels just offshore, snorkeling, crabbing and clamming, and picnicking on the beach, for starters. Lodgings are almost as varied: cabins sleeping one to four, a dormitory, a youth hostel, RV spaces, and campsites. Mike Schultz and his mother manage the whole shebang with the ingenuity and helpfulness that come from 40-plus years of welcoming beach buffs.

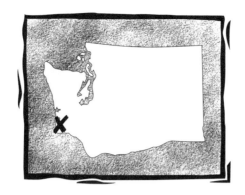

Long Beach Peninsula &
Willapa Bay

En route from Seattle to the Long Beach Peninsula, you drive by the Home of the World's First Tree Farm and by the Largest Estuarine Island on the Pacific Coast. Once on the peninsula—locally proclaimed as the World's Longest Beach (we actually know a longer, 60-mile stretch of beach on New York's Long Island, but never mind), you can devour the World's Largest Hamburger, break the World's Record for Kites in the Sky, or catch the World's Largest Chinook.

We haven't counted, but we suspect the residents of this 28-mile-long peninsula in southwestern Washington, 110 miles northwest of Portland and 180 miles southwest of Seattle, might also claim the world's record for most superlatives. It is easy to poke fun at this peninsula pride. Summertime popularity has spurred on such illustrious attractions as bumper cars, pinball arcades, and T-shirt vendors. Still, behind all the gift shops and the tire tracks on the beach, there is plenty to explore that's wonderful and remarkable.

This southwestern elbow of Washington consists of three distinct environments: the vast beaches of the peninsula; the *eelgrass, shellfish, and migrating birds of Willapa Bay; and the old-growth western redcedar on Long Island.*

The summer invasion of beachbound tourists doubles the prices of lodging, clogs Highway 103 (the peninsula's main artery), and crowds its only state park campground. Increasingly popular festivals make planning ahead at certain times of the summer a must (especially mid-July through August). Instead, try visiting during spring, when the tides are low enough in the daytime for clam digging, or early fall, when the salmon—and charter companies—are still running.

ON THE ROAD

The great thing about **Long Beach** is that you can do almost anything on its hard, flat sands. You can walk, run, sit, drive, fly kites, dig clams, ride horses or mountain bikes, and even drive your car. (There are some limitations, of course.) Beach driving is off limits only at the tip and the tail of the peninsula (Leadbetter Point and Fort Canby State Park). The rest of the beach is open to motorized vehicles year-round, except for a 3-mile section north of Oysterville and a 1½-mile section between Seaview and Long Beach, both of which are closed from April 15 through Labor Day. Vehicular exception is given only to razor-clam diggers when the season is open (usually April to May or October to November).

All **razor-clam diggers** need a license—$5 for residents and $20 for nonresidents (though out-of-staters can get a special two-day license for $6). Again, there are rules and limits. Call the Department of Fisheries

---

Attention Bicyclists

Bring your own: there are no bike rentals on Long Beach Peninsula. The hard, smooth beach, however, is an excellent place for fat-tired mountain bikes. Ride out to the tip of Leadbetter Point State Park and hope that the winds are with you on the return trip.

in Nahcotta for specific dates; (360)249-4628. Sand-Sations, a sand-sculpting contest held each year on the last weekend in July, is a beach-going pursuit of the more artistic kind, attracting artists and gawkers from near and far.

The constant coastal winds make **kite flying** a passion; Long Beach boasts three kite shops. The oldest is Stormin' Norman (205 S Pacific Highway, Long Beach; (360)642-3482), which does a good business with families because of its huge stock of reasonably priced kites. Ocean Kites (511 Pacific Street, Long Beach; (360)642-2229 or 800-KITE-FLY) boosts the ante with free kite-flying lessons. Long Beach Kites (104 Pacific Avenue N, Long Beach; (360)642-2202) stocks kites from all over the world and sells numerous oddball kite parts. The owners, Jim and Kay Buesing, also run the World Kite Museum (3rd Street NW, Long Beach; (360)642-4020), which exhibits Asian fighter kites, a collection of locally made flyers, ancient kites, and exotic shimmering works of flying art. Prices are $3 for families, $1 for adults, and 50 cents for kids; they're open only on weekends, unless you call ahead. In mid-August you can celebrate the International Kite Festival, during which stunt kites, homemade kites, and high-altitude kites compete for flight time; (360)642-2400.

Horseback riding on the beach is the stuff of dreams. An hour ($11) with Kotek Skip (9th Street S and Beach Boulevard, Long Beach; (360)642-3676) gets you a 5-mile beach ride. Bring your own horse and for a small fee you (and your critter) can set up camp at Long Beach's rodeo ground.

It makes perfect sense that **Ilwaco**, where the mouth of the Columbia River meets the Pacific, is the salmon, sturgeon, steelhead, trout, and bottom-fish fishing charter hub. Charter companies vie for your dollars, with the average daily charter price at around $60 (bottom fishing is slightly more). The charter companies are open for fishing

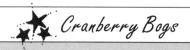

Cranberry Bogs

Between late September and early November, drive Cranberry Road through acres and acres of ripe cranberry bogs. The peninsula hosts a cranberry festival the third weekend in October, when the harvesting begins. You can observe the process of sorting, cleaning, and grading the berries at the Ocean Spray Receiving Station. Festival attractions include performances by a logger poet and Willapa folk dancers; (360)642-2400.

primarily in May through October, with an occasional bottom-fishing excursion at other times of the year. Call ahead for season openings and reservations. There are many charter companies to choose from: A-1 Tuna, Salmon Charter, (360)642-3734; Beacon Charters, (360)642-2138; Columbia Bar Charters, (360)642-2395; Ilwaco Charter Service, (360)642-3232; Pacific Salmon Charters, (360)642-3466 or (800)831-2695; Sea Breeze Charters, (360)642-2300; and Tidewind Charters, (360)642-2111.

With the blessing of three major grants, the newly expanded **Ilwaco Heritage Museum** (115 SE Lake Street, Ilwaco; (360)642-3446) is now an art gallery, community center, and heritage museum, with information on Native Americans, explorers, fishermen, farmers, commercial cranberry growers, and, more recently, local kite flyers.

In 1862, Fort Canby was established to protect the mouth of the river. It's now the 1,800-acre **Fort Canby State Park**, the only state park on the peninsula allowing camping. Not surprisingly, it gets quite full in the summer. Call as far ahead as possible, since August usually fills up by the end of the previous January, or reserve by mail beginning January 1 (PO Box 488, Ilwaco, WA 98624-0488; (360)642-3078). Your only chance of getting drop-in space in July or August is if there is a cancellation. The best tent sites are those closest to the ocean (91–110 or 161–180). There are a few good hiking trails here; one goes to the North Head Lighthouse, another loops through old-growth forest, and a third descends to a white, sandy beach known as Waikiki. **Cape Disappointment Lighthouse**, the West Coast's oldest lighthouse still in use, is, disappointingly, no longer open to the public for viewing purposes but is worth checking out anyway.

Fort Canby contains the **Lewis and Clark Interpretive Center**, (360)642-3029, which details the expedition's travels and documents its scientific and social contributions. You'll also learn about the numerous shipwrecks off the Columbia Bar. The world's only National Motor Life Boat School is located here, where the ocean's treacherous conditions

♫ Water Music

In late October, chamber music concerts flourish everywhere, from the church in Oysterville to the community center in Ilwaco. Each concert runs from $5 to $15, but in the Water Music Festival's spirit of making good music available to all, musicians occasionally perform at no charge; (800)451-2542.

 *Long Island*

Crowning Long Island is the 274-acre Cedar Grove, one of the last remnants of a coastal forest spared from logging, fires, and violent storms. It's a pleasant day hike. Paddle over to the island from the boat launch at the refuge headquarters on Highway 101; (360)484-3482. You can camp on the island at one of five designated sites (available on a first-come, first-served basis). Bring your own boat or rent a kayak from Willapa Bay Kayak Rentals (corner of 270th Street and Sandridge Road, Nahcotta; (360)642-4892 or (360)665-4449).

allow coast guards to practice in the 44-foot motor lifeboats virtually every day. The school offers no organized tours, but if you catch the watch-stander on a good day, you might get to stroll around those unsinkable boats.

Ilwaco has two great places to **chow**. Smalley's Galley (133 Howerton Way, Ilwaco; (360)642-8700) is a bright little spot of sunshine on the pier for fish and chips, strawberry shortcake, and clam chowder served in a bowl of hollowed-out bread. Or buy some excellent fresh seafood at Jessie's Ilwaco Fish (West End and Port Docks, Ilwaco; (360)642-3773), take it to the city park in Ilwaco, and have a fisherman's barbecue.

The attractive, pint-sized Heron and Beaver Pub (SR 103 and N 45th Street, Seaview; (360)642-4142) at the Shelburne Inn is *the* place on the peninsula to sip something with a head on it and dine on a great bowl of sherried mushroom soup or cheese fondue. You'll get more food and less ambience down the road at the American-style 42nd Street Cafe (Pacific Highway 103 and 42nd Street, Seaview; (360)642-2323).

In Long Beach, a three-quarter-mile **boardwalk** stretches along the dunes and the ocean, from the main beach access to South 10th Street. Amid all the kitschy beach shops are a few good places to eat. The Crab Pot (1917 Pacific Highway, Long Beach; (360)642-2524) serves lots of fried fish that is actually quite fresh (the restaurant doubles as a seafood market), and the steamed crab is excellent and reasonably priced. The name says it all at My Mom's Pie Kitchen (285 Pacific Highway, Long Beach; (360)642-2342).

At the end of the Ocean Park beach approach is Kopa Wecoma, (360) 642-4224, a must-stop between volleyball games or foot-tingling forays into the cold Pacific. Dive into the excellent white chowder, feast on a sandwich with housemade bread, and crunch on housemade potato chips. **131**

While most of the peninsula bustles with noisy summer beach-and-sidewalk fun, **Oysterville**, the peninsula's northernmost burg, is an historic town of beachworn homes and quiet streets. Ride your bike, enjoy a dozen oysters at the Oysterville Sea Farm, (360)665-6585, and then continue on to the nature trails of **Leadbetter Point State Park**—the very tip of the peninsula. During spring and fall migration periods, tens of thousands of shorebirds feed and rest on the beaches, tidal flats, and salt marshes.

Other attractions include the Willapa National Wildlife Refuge; (360)484-3482. Long Island in Willapa Bay has 5,000 acres of damp coastal forests, sandy beaches, salt-grass tidal marshes, and muddy tidal flats. On the edge of the island you'll find thriving beds of oysters, clams, and an army of crabs. Farther inland, there is much varied wildlife: Roosevelt elk, black bear, river otter, and pileated woodpeckers, to name a few.

CHEAP SLEEPS

Fort Columbia Hostel
PO Box 224, Chinook, WA 98614 • (360)777-8755

This one is nothing more than a big, drafty hostel set high above the Columbia River in Fort Columbia State Park. The men's dormitory was the infirmary during the Spanish-American War and can get chilly during inclement weather. There's a great beach just a short walk from the hostel, and Long Beach Peninsula is only 6 miles away. A living room and a fully equipped kitchen are available for all to use. Couples should reserve the nice private room ($24).

Sou'wester
Beach Approach Road (PO Box 102), Seaview, WA 98644 • (360)642-2542

Hosts Leonard and Miriam Atkins make lodgers feel like long-awaited guests in this rambling, 100-year-old house near the beach, with a variety of unusual guest quarters. Self-sufficient apartments upstairs are often frequented by artist-musician-writer types. Smaller lodgings on the main floor are available on what the Atkinses call the B&MYODB plan (bed & make your own damn breakfast). That includes kitchen privileges. There are also rustic cabins and a nostalgic assortment of classic trailers, dubbed the "TCH! TCH!" (Trailer Classics Hodgepodge) collection. Fortunate guests may be treated to chamber music or drama evenings or have the chance to participate in a "Teacup T'ink Tank" (not quite a think tank, says Len), exploring matters great and small.

Arcadia Court
N 4th and Boulevard (PO Box 426), Long Beach, WA 98631
(360)642-2613

This modest, crisply appointed motel has small but cozy rooms starting at $39. The principal draws are the perky flower boxes, kitchenettes (in some rooms), location dead-bang in the middle of the Long Beach action, and marvelous proximity to the dunes—there they are right behind you!

The Lighthouse Motel
Route 1, Box 527, Long Beach, WA 98631 • (360)642-3622

In this little beachfront motel, each room feels like your own cabin, and your pooch is welcome too. Old books, small TVs, beach treasures, and salty old trunks remind you of your whereabouts; so do the path to the beach and the uninterrupted view. All eight nautical units face the sunset. Some have one bedroom and others have two, but they all have fireplaces, driftwood-inspired porches, and kitchens.

Our Place
1309 S Boulevard (PO Box 266), Long Beach, WA 98631 • (360)642-3793

This modest motel squeezed between the Long Beach strip and the dunes has 25 rooms (some with kitchens) and a steamy, tiled Jacuzzi, a sauna, and an exercise building. Get a room on the top floor, facing west, and you (and Fido, if you like) will be quite content.

Pacific View Motel
203 Bolstad (PO Box 302), Long Beach, WA 98631 • (360)642-2415

These tidy yellow units have the self-contained feeling of cottages—with kitchenettes, dining nooks, and charming knotty pine interiors. To be inside one, just a stone's throw from the boardwalk and the beach, is to forget you're in a motel in the middle of Long Beach's Coney Island strip. Rates start at $48; pets allowed in some units.

Moby Dick Hotel
Sandridge Road (PO Box 82), Nahcotta, WA 98637 • (360)665-4543

The Moby Dick, which has been around since the '30s, is humble in appearance and generous in spirit. Owners Fritzi and Edward Cohen— who also own the venerable Tabard Inn in the *other* Washington (DC)— have worked hard to pretty up the interior of this nonsmoking hotel. It's a chipper place, splashed with vibrant colors and sophisticated art and punctuated with fresh flowers, hardwood floors, an upright piano, a fireplace, and put-your-feet-up couches. The rooms are simple (and all 10 share a couple of baths), but the outside is big. You'll find an oyster

Summer Vacation

The key to getting a good deal anywhere on the peninsula is to simply avoid summertime. Prices plummet and everything seems affordable before May and after October. Trouble is, summer is when most people really want to be here. For a list of available rental homes, contact the Long Beach Peninsula Visitor's Bureau (corner of Highway 103 and Highway 101, Long Beach; (360)642-2400 or (800)451-2542). Prices are very reasonable, especially for small groups.

farm at the water's edge (Tabard Inn's private reserve), dazzling gardens out front, and walking trails through Leadbetter Point State Park, which is right down the road. A resident chef spins the local bounty into lovely meals—not quite cheap, unfortunately, at $15–$30 for dinner. Neither, for that matter, are the rooms, which can edge up beyond $65 in summer but which, for sheer delightful ambience, are well worth the slight splurge.

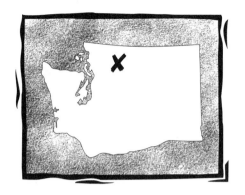

The North Cascades

Some say the glorious granite spires and awe-inspiring glaciers of the North Cascades are unmatched in the lower 48 states. Indeed, when the alpine flowers are at their best in early August, and when the fall colors peak in early October, you should head out over the North Cascades Scenic Highway and return via Stevens Pass to behold some of this country's finest scenery. Get off the highway whenever possible. The high trails (many are easy day hikes) are the most spectacular, reaching glaciers, old lookout shelters, and exhilarating panoramas that overlook the rest of the range. Seekers of solitude will find it here.

ON THE ROAD

The end of **Mount Baker Highway** (Highway 542), which winds through the narrow valley of the North Fork of the Nooksack, doubles as the parking lot for the Mount Baker ski resort in winter. In summer, it is a jumping-off point for some easy day hikes and spectacular views of both Mount Baker and the geographically eccentric Mount Shuksan. Hiking here is extensive and beautiful, especially in the late summer when the foliage is turning, the wild blueberries are ripe, and the days are hot and dry. Experienced climbers ascend Mount Baker primarily in May and June. Permits are not required, but the ranger station prefers that you register at either the Glacier Public Service Center, (360)599-2714, or the Mount Baker Ranger Station in Sedro Woolley, (360)856-5700.

Mount Baker Ski Area, 56 miles east of Bellingham, has good downhill slopes but is equally noteworthy as a cross-country skiing destination. It's open daily from mid-November through January, Wednesday through Sunday till the end of March, and weekends only through May 1 (the longest skiing season in the state). Tickets are about 10 bucks cheaper on weekdays, and the beginner's rope tow is free. Reasonably priced **day care** is available for children (two years and older) on weekends. The mountain seldom lacks for snow, and runs are predominantly intermediate, with bowls, meadows, and trails; (360)734-6771. **Baker Lake**, accessible from Highway 20 via Baker Lake Highway, is a popular camping spot.

In December through March, hundreds of **bald eagles** perch along the Skagit River next to Highway 20 between Rockport and Marblemount. Bring your binoculars. You'll be able to spy a number of them from the road; however, the best way to see them is from the river. The adventuresome may want to canoe downriver from Marblemount to Rockport (an easy 8 miles); the river appears tame but can be deceptively swift. Otherwise, rafting companies will gladly guide you down the river from December 15 through the end of January, when eagle watchers often spot up to 200 eagles. Trips cost around $50. Call Downstream River Runners, (206)483-0335; Northern Wilderness River Riders, (206)448-RAFT; or Orion Expeditions, (206)322-9130. These companies also run the more challenging Wenatchee and Skykomish rivers in spring.

Marblemount is the unofficial gateway to the North Cascades. Hikers veer off the highway onto the 22-mile-long Cascade River Road. Numerous trails branch off this road into the **Glacier Peak Wilderness**, leading ultimately to such places as Hidden Lake and Lookout Mountain.

Canoe Ross Lake

Since the only road access to Ross Lake is south from Hope, BC, the best way to get to the lake—except for a mile-long hike—is by boat via Diablo Lake. Launch your canoe in Diablo Lake at Colonial Creek National Park Campground, and paddle up the pretty lake to the dam. Pick up the phone there, and a truck ports you up and around the dam and deposits you and your gear on the shore of Ross Lake (if only they could do the same for salmon). Ross Lake extends 24 miles across the Canadian border, and you won't have any trouble finding a place to camp.

🎵 Bluegrass

Every summer on the third weekend in July, bluegrass fans from all over the country turn their attention to the town of Darrington, nestled in the Cascade foothills. Terrific foot-stomping, thigh-slapping music is played outdoors by some of the country's best musicians. Tickets are $25, and a $10 fee (per vehicle) buys an on-site camping space (no hookups, though). For more information, call the Chamber of Commerce; (360)436-1177.

The most popular is the 4-mile hike up to Cascade Pass (laden with blueberries come fall), which yields an exceptional view for a minimal effort. See the Lake Chelan chapter for tips on hiking the Cascade Pass from Stehekin to Marblemount. When you're heading east over the North Cascades Highway, the last good grub is found in Marblemount at Good Food. Newhalem, maintained by Seattle City Light to house employees on the Skagit Hydroelectric Project, is the last town on the west side of the North Cascades. Stop at the **Ladder Creek Falls and Rock Gardens** (no charge) for an inspirational walk through a light park (electricity is in abundance up here).

In the next 10 miles, you'll pass three dams providing power to Seattle. Built by a visionary engineer named James Delmage Ross, the dams are worth visiting. Seattle City Light's Skagit Tours, (206)684-3030, offers 4½-hour journeys (lunch included) through the Skagit Project, including an informative slide presentation, a 560-foot ride up an antique incline railway to the top of Diablo Dam, and a boat ride along the gorge of the Skagit to Ross Dam, a construction of daring engineering in its day. Those not wishing to splurge on the full tour can take a shorter version, which includes the slide show, railway ride, and brief walking tour, at a far lower price.

Between the dams and Washington Pass (the highest point on this route is marked by the highly visible Liberty Bell), numerous **hiking trails** offer opportunities for day hikes (and longer). The shortest hike, and also the most challenging, is the 1-mile path to Rainy Lake, with views of waterfalls and glaciers. Blue and Cutthroat lakes also make excellent day hikes—both are surrounded by granite spires and are no more than 2 miles off the highway. The ambitious might continue another 4 miles up from Cutthroat Lake to a North Cascades vista from Cutthroat Pass. The Canada-to-Mexico Pacific Crest Trail crosses Highway 20 at Rainy Pass.

Relay Races

Summer begins in the North Cascades with two grueling five-event relay races. Two thousand athletes (and wannabes) head over to Wenatchee in April to ski (cross-country and downhill), run, bicycle, and canoe from Mission Ridge to Wenatchee's Riverfront Park. A month later, over Memorial Day weekend, teams blast up to Bellingham to complete an 80-mile-plus race that includes skiing, running, cycling, canoeing, and sailing. Contact Ridge-to-River, (509)662-8799, or Ski-to-Sea Festival, (360)734-1330.

For a panoramic view without getting out of your car, drive east to the upper Methow Valley and turn left on Hart's Pass Road. It climbs to over 7,000 feet in 22 miles, reaching **Washington's highest point** accessible by car, where it intersects the Pacific Crest Trail. (For more information on this area, see the Methow Valley chapter.)

The Pacific Crest Trail crosses Highway 2 (the next route south over the Cascades) at **Stevens Pass**, (360)973-2441, a challenging downhill ski area at the top of Highway 2. Eleven chairs lead to over 30 runs, and the Double Diamond and Southern Cross chairs take you to some daunting expert slopes on the back side. Mondays and Tuesdays are the days to go ($12); Wednesday through Friday it's $18, and on weekends, why bother?

The old railroad towns along Highway 2, on the west side of the Cascades, offer little more than some big ice cream cones and camping provisions. Rock climbers know **Index** for its challenging cliffs, just outside the tiny town, and the hefty portions at the Index Cafe on Highway 2. There are plenty of hiking trails that lead off from the pass or from near Lake Wenatchee.

On the dry side of the mountains, approximately a half hour east of the pass, sits **Leavenworth**. This former railroad yard and sawmill town, with a stunning alpine setting, decided a few decades back to recast itself as a Bavarian-style village with tourism as its primary industry. The architecture in the city center features some excellent craftsmanship in the Bavarian mode. Popular events are the Autumn Leaf Festival, held the last weekend in September and the first weekend in October, and the Christmas Lighting Festival, held the first two Saturdays in December.

Outdoor activities include river rafting on the Wenatchee; fishing and hiking at Icicle Creek; touring the national fish hatchery (12790 Fish Hatchery Road, Leavenworth; (509)548-7641) on Icicle Creek to watch the Chinook salmon run (June and July) and spawn (August and

September); and golfing at the scenic 18-hole Leavenworth Golf Club (on Icicle Creek Road just past the fish hatchery; (509)548-7267). In winter, you'll find fabulous cross-country skiing on the golf course and at the Leavenworth Nordic Center; (509)548-7864. And there's more—horseback riding at Eagle Creek Ranch, (509)548-7798; walking along the river on the new city-center trail system, which leads to Blackbird Island via wheelchair-accessible ramps; mountain biking (rentals available at Leavenworth Ski and Sports Center at the Leavenworth Nordic Center; (509)548-4566 or (509)548-7864); and rock climbing in the new **Peshastin Pinnacles State Park**, just 10 miles east of Leavenworth (no camping, just climbing).

Locals meet at Katzen Jammers (221 Commercial Street, Leavenworth; (509)548-5826), a steak-and-seafood joint, to hoist a brew. Homefires Bakery (13013 Bayne Road, Leavenworth; (509)548-7362) fires up some formidable dark German rye in its wood-burning oven. Oberland Bakery and Cafe (703 Front Street, Leavenworth; (509)548-7216) also bakes substantial whole-grain breads. Try some with chicken salad.

Hikers are especially fond of the lake-laden Enchantments within the **Alpine Lakes Wilderness Area**, which lies east of Leavenworth (main access off Icicle Creek Road). Permits are required in late spring, summer, and early fall, and they're in high demand, so it is best to write the Leavenworth Ranger Station far in advance (600 Sherbourne Street, Leavenworth, WA 98826; (509)548-6977). The wilderness area can also be approached from Cle Elum and Stevens Pass.

Wenatchee, in the heart of apple country, celebrates its good fortune with an Apple Blossom Festival during the first part of May—a good time that lasts for 11 days. In winter, skiers come for the powder at **Mission Ridge**, 13 miles southwest of town; (509)663-7631. The four chairs lift downhillers to challenging and intermediate slopes. Tickets are $13 weekdays and $26 on weekends, but call ahead about special promotions.

CHEAP SLEEPS

Cougar Inn
23379 Highway 207, Leavenworth, WA 98826 • (509)763-3354

Most people come to this inn on Lake Wenatchee for the all-you-can-eat prime rib on Friday nights or the champagne brunch on Sundays. What many of them probably don't know is that if you purchase a weeknight dinner, you can stay in the lodge for half price—and even full price ($45) ain't bad. Four of the six rooms share a bath (enjoy the gigantic tub), so if you insist on your own, check out one of the three cabins. Even if the lake weren't at your doorstep, you still wouldn't be twiddling your thumbs. What with tennis, horseshoes, volleyball nets, and the mountains, summer reservations should be made six months in advance. Open year-round.

Edelweiss Hotel
843 Front Street, Leavenworth, WA 98826 • (509)548-7015 or (509)548-5010

This Front Street hotel, the first building in town to go Bavarian, is now owned by Eva Rhodes. Her son, John Rhodes, oversees the 14 rooms (5 with private bath) and keeps the prices more than reasonable (less than $20, or just over $50).

Ingall's Creek Lodge
3003 US Highway 97, Leavenworth, WA 98826 • (509)548-6281

Built in 1960, Ingall's Creek sports four little rooms with cable TV and private baths. It makes a good base camp for skiing any of the 210 miles of trails in the winter or for heading into the Enchantments via the Ingall's Creek Trail in summer.

Mrs. Andersen's Lodging House
917 Commercial Street, Leavenworth, WA 98826 • (509)548-6173 or (800) 253-8990

Though it's been through several incarnations (it originally opened in 1903 as a boardinghouse for sawmill workers), this 10-room inn right in the center of Leavenworth has charm to spare. The rooms are basic boardinghouse—minimally furnished—but sparkling clean, with pristine whitewashed walls and lace curtains. All have cable TV, eight have private baths, and two upstairs rooms with shared bath offer one of the cheapest sleeps in Leavenworth ($49 and $55).

Hillcrest Motel
2921 School Street, Wenatchee, WA 98801 • (509)663-5157

Hillcrest has 16 rooms up on Sunny Slope Hill above Wenatchee. The owners have been slowly refurbishing each room over the past few years, and each keeps getting better. There's also an outdoor pool (summers only).

Orchard Inn Motel
1401 North Miller, Wenatchee, WA 98801 • (509)662-3443 or (800)368-4571

Smack in the middle of Wenatchee, with 103 rooms, the Orchard Inn does good business and keeps its prices real low. (Okay, so one May weekend during the Apple Blossom Festival, prices sneak above $50.) A big bubble covers the heated pool in the winter, but you can swim under the stars in the summer. Pets okay with a deposit. Mission Ridge ski packages are available.

North Cascades Inn
4284 Highway 20, Concrete, WA 98236 • (360)853-8870

Kids are free and the pie is perfect (sometimes we wish it were the other way around) at Larry La Plante and Einar Storaker's roadside inn. These are the two who made the Skagit Valley's Conway Tavern a success. Now they're making the North Cascades Inn the same kind of place . . . a place where people congregate. Stop in anytime for housemade pie and coffee, Wednesdays for a Mexi-meal, or Sundays for prime rib. Stay in one of their 14 motel rooms ($35) and order a slice of you-know-what for breakfast.

Clark's Skagit River Cabins
5675 Highway 20, Rockport, WA 98283 • (360)873-2250

The Clark family has been in the resort business long enough to have worked all the bugs out of their 25-unit operation. Located near the entrance to the North Cascades National Park, Clark's borders the Skagit, offering plenty of possibilities to keep hikers and fishers happy. The standard cabins are cozy, clean, and authentic—in stark contrast to the newer cabins, which fancifully attempt to re-create, say, an Indian longhouse, a Mexican hacienda, or a mountain sawmill. Who *really* needs contrived atmosphere when a night in one of the standard cabins will have you expecting Bogey to tag along for some early fly fishing?

Home Away from Home

Don't own a vacation home? You can always rent one. Mt. Baker Chalet, Inc., (360)599-2405, offers accommodations in privately owned cabins, chalets, and condos near Mt. Baker National Forest and the North Cascades National Park. Located just outside the village of Glacier, these lodgings range from small, rustic A-frame cabins (perfect for a weekend à deux) to deluxe four-bedroom chalets (which sleep up to 10). Some have creek or mountain views, and all are set in wooded locations, with playgrounds, swimming pools, tennis courts, and hiking trails nearby. Rates vary, but you can get a good deal on weekly rates in summer.

We'd like to let you in on a little secret about some free lodgings. Roughly 500 fire lookouts were built in the '20s and '30s in Western Washington alone. Each accommodated the lifestyle of one or two very solitary people, who would live there for a couple of months and report forest fires to the Forest Service. By virtue of their function, these lodgings usually had amazing views. Some were abandoned, some destroyed, and some left to the ravages of wind and snow. Yet a handful have been maintained by local hiking and mountaineering groups.

You'll need to bring sleeping bags and, to be safe, a stove, and you'll need to keep in mind that the lookouts are run on a first-come, first-served basis. They are very special places, a slice of Northwest history in a corner of the beauty they were designed to protect. Please respect them.

• The **Park Butte Lookout**, with its close-up view of Mount Baker's Easton Glacier and surrounding mountains, seems much higher than its 4,052 feet. Bring a stove, or some wood for the wood stove. The Skagit Alpine Club maintains this lookout and has priority use. The hike to the lookout is a fairly easy 3½ miles. In the winter, make sure it's closed and shuttered when you leave. Call the ranger station in Sedro Woolley for directions; (360)856-5700.

• **Three Fingers Summit** has, by far, the most dramatically situated lodging options in the Northwest. The Three Fingers south summit, at 6,854 feet, affords breathtaking (and vertigo-inducing) views from all sides. To the west is a 500-foot drop into a crevasse; to the north, a 1,000-foot descent to a lake; and to the east, a straight drop of 2,400 feet. Sleepwalkers beware. The lookout, refurbished by the Everett Mountaineers, sleeps as many as eight people, though it has only one bunk. The hike is 7½ miles—long miles—and requires some knowledge of snow travel, as you'll cross a small glacier. Call the Darrington Ranger Station in the Mount Baker-Snoqualmie National Forest for information and directions; (360)436-1155.

• The **Hidden Lake Lookout**, at 6,890 feet, is surrounded to the west and north by 7,000-foot peaks and the nearby namesake lake. The lookout is a 4-mile hike from Forest Road 1540 off Cascade Pass Road. Call the ranger station in Sedro Woolley for information; (360)856-5700.

• **Winchester Mountain**, with its panoramic view of Mount Shuksan and Mount Baker, greets hikers a couple of miles south of the Canadian border. This lookout is maintained by the Mount Baker Hiking Club. From the trailhead it's 2 miles to the lookout. Call the ranger station in Sedro Woolley for information before checking in for the night; (360)856-5700.

Circle F

2399 Mount Baker Highway, Bellingham, WA 98226 • (360)733-2509

Five and a half miles east of Bellingham, Guy Foster runs this castlelike farmhouse with three rooms for rent under $50 (including breakfast) on 330 acres with cows, horses, pigs, chickens, cats, dogs, and probably a few more creatures we never met. It's a comfortable spot (as long as you like animals) where everyone tends to gather and chat near the kitchen fireplace. It's a great location for hikers and skiers; Mount Baker's a short hour east.

Glacier Creek Motel & Cabins

PO Box 5008, Glacier, WA 98244 • (360)599-2991

On Mount Baker Highway, in the tiny town of Glacier ("Gateway to Mount Baker"), 11 cozy cabins and 9 motel units nestle among tall firs next to a rushing stream. (You can actually *hear* the stream from the cabins, and yes, it does rush.) Skiers and hikers will love the proximity to slopes and backcountry—and they'll appreciate soaking tired bones in the motel's hot tub at day's end. The cabins are simple but pleasant; some have kitchens. Barbecue areas dot the woodsy grounds, an espresso bar in the main building pumps caffeine, and within walking distance are other amenities, including a strikingly good restaurant and the local ranger station.

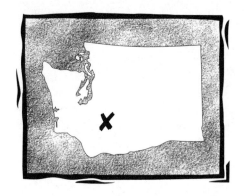

The South Cascades

Three volcanoes battle for attention in the South Cascades. *Mount St. Helens, the most recently verbal one, erupted on May 18, 1980, leaving a huge, gaping scar on its north side. Mount Rainier calls out to climbers with its massive, glacier-covered 14,410-foot cone. Mount Adams stands peacefully to the south—a shorter (12,276 feet), well-mannered kid brother to Rainier. While a few hearty souls aspire to climb one or all of these, most weekenders use them for photo backdrops, and spend time hiking and skiing near the less challenging and more accessible Snoqualmie Pass, an hour east of Seattle on I-90. Another favorite playground, tucked inconspicuously between Mount Rainier and Mount Adams, is the sawtooth-ridged Goat Rocks Wilderness.*

ON THE ROAD

In summer, the ski runs thaw into mountain meadows, and melting snows unveil crystalline lakes and hiking trails galore. But it's winter that really draws the crowds. At the top of **Snoqualmie Pass** is the ski-resort quad of Snoqualmie, Alpental, Ski Acres, and Hyak; (206)232-8182 or (206)434-6161. The resorts are very popular (especially on weekends and at night) due to their proximity to Seattle.

The wide-open slopes of Snoqualmie are a great place to learn to ski. Alpental's challenging slopes are known as the home mountain of Olympic gold medalist Debbie Armstrong. Ski Acres has a number of bump runs, and Hyak, the smallest of the four areas, is your best bet if you want to avoid the lines and try telemark turns (you won't be alone). The cheapest days are Mondays and Tuesdays ($12). As the week progresses, so does the price. By the weekend, lift tickets peak at $26. Ski Acres gives you the most runs for your money.

Save gas and avoid snow perils by taking the **I-90 Ski Bus** up to Snoqualmie Pass. On Saturdays and Sundays, the bus leaves from four locations in Seattle and the Eastside for $17 round trip. It operates in conjunction with the Seattle Times Ski School, but you don't need to take lessons to get a ride up to the pass; call the ski school, (206)232-8182 or (206)434-6363, for information and reservations.

A wonderfully groomed cross-country loop around Mount Catherine connects Hyak and Ski Acres. It's a pleasant 12½-mile day loop with a warming hut halfway out. Ski Acres' lower trail system has 1½ kilometers of lit trails for night skiing Wednesdays and Saturdays; (206)434-6646.

Twenty miles east of the pass is **Roslyn**, once a thriving coal-mining area. Today, the charming rough-and-tough town is the somewhat bustling set for the TV series "Northern Exposure." If that's not enough, modest turn-of-the-century homes have become weekend places for city folk, and the former mortuary is now a video store and movie theater. And yet, a few mementos of yesteryear remain, one being the water-fed brass spittoon of the old stone tavern, the Brick (1 Pennsylvania Avenue, Roslyn; (509)649-2643). Hikers should pick up some beef jerky or pepperoni at Carek's Market (510 South A Street, Roslyn; (509)649-2930). There's excellent hand-thrown pizza at Village Pizza (6 Pennsylvania Avenue, Roslyn; (509)649-2992) and buttermilk waffles for breakfast at the Roslyn Cafe (28 Pennsylvania Avenue, Roslyn; (509)649-2763). The Roslyn Brewing Company (33 Pennsylvania Avenue, Roslyn; (509)649-2232) has a taproom, open on weekends from noon to 5pm, where you can have a free taste of their flagship brew, a full-bodied lager, and buy a quart to take home. Roslyn Beer can also be quaffed at Village Pizza, the Roslyn Cafe, and the Old #3 (in Ronald).

A few miles east is **Cle Elum,** another former coal-mining town (which doesn't have quite the charm of Roslyn). Cle Elum Bakery (501 E First Street, Cle Elum; (509)674-2233), a longtime local institution with one of the last brick-oven hearths in the Northwest, is doing as much business these days with travelers as with locals.

Lake Cle Elum is a recreation hub for boaters. In June, the Cle Elum

River just above the lake is filled with swiftly paddling racers in their brightly colored kayaks from all over the Northwest. For access to the lake, stay at the Wishpoosh or Salmon La Sac campgrounds, beyond the Last Resort in Ronald. The Forest Service land is laced with trails for mountain biking in the spring and summer (the Ronald General Store rents mountain bikes) and is groomed for cross-country skiers and snowmobilers in the winter. It's the snowmobiling that draws the crowds. You can rent a snowmobile from Pioneer Rentals on Sparks Road in Easton ($100 per day); (509)656-2302.

On Highway 410 in the Mount Baker/Snoqualmie National Forest, **Crystal Mountain,** believed by many to have the best skiing in the state, draws outdoor aficionados in the summer for mountain biking and that up-close Mount Rainier view. Off season you can ride the chair lift (with your bike if you like). During the ski season, midweek tickets are substantially discounted; (206)634-3771. After a particularly satisfying day of skiing, stop at the Naches Tavern (Highway 410, Greenwater; (360)663-2267) for a respectable double burger and a shift in front of the fireplace. On the way *to* Crystal, try the Black Diamond Bakery (32805 Railroad Avenue, Black Diamond; (360)886-2741) for breakfast, or just grab one (or two) of the 26 kinds of bread made in the wood-fired oven and devour it (or them) in the car.

Elbe, on the western approach to Mount Rainier, was once a sawmill town. It is on the verge of becoming a museum for antique cabooses thanks to the advent of the Cascadian Dinner Train (and an enterprising restaurateur). The four-hour ride—on a fully restored 1920s passenger train, with dinner served by tuxedoed waitstaff—is expensive. Instead, hop on the **Mount Rainier Scenic Railroad** for a 90-minute trip (to tiny Mineral and back) whose scenery is equally attractive. Offered only in summer, the ride costs $7.50 for adults and a few bucks less for kids; (360)569-2588. If you insist on eating on a train, try the stationary Mount Rainier Railroad Dining Company (54106 Mountain Highway, Elbe; (360)569-2505). One car is a dining room; the other (the Sidetrack Room) is a bar with a dance floor.

Better eats (and sleeps) can be found a couple of miles closer to the mountain in **Ashford**. The beloved Copper Creek Inn (35707 State Route 706, Ashford; (360)569-2326) helps you attain paradise with heavenly, housemade blackberry pie, grilled trout, chicken soup, and burgers served between two grilled slices of housemade bread. It's closed, unfortunately, from the end of October through winter.

A few miles inside the southwestern border of Mount Rainier National Park lies the little village of Longmire, with an inn, a small wildlife museum, a hiking information center, a cross-country skiing rental outlet, and the only gas inside park limits. The folks at Rainier Ski Touring can recommend slopes and trails; (360)569-2211, ext. 237.

Ahead is **Paradise**. At 5,400 feet, Paradise is the most popular destination point on the mountain. On the way to the visitors center, you'll catch spectacular views of Narada Falls and Nisqually Glacier. The visitors center, housed in a flying-saucer-like building, has a standard cafeteria and gift shop, nature exhibits and films, and a superb view of the mountain from its observation deck. Depending on the season, you can picnic among the wildflowers, explore some of the trails (the rangers offer guided walks), let the kids slide on inner tubes in the snow-play area, try a little cross-country skiing, or even take a guided snowshoe tromp from the folks at the Park Service. The tour lasts two hours and is free ($1 suggested donation for equipment); there are two trips per day on weekends. Be warned that entering the ice caves (3 miles northeast of Paradise) in their deteriorating state has become extremely dangerous.

Open only during the summer months, the Sunrise Visitor Center on Mount Rainier's north side (6,400 feet) is the closest you can drive to the peak. The old Sunrise Lodge has no overnight accommodations, but it does offer a snack bar and exhibits about the mountain. Dozens of trails begin here, including a short one leading to a magnificent viewpoint of Emmons Glacier Canyon.

Majestic **Mount Rainier** is the abiding symbol of natural grandeur in the Northwest. The best way to appreciate the mountain is to explore its flanks: 300 miles of backcountry and self-guiding nature trails lead to ancient forests, dozens of massive glaciers, waterfalls, and alpine meadows lush with wildflowers during the short summer. There is a 98-mile hiking trail around the mountain. Or you can simply loop the mountain in a car via Chinook or Cayuse Pass (open only May through October).

There are two ways to climb the mountain: with a guide service or on your own. Unless you are qualified to climb it on your own—and this is a huge, difficult, and dangerous mountain on which many people have been killed—you must climb with the guide service. A number of outdoor organizations sponsor trips up the mountain, but the best elevation for your dollar is with Rainier Mountaineering, the concessionaire guide service. (Call Paradise in the summer, (360)569-2227, and Tacoma in the winter, (206)627-6242.) If you plan to climb with your own party, you must register at one of the ranger stations in Mount Rainier National Park; (360)569-2211. Generally, the best time to climb the mountain is from late June through early September.

South of Paradise is **Packwood,** a great hub for a trip to Rainier or Goat Rocks. Here, locals favor Ma and Pa Ruckers (304 US Highway 12, Packwood; (360)494-2651), an old drive-in (with inside seating too)

Northwest Trek

Northwest Trek is a "zoo" where animals roam free while people tour the 600-acre grounds in small, open-air trams. The 5-mile tour passes by a large collection of native northern beasts, from caribou to mink. The buffalo herd steals the show. The entire tour is impressive for kids and adults alike. The park is open daily February through October, and weekends only the rest of the year. Ticket prices are $3.25/$5.25 for kids and $7.75 for adults; group rates are available (11610 Trek Drive E, Eatonville; (360)832-6116).

serving housemade ice cream, good pizza, and burgers; especially good, they say, is the Ma Burger.

The **Pacific Crest Trail,** which winds down from Canada to Mexico through Washington's Cascades, cuts right through the Goat Rocks Wilderness, crossing higher-elevation terrain (4,200–7,500 feet). It's not an easy hike (allow two or three days to get from one end of Goat Rocks to the other), but the views of jagged ridges from the year-round snowfields are stunning.

For the less hard-core hiker, the wilderness area offers plenty of easier trails for day hikes and two-day trips. Call the Packwood Ranger Station for information; (360)494-5515. There are no campgrounds in the wilderness proper (although you're welcome to camp in the back-country), but plenty of campgrounds with facilities are available farther south, at Walupt Lake and at White Pass (Naches District of Wenatchee Forest Ranger Station; (509)653-2205). You can enter Goat Rocks from either White Pass or Packwood.

The drive over White Pass is scenic and virtually unknown to many Western Washingtonians. You might miss the **White Pass Ski Area,** (509)672-3100, if you drive by it too quickly. Four lifts, a general store/post office, and some condos are all there is to it. Backcountry skiers like to take the lift up and ski into the Goat Rocks Wilderness, while intermediate alpine skiers command a majority of the runs. Lift tickets are $17 Monday, Tuesday, and Friday, and $26 weekends and holidays. The real deal days are Wednesday and Thursday, when the price of a lift ticket (10 bucks!) can't be beat.

Beyond White Pass, the forests part for the waters of Rimrock Lake, a human-made lake lowered for irrigation in late summer. When the lake is up, boaters flock to the blue-green waters (watch Highway 12 for public boat launch signs). When the Tieton Dam is opened, the walls of the lake emerge from under the waters like the walls of a canyon, adding an aura of natural mystery. That's when the Tieton River really roars.

During the first two or three weekends in September, **whitewater rafters** come in search of downriver thrills. Try Wild and Scenic River Tours (PO Box 22606, Seattle, WA 98122; (206)323-1220) for one of the longer runs—20 miles and four hours ($55). Orion Expeditions (4739 Thackeray Place NE, Seattle, WA 98105; (206)547-6715 or (800)555-7466) will set you up with all the gear you'll need—including lunch ($60 for a four-hour trip). If you have your own equipment (wet suit, booties, paddle jacket), Adventures with Wenatchee Whitewater (PO Box 12, Cashmere, WA 98815; (509)782-2254) charges less for the trip—they also rent equipment on the side. Other rafting companies include Downstream River Runners (12112 NE 195th Street, Bothell, WA 98011; (206)483-0335), one of the oldest in the area, and Wildwater River Tours (PO Box 3623, Federal Way, WA 98063; (206)939-2151).

The temperamental **Mount St. Helens** simmers to the south. On a clear summer day it is well worth the 37-mile trip from Randle to Windy Ridge (closed in winter) to see the 8,365-foot remains, and to witness the rebirth of the ecosystem destroyed by the forceful 1980 eruption. The explosion carved out a crater 2 miles across and a half mile deep; created a blast zone of fallen, scorched timber; and dumped oceans of mud and logs into nearby Spirit Lake. Many of the trails have been created or reconstructed to allow for further exploration.

To climb St. Helens, take one of two trails (Butte Camp or Monitor Ridge) up the south face—more of a rugged hike than real alpine climbing, but an ice ax is still recommended. The all-day climb (8 strenuous miles round trip) is ideal for novice alpinists; the only big dangers are some loose-rock cliffs and the unstable edge around the top of the crater. Permits are required mid-May through October. Only 100 people per day are allowed to climb the volcano, and 60 of those permits are allotted by mail. It's best to write and reserve ahead of time, since obtaining a permit in person is a full day's job. Call or write for an application after February 1: Mount St. Helens National Volcanic Monument, 42218 NE Yale Bridge Road, Amboy, WA 98601; (360)247-5800 or (360)247-5473.

Five miles east of I-5 on Highway 504, the U.S. Forest Service **Visitor Center** (3029 Spirit Lake Highway, Castle Rock; (360)274-6644 or (360)274-2103) sits near Silver Lake. Though it's quite a distance from St. Helens, there's a stunning view of the mountain on a clear day. The center commemorates the blast with excellent exhibits, a walk-through volcano, hundreds of historical and modern photos, geological and anthropological surveys, and a documentary about the volcano's destruction and recovery. A network of trails, some wheelchair-accessible, are good for short, scenic strolls. Cover the area on horseback through either EZ Times Outfitters (18703 Highway 706, Elbe; (360)569-2449) or Indian Creek Corral (40911 Highway 12, White Pass; (509)672-2400). Both are open year-round; reservations are advised.

For information on Mount Adams, see the Columbia River Gorge & Mount Adams chapter.

CHEAP SLEEPS

Wardholm West Bed and Breakfast
861 Yellowstone Road (PO Box 143), Snoqualmie Pass, WA 98068
(206)434-6540

This red chalet on a quiet road offers rooms with a sort of country-house clutter about them—but they're comfortable and pleasant and $45 a night (ask about the hiker's special). Your continental breakfast might be brought to you in bed. Owners Bob and Peggy Ward know all about fishing in nearby Lake Keechelus or Denny Creek, hiking on the Pacific Crest Trail, and getting cheap lift tickets.

Hobo Inn
54106 Mountain Highway E (PO Box 10), Elbe, WA 98330
(360)569-2500

We like this place, if only because it's fun to stay in a caboose. So what if it's right on the road to Rainier and rooms are $70 during high season—squeeze in four and you've got a genuine train experience. Eat breakfast in the train next door or get sidetracked in the lounge.

The Lodge Near Mount Rainier
38608 State Route 706, Ashford, WA 98304 • (360)569-2312

This place is best for big groups of, say, 25. The lodge has other, smaller cabins, but it's best to hold out until you've found a great reason for two dozen friends to rent the largest lodge. You bring your own sleeping bag and towel; all kitchen supplies are provided. There's a big outdoor lawn for games or a barbecue, and a large fireplace in the living room for winter months.

Mount Rainier National Park
Mount Rainier Guest Services, PO Box 108, Ashford, WA 98304
(360)569-2275

The only two lodges located within Mount Rainier National Park are Paradise Inn and National Park Inn. You can't get any closer to Mount

Rainier than these lodges, unless you stay in a tent. Neither inn is particularly cheap, but both have inexpensive rooms. The cheapest rooms ($56) are at the modest National Park Inn. At Paradise they start at $60. (You can pay up to $100.) Be aware that at both places, the least expensive rooms are very small and bathrooms are shared. If you plan to stay at either, check at Paradise first; the up-front location and huge fireplace in the lobby are worth the extra few bucks.

Mount Tahoma Ski Huts
PO Box 206, Ashford, WA 98304 • (360)569-2451

Just off Highway 7 is Western Washington's first hut-to-hut ski system. The Mount Tahoma Scenic Ski Trails Association (MTTA) has cut almost 90 miles of trails through a spectacular area south and west of Mount Rainier National Park. There are two 8-person huts in the South District (built by MTTA members) and one 12-person hut in the Central District. The reservation policy requires a three-night maximum at each hut (and a $25-per-person-per-night refundable deposit for damage and usage). Reservations are taken on a first-come, first-served basis between December 15 and April 1.

Hotel Packwood
104 Main Street (PO Box 130), Packwood, WA 98361 • (360)494-5431

The oldest building in Packwood (a 1912 hotel with a wraparound porch) is by far the best and the cheapest place to stay this side of Paradise. Two can stay in the bunk room for $25 (which has a view of Rainier) or fork out all of $30 for a double; a room with private bath is $38. Many of the nine spartan rooms have cast-iron beds, and all have cable TV and the homey aroma of wood-fired heat. During the summer, the Packwood becomes a hub for hikers venturing to Mount Rainier and the South Cascades.

Tatoosh Motel
12880 US Highway 12, Packwood, WA 98361 • (360)494-5321

Kathie and Richard Sharp have put almost as much care into their motel as most bed-and-breakfast owners invest in their inns. Amenities include handmade quilts on the beds, dried flower arrangements in many of the rooms, an outdoor hot tub, and often, upon arrival, a complimentary package filled with the fixings for lentil salad (straight from Kathie's parents' farm). If you have a group, ask for the cabin, and be sure to say hello to the pet llamas.

Alpine Inn

34800 Crystal Mountain Boulevard, Crystal Mountain, WA 98022
(360)663-2262

The bunk rooms in the Alpine are by far the least expensive option at Crystal Mountain. A room with private bath costs you $50. The Snorting Elk, a great aprés-ski spot, is downstairs.

Skiers' Cabins

The Mountaineers, Washington's venerable outdoor club, runs **four winter lodges** in the Cascades. The dormitory-style cabins—on Snoqualmie Pass, Stampede Pass, Stevens Pass, and Mount Baker—are located very close (sometimes within skiing distance) to the respective ski areas. (Meany Lodge at Stampede Pass is the only one not adjacent to a downhill area.) You don't have to be a member to stay at the lodge (though nonmember rates are slightly higher); you just need a reservation by the Thursday before the weekend.

The large lodges hold 55 to 105 skiers. They're open only on winter weekends, except during the holidays. All you need to bring are a sleeping bag and a flashlight (electricity is turned off at 10pm). Prices range from $24 at Snoqualmie to $39 at Meany (which includes a Sno-Cat ride to the remote lodge). Some or all of your meals may be included with the rates (it varies with each lodge). Reportedly, the Snoqualmie and Stampede Pass lodges are better set up for families (preschool children may stay overnight with permission of the lodge chairperson, though you're encouraged to leave toddlers at home). Nighttime activities include folk dancing, games, and slide shows. For reservations or membership information contact the Mountaineers, 300 3rd Avenue W, Seattle, WA 98119; (206)284-8484.

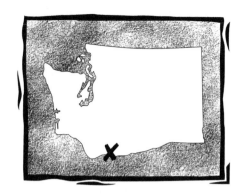

Columbia River Gorge & Mount Adams

Mother Nature pulled out all the stops here. Basalt columns, whitewater rivers, snow-covered peaks, alpine lakes, lava tubes, and the windy gorge provide a panoply of outdoor activities unparalleled in the Northwest. In addition, the sheer bulk of Mount Adams (at 12,276 feet, the second-highest peak in the state) casts a welcome rain shadow over the area. It's not unusual to leave Portland on a rainy day and emerge an hour later into a breezy, sun-drenched playland.

This is nirvana for the recreation-obsessed vacationer who can never pack enough outdoor activities into a day—maybe some cross-country skiing in the morning, some midday cave exploring or mountain biking, and then a few hours of board sailing squeezed in before dinner. Or maybe rock climbing in the afternoon, and an after-dinner hike by full moon to a natural hot springs—you get the idea.

On the other hand, the less ambitious can spend the day reading a book and contemplating views of snowcapped volcanoes—and then spend the evening at the Goldendale Observatory gazing at the celestial scenery.

ON THE ROAD

Legend has it that when Mount St. Helens took a fancy to Mount Adams, the jealous Mount Hood bashed Adams on the head and flattened his top for good. (Who knows what part Mount Hood played when Mount St. Helens lost her top?) Of course, there's no better place to admire the scenery surrounding Mount Adams than from atop the volcano's massive, rounded dome. If you harbor a yen to reach Mount Adams's summit, you must check in for a permit from the **Mount Adams Ranger Station** (Gifford Pinchot National Forest, Trout Lake, WA 98650-9724; (509)395-2501). If you want to see wildflowers, the best time to visit is usually mid-July to early August; a highly recommended destination is Bird Creek Meadows, on the southeast side of Adams and partly on the Yakima Indian Reservation.

The Mount Adams area is riddled with **lava tubes**, which white settlers used as a source of ice and as a place for storing cheese in summer. Best known is Ice Cave, near Trout Lake, a lava tube with ice stalactites and stalagmites. You can spelunk it from end to end with a good flashlight and a willingness to squeeze through some narrow passages. The Big Lava Bed, southwest of Trout Lake, is a vast area of moss-covered lava formations. Bordering it to the northwest is **Indian Heaven Wilderness**, a 20,000-acre wilderness plateau studded with more than

Hot Mineral Baths

At the weathered Carson Hot Mineral Springs Resort (on Wind River Highway, 2 miles from the junction of Highway 14 and Carson; (509)427-8292), slip back in time as the attendant draws the curtains around your steaming claw-footed bathtub in the dimly lit bathhouse. A soporific soak at Carson has become a requisite ingredient of many a visit to the Columbia Gorge—so plan ahead if you want a massage after you take the waters. It's suggested you reserve six to eight weeks in advance for a rub on weekends ($32 an hour). Eight dollars buys a hot mineral bath (request an extra-long tub) and an after-bath wrap (half an hour of sweating out your impurities—just try to stay awake). Baths are open from 8:45am to 7pm every day. The adventurous may want to hike to the source of the springs. Ask for directions from the front desk, wear sturdy shoes, and be careful, since the trail can be quite slippery.

Stargazing

The Goldendale Observatory (1602 Observatory Drive, Goldendale; (509)773-3141) has the largest telescope in the nation available for public use—and it's free! The observatory is open afternoons and evenings (Wednesday through Sunday in summer; Saturday and Sunday in winter). Hours vary, so call ahead.

150 lakes and ponds among subalpine forests and meadows. For information on the wilderness areas, lakes, and waterfalls in the national forest, and winter activities, contact Mount Adams Ranger Station (see above).

After snow blankets the area, you'll find groomed **cross-country ski trails** from three Sno-Park sites off the Wind River Road north of Carson; the first is at Oldman Pass, 25 miles north of Highway 14. For a map and information, contact the Wind River Ranger Station (Milepost 1.23R, Hemlock Road, Carson, WA 98610; (509)427-5646). Other ski trails from Sno-Park sites around Mount Adams include Pine Side Sno-Park, 5 miles northeast of Trout Lake on Road 82, with 2½- and 5-mile groomed cross-country loops; and Smith Butte Sno-Park, with backcountry routes.

When the weather's been below freezing and the precipitation light, you can ice-skate on area lakes such as Bench Lake and Bird Lake. Check with the Mount Adams Ranger Station in advance regarding weather and ice conditions.

Three companies offer **whitewater-rafting trips** from March through October on the White Salmon National Scenic River, on an 8-mile stretch of glacial runoff shooting through a lava gorge, with plenty of challenging rapids from Class 1 to Class 4. Spring trips offer the most excitement. The following three outfitters offer essentially the same three-hour trip, from BZ Corners to Northwestern Lake ($45): Phil Zoller's Guide Service in White Salmon, (509)493-2641; Whitewater Market in Husum, (509)493-2511; and Whitewater Adventure in BZ Corners, (509)493-3121 or (800)366-2004.

Boardheads can check out the scene at several **windsurfing sites** along the Washington side of the gorge, where the wind really blows. To see the hottest surfers dodging barges, doing endos on waves, and tacking on a dime, take Route 14 and look for parked vehicles at Swell City, 4 miles west of the Bingen Marina (a good spot for spectators); the fish hatchery a little farther east; Doug's Beach, a few miles east of Lyle; or farther east at Maryhill State Park and Roosevelt Park.

Foraging

The country bordering the Columbia Gorge has long offered an abundance of delicious foods for the taking; Lewis and Clark noted as much in 1805, after arriving in the area half-starved. Before the Columbia was dammed, Indians caught monster-sized salmon each spring; today the fish still run, though they're greatly diminished in number and size. During salmon season you can venture just north of Lyle on the Klickitat River to watch Native American fishermen **dip-netting for salmon** from precarious wooden platforms, just as their ancestors have done for generations.

Picking huckleberries from the abundant fields at the base of Mount Adams is a tradition practiced by countless jam and pie lovers each year from mid-July to mid-September. The Mount Adams Ranger Station in Trout Lake offers an excellent brochure on huckleberry harvesting in the Gifford Pinchot National Forest, complete with a map of the best fields; (509)395-2501. The Trout Lake Grocery (2383 Highway 141, Trout Lake; (509)395-2777) pays pickers $8–$12 per gallon and sells the berries for $3–$4 more. Most of the berries are then frozen and distributed all over the country.

The hills around White Salmon are covered with **orchards**, including cherry, apricot, apple, and pear trees, and many farmers offer the U-pick option. You can tour and taste the fruits of **two area wineries**: the Charles Hooper Family Winery (on the north fork of Spring Creek Road, off Route 141 just north of Husum; (509)493-2324), which specializes in white riesling, and Mont Elise Vineyards (State Route 14, Bingen, (509)493-3001), which consistently wins regional awards for its gewürztraminer.

Beginning and intermediate sailors are advised to stick to more sheltered spots like Stevenson Park, Home Valley, Drano Lake, Hood Vista Sailpark, Bingen Marina, and Horsethief Lake State Park—but be aware that beginner sites in the gorge are for intermediate lake board sailors. For information on the wind speed, call (509)427-5484.

The paved roads around Mount Adams and points east are ideal for **bike touring**, with little traffic, gentle grades, and stunning views. Bike from Goldendale or Trout Lake to the 5,654-acre Conboy Lake National Wildlife Refuge, (509)364-3410, a marshy oasis for waterfowl—swans, geese, ducks, and sandhill cranes—at the foot of Mount Adams. Well worth the effort of shuttling cars is the exhilarating, mostly downhill ride from Glenwood, heading east on the Glenwood-Goldendale Road and then south on Route 142 to Lyle. The route follows above the canyons of the Klickitat River and gradually drops down into the river valley to join up with the Columbia. (If you can't swing this by bicycle, don't miss it by car.)

Visit the **Maryhill Museum of Art** (35 Maryhill Museum Drive, 13 miles south of Goldendale; (509)773-3733) in the 1914 mansion of financier Sam Hill, who never moved in to enjoy the spectacular Columbia River vistas. The museum (open mid-March through mid-November; $4 for adults) houses an eclectic mix of art and artifacts such as Rodin sculptures, Russian icons, and Native American baskets. Just up the road a piece is a life-sized replica of **Stonehenge**, constructed by Sam Hill as a memorial to the soldiers from Klickitat County who died during World War I.

You can build up an honest hunger after so much activity, and plenty of places here serve straightforward, satisfying fare. You can pick huckleberries in the summer (see box), but to enjoy local huckleberries any time of the year, try the treats at Bonnie's Place Cafe (Highway 141, Trout Lake; (509)395-2747). Healthy sandwiches and that long-lost espresso can be found at Tsulgali's (Highway 141, Trout Lake; (509)395-2622). The Logs in BZ Corners (1258 Highway 141, White Salmon; (509)493-1402) is a tavern and restaurant that has been run by the same family since 1930. Great fried chicken, hickory-smoked barbecued ribs, and local color—just don't bring up the plight of the spotted owl.

The hangout for boardheads on a budget is Guido's (104 E Steuben Street, Bingen; (509)493-3880), a tiny Italian take-out spot with a handful of tables and big tumblers of wine for $1.25. Next door, noisy Fidel's (120 E Steuben Street, Bingen; (509)493-1017) serves pretty good Mexican food—get there between 5pm and 6pm for the early-bird dinner special. Afterward, head to the Gorge Theater (206 N Oak, Bingen; (509)493-3660) for a $2.50 movie (current releases too).

CHEAP SLEEPS

Lyle Hotel
7th and Lyle streets, Lyle, WA 98635 • (509)365-5953

A stylish restaurant anchors owner Cal Wood's hotel in decidedly unstylish Lyle. Although the affable owner puts most of his energy into his eatery, it's obvious he cares about the whole hotel. The rooms are spotless and cost considerably less than dinner for two. One drawback: this 1905 inn is situated at the confluence of the Klickitat and Columbia rivers, a peaceful setting interrupted periodically by passing freight trains (complimentary earplugs in every room). Fortunately, the morning coffee is strong. Open March through December.

The Inn at Bingen School

Humboldt and Cedar streets (PO Box 155), Bingen, WA 98605
(509)493-3363

No more pencils, no more books, no more teachers' dirty looks. When John Newman reopened the local grade school, he filled the classrooms with beds (doubles and bunks), the cafeteria with a big-screen TV, and the gymnasium with a climbing wall. Board sailors, mountain bikers, and climbers from all over the world now hang out at this hostel-like dwelling. No wonder so many big kids find themselves returning—big-kid toys in tow—to Bingen School.

Orchard Hill Inn

199 Oak Ridge Road, White Salmon, WA 98672 • (509)493-3024

This comfortable country B&B, surrounded by apple and pear orchards, is rare in that children are welcome and will find plenty to do—with or without their parents. There are a big tree house, croquet, badminton, horseshoes, and a pitch-and-chip golf course on the grounds. The property slopes down to the White Salmon River, where you can watch rafters and kayakers negotiating the rapids or trying to catch dinner. In the evening, take your pick of games and books to enjoy by the fire.

Trout Lake Grocery

2383 Highway 141, Trout Lake, WA 98650 • (509)395-2777

There are two sleeping rooms above and one below this country store—the focal point of Trout Lake's social life. Lodgings are clean and basic, with queen-sized beds in two rooms and three twins in the third. The upstairs guests share a bath. Hunters book a year in advance for the mid-November deer season, and foragers crowd the place in huckleberry season, but at other times hikers and skiers can count on an opening with little notice. And the price is right: all the people you can fit in a room (within reason, says the owner) for $25 a night.

Flying L Ranch

25 Flying L Lane, Glenwood, WA 98619 • (509)364-3488

Rooms at the Flying L are a bit of a price stretch—the cheapest double is $65 a night—but proximity to area activities, a big ranch breakfast, a hot tub in the forest, and the Lloyd family's extensive knowledge of Mount Adams and the surrounding area make it a value. The Lloyds have owned the 160-acre ranch since 1945, and there's plenty of history here—ask Darvel to show you the bullet holes in the door of the spacious, comfortable living room, where his father shot his gun during a family theatrical presentation. If you have a party of four, opt for one of the two cabins in the woods. Breakfast, served in the cookhouse, invariably includes huckleberry pancakes. The kitchen is open for your use at lunch and dinner. Bikes are included in the price of your room.

Far Vue Motel

808 E Simcoe Drive (Highway 97), Goldendale, WA 98620
(509)773-5881

Here is a motel of the best sort: new, clean, and private, with little personal touches that show it is not a chain. In addition, there's a pool, cable TV, and a view of Mount Adams or Mount Hood from every room ($48.50 for two). In the summer you need to reserve a few days in advance; at other times you can just appear. After church the locals gather at the motel's Homestead Restaurant and Lounge, reputedly the best place for a meal in Goldendale.

 *Camping*

There are numerous summertime **scenic campsites** near Mount Adams, such as those at Takhlakh Lake and Horseshoe Lake, both with breathtaking reflections of the snow-covered volcano. You can obtain a list of 26 campgrounds in Gifford Pinchot National Forest's Mount Adams Ranger District (out of Trout Lake; (509) 395-2501) and Wind River Ranger District (out of Carson; (509)427-5645). Along the gorge, Horsethief Lake State Park, (509)767-1159, boasts **Indian petroglyphs**, a boat launch, and a dozen campsites available from April through October; farther east, Maryhill State Park, (509)773-5007 has 50 campsites close to the Columbia.

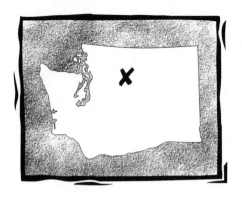

Lake Chelan

The 55-mile-long Lake Chelan carves its way through rough and barren hills, curving into the North Cascades. It's deep, cold, and clear—great for water skiing or fishing or taking a refreshing dip. The town of Chelan sits on the southern tip, where a dam keeps the lake from cascading into the Columbia River.

Orchards surround the town and dot the sides of the lake, filling the air with the scent of blossom nectar in the spring and the sweet pungency of harvest in the fall. It's dry and hot here as summer approaches, and it stays that way long after the kids have returned to school. In winter, with luck, snow sticks to the hills around the town and cross-country skiers find miles of trails to roam.

Chelan's population of 3,000 fluctuates during the year, what with time-share condos coming into fashion and migrant farmworkers arriving for the picking season. Tourism now fuels the economy for many months of the year because, at its root, Chelan is a resort town with recreation in abundance. Fortunately, it remains a small, idyllic place, with a wide main street lined with benches to rest on and at least three well-equipped hardware stores.

ON THE ROAD

Opportunities for getting wet abound at Lake Chelan. In Chelan proper there are two parks for **swimming**: the Don Morse Memorial City Park, just past the Red Apple Market on Manson Highway, and Lakeside Park, as you enter town on Highway 97A from the west. Both are located on the eastern side of the lake, so that afternoons feel long and hot. Don Morse also has a boat launch, marina, trailer park, and campground, so it is usually a bit more crowded than Lakeside, which is mainly a swimming and picnicking park. Lake Chelan State Park, on the west side of the lake, has a large swimming area and boat launch. We like it because it's a bit away from the bustling south end.

Riverwalk Park is a pleasant mile-long promenade that skirts the shores of the lake. You can, of course, forget the stroll and get on a jet ski like everyone else. Launch from any of the previously mentioned parks, or rent a jet ski (starting at $30 an hour) from Chelan Boat Rentals Inc. (1210 W Woodin Avenue, Chelan; (509)682-4444). This is also the place to rent water toys: ski boats, fishing boats, Hobie Cats, sailboards, and, for the road, mopeds and bicycles. Try Ship 'n' Shore Drive Inn (1230 W Woodin Avenue, Chelan; (509)682-5125) for rentals: jet skis ($30 an hour), ski boats ($50 an hour including gas), and canoes and rowboats ($10 an hour).

In summer, stop by the Chelan-Gri-La espresso cart at Safeway (corner of Columbia and Johnson), which serves Starbucks coffee, or check out Flying Saucers Espresso (116 S Emerson Street, Chelan; (509)682-5129), which has retro-Jetsons decor and innovative espresso drinks plus morning muffins. For great burgers and beer, try Goochi's (104 E Woodin Avenue, Chelan; (509)682-2436). It's comfy and has a

Plan Ahead

When confronted a few springs ago with hordes of Memorial Day weekend sun-seekers, Chelan responded by setting up roadblocks, issuing passes to locals, and throwing any drunken road trippers in the pokey. It worked. The influx of tourists these days consists predominantly of families and older folks in RVs. And that suits the locals just fine. If you're thinking of a summer weekend at Lake Chelan, be warned that it fills up months in advance (call in January for a summer reservation).

Remote Campsites

Those who roll into town without a reservation might have better luck at some of the remote campsites around the lake. There are eight sites available near Stehekin even in the height of the summer. Reservations aren't accepted for them, and there is no way of knowing whether they are full until you get there, so it's a bit of a crapshoot. Take the boat and arrange for a National Park Service van from Stehekin to drop you off and pick you up at one of the campsites up the lake. For more information on these sites (or to make a reservation on the van), contact the Golden West Visitors Center at (206)856-6055, ext. 14.

nice bar and 18 microbrews on tap. Golden Florins General Store (125 E Woodin Avenue, Chelan; (509)682-5535) carries a wide selection of natural and bulk foods. Try the Muesli Lite. This is a good place to stock up before you head into the wild.

Seven miles up the east side of the lake is the little town of **Manson**, where El Vaquero (75 Wapato Way, Manson; (509)687-3179) supplies the hungry and the sunburned with authentic Mexican food. After your meal, take a drive along Manson's scenic route and get a better look at this interesting landscape. Orchards are carved into impossible hills sprinkled with hidden lakes and enticing views.

Because much of the lake is inaccessible from the land, a good way to get around is by boat. For years, the *Lady of the Lake*, known by the townspeople as the Mail Boat, has made her way slowly up the lake each day to deliver mail, supplies, and people to the various ports of call. The *Lady* remains a vital part of life on the lake, sailing daily from Chelan in May through October. Round trip on the *Lady* ($21) is an all-day journey; she leaves Chelan at 8:30am and arrives back at 6pm, with a 90-minute layover in Stehekin.

For those interested in a shorter boat trip, there's the *Lady Express*, which runs year-round. In summer, the *Express* leaves at 8:30am and is back in Chelan by 2pm. Or sail the *Express* in the morning and make your return trip on the *Lady*, which affords you a three-hour stay in Stehekin and the chance to check out both boats. The *Express* ($39) is the only option in the winter (it sails on Monday, Wednesday, and Friday). Call Lake Chelan Boat Company for a current schedule of departures; (509)682-2224.

Much of the good **hiking** is accessible by boat too. Check with the ranger station, because the *Lady of the Lake* makes a number of stops at lakeside trailheads along her daily route. These are excellent jumping-off points to backcountry and trails. The town of Stehekin offers the best in hiking opportunities, being a base camp, so to speak, for the North Cascades. For specific information about trails and their access, call the National Park Service; (206)856-5700.

Bike trails are limited in this area (and mountain biking is not allowed in the national forest), but the road on the west side of the lake that dead-ends at 25-Mile Creek is wide and flat—great for an **afternoon bike ride**. Reportedly, north of Manson are a number of trails for mountain bikers and motorcyclists (which may be a nightmare in the making). Call the Forest Service for directions; (509)682-2576. Bicycling is limited at Stehekin, and the cost to transport your bike on the *Lady* is $13 round trip. It's cheaper to rent one in Stehekin.

Cascade Pass

One of the most stunning hikes through the North Cascades traverses Cascade Pass, crowned with granite spires, backed by glaciated peaks, and softened with blueberry and wildflower meadows. The trail is 9 miles (one way) and easily hiked in a day. Trouble is, you end up a good 150 miles (by boat and road) from your car. It is, however, possible to turn this into a great two-day loop.

Arrange your trip with another couple. Party 1 begins at the northern trailhead in Marblemount; Party 2 starts in Chelan. Party 1 hikes across the pass to Cottonwood Campground. Party 2 takes the *Lady of the Lake* to Stehekin at the head of Lake Chelan (Lake Chelan Boat Company; (509)682-2224), and then rides the shuttle bus 23 miles up the Stehekin Valley Road to meet Party 1 at Cottonwood. Next morning, exchange car keys. Party 2 hikes to Marblemount via Cascade Pass, and Party 1 takes the shuttle bus and boat back to Chelan.

Hint: Lighten your load by having Party 2 bring all the gear to Cottonwood; Party 1 takes it back to Chelan. More ambitious adventurers can opt to ride mountain bikes up the primitive Stehekin Valley Road instead of taking the shuttle bus. Bike rentals are available in Stehekin, or bring your own. The shuttle bus runs mid-May through mid-October; reservations required. Write Shuttle Bus Reservations, National Park Service, PO Box 7, Stehekin, WA 98852; or call (206)856-6055, ext. 14.

During the winter, 55 kilometers of groomed **cross-country ski trails** surround the 5,500-acre Bear Mountain Ranch (5 miles west of Chelan off Highway 97A; (509)682-5444). Elevation ranges from 1,500 to 3,500 feet, and the terrain spans all levels of difficulty.

CHEAP SLEEPS

Apple Inn Motel
1002 E Woodin Avenue, Chelan, WA 98816 • (509)682-4044

Across the street from the high school football field is a clean, well-lighted roadside motel that's also one of the least expensive places to stay in the area, probably because it's located 10 blocks from town (a very pleasant stroll). The Apple Inn has three sections. The first (and oldest) has the best deals ($49 in summer) and most charm, with its knotty pine paneling. Rooms with kitchenettes and living rooms run about $55. The rooms in the second building are short on charm but have bigger beds and newer plumbing. The third building contains 20 units—called "deluxe" because they've got wet bars and bigger beds ($59). But you'll find us in the knotty pine rooms. Or maybe in the hot tub and pool.

Parkway Motel
402 N Manson Road (PO Box 1237), Chelan, WA 98816
(509)682-2822

The wagon wheel and the brick fence around the grassy play area are a dead giveaway that this is a fun, family place. The low-lying motel is tucked beneath shade trees that give it the feel of a retreat, even though it's on the main thoroughfare east of the lake. It's a great location—

Lake Chelan State Park

Camping at Lake Chelan can be as difficult as trying to find a vacant room in July sans reservation. One of the better parks is Lake Chelan State Park (Route 1, Box 90, Chelan, WA 98816; (509)687-3710), 10 miles up the west side of the lake, which offers 127 campsites, great facilities, a fine swimming area, boat launches, and a stargazing dock. Reservations are important. Call the Washington State Park Headquarters in Olympia for a reservation application; (360)753-2027. It must be postmarked at least 14 days in advance of the first camping date requested.

directly across the street is a park, around the corner there's a burger joint, and next door is a market. The units are rustic and knotty pine-paneled, with small bedrooms. The rooms facing the grass all have kitchens and living rooms with hideabeds ($60 peak). Sleeping rooms in the rear of the motel are small, with double beds—charmingly cramped at $35 a night. They can be adjoined with the front unit into a big two-bedroom affair (sleeping six).

Ship 'n' Shore Drive Inn

1230 W Woodin Avenue, Chelan, WA 98816
(509)682-5125; (509)946-6407 in winter

If you've got a gang that likes barbecued beef and fresh-fruit shakes (and maybe has a boat that needs moorage), this is the place. Here's the scoop: the Ship 'n' Shore has two mobile homes situated smack-dab beside the drive-in on the town's main drag. The convenience (and the cleanliness) of the units overshadows the feeling that you're visiting your Aunt Mabel at the trailer park in Fife. They sleep six (with plenty of sleeping-bag space) and are close to a picnic area that juts into the southern tip of the lake. Tie up your boat behind the drive-in, or if you're without one, rent some water toys. Ask for the unit closest to the lake.

 *Holden Village*

At the Lucerne stop on the *Lady of the Lake*'s run is Holden Village (Holden Registrar, Holden Village, Chelan, WA 98816; (509)687-3644). Once a copper, gold, and zinc mine, it's now a Lutheran Church-owned year-round resort. Holden Village is 11 miles from the boat drop in Lucerne. In the winter, snowmobiles meet you at the dock and transport you up to the village. There are plenty of hiking and cross-country ski trails here, though many people come to this remote place to immerse themselves in politically challenging discussions and politically correct meals. A three-night stay is about $120 per person and includes all meals. Lodging is dormitory-style, though there are facilities for families.

The Methow Valley

The North Cascades Highway (Highway 20) flirts along the granite walls of Liberty Bell, elbows round the sawtoothed Early Winters Spires, and dips down into the broad, open valley of the Methow River. In the summer, deep green ponderosa pines line rocky-bottomed rivers that meander through sun-baked meadows. Hikers stock up on provisions for a long trek on the Pacific Crest Trail, fly fishermen cast into the Methow or Chewack rivers, mountain bikers traverse the valley floor, and horseback riders head for the Pasayten Wilderness. RVs refuel in Winthrop, snap photos of the Westernalia, and move on to the next camping spot.

In the winter, four-wheel-drive Jeeps and Subarus replace RVs, and cross-country skis take the place of mountain bikes. The dormant farmlands become a playground for the skier who gets everything: blue sky above, squeaky-dry snow below, and more than 175 kilometers of groomed trails webbing the valley, where one-piece Lycra outfits are almost de rigueur.

ON THE ROAD

You can call it MET-how or you can call it MED-ow, but you'll never call it dull. Pick your mode of transport—mountain bike, horse,

🎵 Winthrop Rhythm and Blues Fest

This late July festival has attracted such national performers as Mick Taylor and John Mayall, as well as the best of the local bands. Now it's expanded to three days. Events include a New Orleans-style street dance in the boot-kick town of Winthrop and a full day of steamy blues under the blazing sun at Twin Lakes. A popular event with the Harley crowd. Call (509)996-2125 for information.

hiking boots, skis, wading boots, or steel-belted radials—this 50-mile-long, glacier-carved valley is every outdoor enthusiast's dream.

The first stop off the North Cascades Highway is **Mazama**—which consists primarily of the recently renovated Mazama Country Store; (509)996-2855. You'll find everything here from fishing lures to trail mix, pile jackets to pasta salad, wading boots to wine. Fuel up on caffeine at the espresso bar while you fuel up your car and gather provisions for that backcountry adventure.

You can't miss **Winthrop**—it's the Western-motif town thronged with tourists. If you can find a parking spot, stop at the Shafer Museum, housed in pioneer Guy Waring's 1897 log cabin on the hill behind the main street. Exhibits tell of the area's history and include old cars, a stagecoach, and horse-drawn vehicles. It is said that Waring's Harvard classmate Owen Wister came to visit in the 1880s and found some of the material for *The Virginian* here. Believable enough perhaps, but don't be tricked into thinking the whole town is a relic. The Western storefronts, old-fashioned signs, and well-worn hitchin' posts were planned by the wife of a Twisp lumber-mill operator in the early 1970s to entertain the travelers crossing the newly opened North Cascades Highway.

Eats are good and plentiful in Winthrop. Down a beer and burger at Three-Fingered Jack's Saloon (176 Riverside Avenue, Winthrop; (509)996-2411), or split a burrito especial (or any other dish—they're all terrific and *huge*) at the Duck Grand Cantina (256 Riverside Avenue, Winthrop; (509)996-2192).

When you're tired of bumping shoulders with tourists and cowboy wannabes in Winthrop, continue the short 8 miles south to **Twisp**. Here is where genuine Methow Valley residents come for horse food, auto parts, or groceries. Tucked away in this utilitarian town is the Queen of Tarts and Confluence Gallery, which houses the best arts and crafts in the valley (104 Glover Street, Twisp; (509)997-1335). View World War II memorabilia, order a hearty breakfast, and bowl a few

Hut-to-Hut Skiing

Rendezvous Outfitters; (800)422-3048

In the Rendezvous Hills between Winthrop and Mazama are five spartan huts. Each plywood hut bunks up to eight people and comes equipped with a wood stove, a propane cookstove, and basic cooking utensils. Come with just one or two others and join new friends for the night, or round up eight others and reserve an entire cabin. Pack in your needs or have them hauled up on a skimobile (adds a $70 surcharge to the otherwise rock-bottom rates). All the cabins are opened as a warm, dry lunch stop for day skiers.

lines at Bombers Restaurant and Bowling Alley (607 Canyon Street, Twisp; (509)997-2525). There are lemon bars and more to die for at the Cinnamon Twisp Bakery (116 Glover Street, Twisp; (509)997-5030). Or get totally decadent and indulge in baby back ribs and a bloody Mary in a mug at the Roadhouse Diner (Highway 20; (509)997-4015); they offer a wide variety of satisfying dishes for any time of the day. At the city park you can swim in the pool for a thin buck, or inner-tube the river for free.

Last stop in Methow Valley (or first—depending on which way you're going) is the namesake town of **Methow**. Don't blink or you'll miss Cafe Bienville (Highway 153, Methow; (509)923-2228)—the cafe's about all there is in town except for a grocery store and the post office. Hours are limited, but you can catch dinner Wednesday through Saturday.

Nothing better than **Nordic skiing**? For a mere $10 a day or $25 for three days, kick-and-glide your way around the second-largest groomed system in the United States—175 kilometers of trail that slices through feather-light snow over hill, dale, and even river (via suspension bridges). Maintained by the Methow Valley Sports Trails Association (MVSTA, PO Box 147, Winthrop, WA 98862; (509)996-3287 or (800)682-5787), the system links the three major areas of Mazama, Sun Mountain, and Rendezvous, and the smaller Methow Valley Community Trail. Depending on your route, you can ski quiet forests and meadows or link inns, restaurants, and shops. Purchase passes at most lodgings or mountain shops, enter at the most convenient point, and ski your heart out. If you need to rent skis, contact Mazama Country Inn, (509)996-2681; Winthrop Mountain Sports, (509)996-2886; or Sun Mountain Lodge, (509)996-2211.

If you're looking for the best skiing take-off points, Mazama Ski Trails, (509)996-3287, offers 35 kilometers of pleasant valley skiing, starting at either Mazama Country Inn or the North Cascades Basecamp (both located on Lost River Road in Mazama). The trails of Sun Mountain (70 kilometers) run around the lodge's namesake mountain and pamper you with such perks as a pro shop, rental shop, and lessons. For high-country adventure, huts to warm body and soul, and good access to backcountry skiing, start your adventure with Rendezvous Ski Trails (45 kilometers; contact the local ranger station for backcountry information).

For **alpine** (or telemark) skiing without the hype, crowds, and cost, drive to Loup Loup Ski Bowl (PO Box 1686, Omak, WA 98841; (509)826-2720), just off Highway 20 between Twisp and Okanogan. Two poma lifts access surprisingly challenging runs. The lodge is home-spun, and you can stash your brown-bag lunch and gear without fear. You share the slopes with old-timers who will never make the fashion pages of *Ski Magazine*—but they'll ski your Lycra pants off. Nice prices: a regular full day costs $16, and Fridays are just $10. The destination ski resort that was planned for the Early Winters area failed to survive all the controversy. Rumor has it that instead there will be a posh Nordic ski resort built at the site of the Early Winters cabins. Stay tuned.

And when it's not snowing? In the high waters of spring, the heat of summer, or the aspen colors of fall, **raft** the Methow or nearby Columbia via Osprey River Adventures; (509)997-4116. Lace up your hiking boots and step out on the **Pacific Crest Trail** for spectacular alpine hiking north or south from Hart's Pass, or drop into one of the Pasayten Wilderness valleys for deep forests, fishing, and maybe a bear or two. Take a pack trip via horse with Early Winters Outfitting and Saddle, (509)996-2659, or North Cascades Safaris, (509)996-2350, or via llama with Pasayten Llama Packing, (509)996-2326. Prefer your car? Slate Peak is the **highest point in Washington** accessible by automobile—over 7,000 feet, with stunning alpine terrain and views—well worth the bumpy ride up 22 miles of gravel and hairpin turns.

Fat-tire bikers will find ample road and trail travel in the Methow. Pedal and coast your way down Pipestone Canyon or up and over Rendezvous Hill. If you've a yen for fishing, cast your lure over the still waters of the Methow or Chewack and perhaps hook the elusive (and endangered) Methow bull trout. For specific information about all local activities, contact the Winthrop, Early Winters, or Twisp ranger districts; (509)996-2266, (509)996-2534, or (509)997-2131.

CHEAP SLEEPS

Idle-a-While Motel
PO Box 575, Twisp, WA 98856 • (509)997-3222

On Highway 20, at the north end of Twisp, is this simple white motel, with sunny yellow doors and a broad expanse of lawn (or snow). It's half the price of any equally pleasant spot in Winthrop. Idle a night or two—with your dog if you wish. You can stay in one of the standard rooms or get a cabin with a kitchenette. Relax in the hot tub or sauna, have an afternoon barbecue, or play tennis (chase your own balls—there's no fence around this court). The river is a short walk away, and ski trails run by the back of the motel in the winter.

Methow Valley Inn
234 2nd Avenue, Twisp, WA 98856 • (509)997-3014

A big, comfortable old house, a delicious country breakfast, and Audrey and Bill Hoskins. Nothing elegant or fancy about this B&B, but the historic 1904 building, located just off the main street, definitely has character—as do the hosts. Choose from among seven rooms (most share baths), and bring an appetite to the breakfast table. Audrey serves up ham or sausage, housemade jams, blueberry pancakes, and—if you're really lucky—fresh peach cobbler, still warm. Sit on the enclosed porch and get all the Twisp news, past and present.

Chewack River Guest Ranch
E Chewack Road, Winthrop, WA 98862 • (509)996-2497

You're in cowboy country, pardner, so why not stay at a real working ranch? Right across from their riding stables and on the edge of their 2,000-acre cattle ranch, Chris and Don Lundgrin offer a piney "ranch house" for groups (four can stay for $100) and a few standard rooms for

Methow Valley Vacations

Take time out and stay for a while. Methow Valley Central Reservations (PO Box 505, Winthrop, WA 98862; (509)996-2148 or (800)422-3048) is the clearinghouse for approximately two dozen cabins in the valley from Twisp to Mazama. Bring an armful of good friends, cabin games, and a couple of bags of food and you're set for a long (and cheap) weekend in a place you can call your own.

two- or threesomes ($55). Bring your own horse or rent one of theirs. Go mountain biking or skiing or, better yet, sign up for the Cowboy Dinner Campout. Then come back to soak in the hot tub and hum "Git Along, Li'l Doggie . . ."

The Farmhouse Inn and the Duck Brand Hotel & Restaurant
PO Box 118, Winthrop, WA 98862 • (509)996-2191

The inn is in a charmingly restored farmhouse just outside Winthrop. Three of the rooms are small (but so is the price). The other three have their own baths. There's a hot tub and cable TV. Registration is at the Duck Brand, downtown Winthrop, where you can get slightly more expensive rooms (with private baths) upstairs from the popular restaurant.

The Virginian
808 North Cascade Highway (PO Box 237), Winthrop, WA 98862 (509)996-2535

Hitch up your mountain bike or mount your skis; here's a motel with personality. A sprawling complex with Western flair to match the name, the Virginian offers standard, cedar-lined motel rooms and moderately priced cabins (the latter are great for groups). Ski and bike trails cross the property; there's a volleyball court, an outdoor pool (summer), and a hot tub (anytime), as well as a restaurant. Some nights the Bicycle Bar really spins.

Winthrop Mountain View Chalets
Highway 20 & KOA Road (PO Box 280), Winthrop, WA 98862 (509)996-3113 or (800)527-3113

Just off Highway 20, with quick access to everything the valley has to offer. Don't let the nearby KOA put you off: these six attractive little cabins—designed for two people only—are not just cozy, they're even a bit romantic. Each offers pine interior, private deck overlooking the valley, full-size bath, and thoughtful touches such as window boxes, art, and reading material. The cooking facilities fall somewhere between a kitchenette and a wet bar, so bring your favorite electric cookware to supplement. A great deal ($55) for a miniature hideaway.

WolfRidge Resort
Route 2, Box 655, Winthrop, WA 98862 • (509)996-2828 or (800)237-2388

On Wolf Creek Road outside of Winthrop are three stunning, hand-crafted log lodges, with cathedral ceilings, warm wood interiors, private balconies, and log furnishings—all beautifully situated on 50 acres of meadow, aspens, and pines. Can this possibly be a cheap sleep? Amazingly, yes. Lou and Gabrielle Childers have built a top-flight resort without the top-flight prices. Choose a small hotel-style room for two, complete with balcony and log-beam ceiling. Or pay $10 more ($65) for a little more space and a kitchenette—that way, you never have to leave the beautiful premises. Better yet, gather a group together and rent a one- or two-bedroom suite with a large private deck, cathedral ceilings, and a kitchen with everything—right down to the dishwasher. There's a Jacuzzi, heated pool, children's play area, recreation center (which becomes a warming hut in the winter), trails linked to the valley's main ski trail system, and the river only steps away. You won't do better anywhere else.

Lost River Resort
672 Lost River Road, Mazama, WA 98833 • (509)996-2537

This place has cheap sleeps written all over it. First of all, we like the location way at the end of the road (well, about as far as the road gets plowed in the winter, anyway). From here you can connect to Monument Creek Trail or ski up to Yellowjacket. Jim and Sharon Sandon are mighty knowledgeable about all the fun things to do. Everyone gets a wood stove and full kitchen. The least expensive sleep is in the thin-walled duplex. But for $5 more, you can stay in the cabin and talk without fear of eavesdroppers.

North Cascades Basecamp
255 Lost River Road, Mazama, WA 98833 • (509)996-2334

Dick and Sue Roberts have built not a base camp but a home-style retreat. Come in the summer for the best rates and bring the whole family to this perfect gathering place. The beautifully designed, secluded main house—all wood and glass and dramatic angles—has six rooms (shared baths), a comfortable living room, a hot tub, and a glassed-in entry hall overhung with a grape arbor. Sue serves delicious breakfasts, included in the price, but to enjoy some of the best cooking in the valley, spring for the three-meal package (which, alas, takes this place out of the realm of cheap sleeps). Admire the huge vegetable garden, stroll the woodsy trails to trout ponds and beaver dams, or just relax on the shaded patio. In the winter (when rates are higher), this is one of the starting points for the Mazama Ski Trails.

Yakima Valley & Beyond

The Yakima Indians thrived for thousands of years in the arid Yakima Valley. They fished in the Yakima River during the spring and fall and moved to the foothills around Mount Adams to hunt for deer and other game during the summer. The first white visitors to the Yakima Valley, however, were unimpressed. Compared to the giant Douglas fir forests west of the mountains and the fish-filled waters of the Columbia Gorge, the desert valley had no appeal whatsoever. But with the coming of the railroad in the 1880s and the construction of irrigation canals in the early 20th century, the region became almost entirely the domain of white settlers, and Native Americans were relegated to a million-acre reservation.

The economy of the Yakima Valley is driven by agriculture. Crop reports and frost warnings headline the local radio news. Trucks roar through carrying apples, pears, beans, asparagus, and a dozen other products of the harvest. While area wines have found national fame, most of the vineyards are still supported by the traditional, predictable income from less exotic crops. In fact, if you've ever had a stick of spearmint gum or a bottle of Budweiser, you've helped bring economic wealth to this corner of Washington State, a prime growing area for both mint and hops.

There are over 20 wineries in the Yakima Valley and several more in the Tri-Cities area. The number's not surprising, according to the valley's winemakers, who proudly point out that the area's latitudinal coordinates (and thus the climate) are the same as some of France's finest winemaking regions. Touring the valley in September and October reveals the processes of harvest and winemaking and gives you a real taste of the agricultural and viticultural life.

ON THE ROAD

Interstate 82 provides an east-west thoroughfare from Yakima straight through the valley to the Tri-Cities. Take I-82 off I-90 in Ellensburg, but once you get to Yakima, abandon I-82 whenever possible in favor of more scenic routes and stopovers. A first stop in wine country should be a **brewery**: perhaps the Yakima Brewing Company (1803 Presson Place, Yakima; (509)575-1900), in the old train station. This home of Grant's Ale and the birthplace of Northwest microbrewing is a hallowed shrine for many of those who eschew light beers for the heartier flavors of hops and malt, a game of darts, and some pub grub. Across the street is the original operating brewery as well as the Thurston Wolfe Winery (27 N Front Street, Yakima; (509)452-0335), where dessert wines are the specialty. Here you'll also want to pick up a Yakima Valley Wine Growers brochure to aid your navigation to **wineries** down the road. Stop by the Wine Cellar (15 W Yakima Street, Yakima; (509)248-3590) for an overview of the local vintages. The nearby Deli de Pasta (7 N Front Street, Yakima; (509)453-0571) is the darling of the western Yakima Valley—an excellent place to pack a picnic or grab a sit-down lunch if the weather doesn't look promising.

As you head down the highway through the gap between the Rattlesnake Mountains, the vista of the valley opens up. A quick stop at the cedar-and-glass Staton Hills Winery (71 Gangl Road, Wapato; (509)877-2112) reveals a beautiful facility with a view of Union Gap, a neat picnic area, and a wide selection of whites and reds. In Toppenish, the **Yakima Indian Nation Cultural Center** (Highway 97 and Fort Road, Toppenish; (509)865-2800) documents the enlightening (and sobering) history of the Yakima Indians.

In Zillah, the wine scene hits fast and furious. A decade ago the Exit

 *Yakima River*

An alternative to driving I-82 between Ellensburg and Yakima is to take Canyon Road (State Highway 821) along the Yakima River from roughly the same starting and ending points as the freeway route. The scenery along the twisted, slow-flowing river is attractive, and the route doesn't take that much longer than the freeway. The tranquil water of the Yakima River offers a perfect summer's-day float. It's an easy Class 1 river, so bring beer, oversized inner tubes, and plenty of sunscreen, and drift on down to your favorite swimming hole or picnic area.

52 turnoff led to only one winery. Now **seven wineries** make their homes here: Covey Run Vintners (1500 Vintage Road, Zillah; (509)829-6235), one of the first wineries in the valley, with an expansive tasting room and picnic grounds; Bonair (500 S Bonair Road, Zillah; (509)829-6027), a small, family-run winery with a flair for chardonnay; Horizon's Edge (4530 E Zillah Drive, Zillah; (509)829-6401), where a spectacular view indeed stretches to the horizon from the tasting room; Hyatt Vineyards (2020 Gilbert Road, Zillah; (509)829-6333) for fine, dry white wines; Portteus Vineyard (5201 Highland Drive, Zillah; (509)829-6970), an estate winery specializing in reds—cabernet, merlot, and lemberger; Zillah Oakes (1001 Vintage Valley Parkway, Zillah; (509)829-6990), right on the highway, with a gift shop and Victorian-motif tasting room; and Eaton Hill (530 Gurley Road, Granger; (509) 854-2508), in an old cannery. Most of these operations are open daily for tasting, tours, and sales. Winter hours are sometimes abbreviated, so call ahead.

Before the wine boom, Zillah was best known for the **restaurant-cum-tortilla factory** El Ranchito (1319 E 1st Avenue, Zillah; (509)829-5880). This landmark features a variety of enterprises. A fast-food operation serving authentic Mexican fare is still the most popular, but the south-of-the-border gifts, cooking ingredients, folk remedies, records, tapes, magazines, and more are a browser's paradise. The on-premises bakery creates a variety of filling, colorful treats. Another local favorite is the Squeeze Inn (611 1st Avenue, Zillah; (509)829-6226), a steak house where you can get a beer or a glass of wine to accompany your meal (El Ranchito has always been dry in deference to its broad family trade). Stewart Vineyards (1711 Cherry Hill Road, Granger; (509)854-1882) is perched on the side of Snipes Mountain in the middle of a beautiful cherry orchard that provides a fabulous blossom display in mid-April. Try a riesling or cabernet.

The importance of agriculture becomes more and more apparent as you travel east, deeper into the heart of the valley. **Orchards, vineyards, and hop yards** line both sides of the highway. You'll recognize the hop yards by what look like planted rows of telephone poles. (Hops, a relative of the marijuana plant, have flower clusters used to flavor beer.) You can tell the older, Concord vineyards (whose fruit is used in Welch's grape juice) from the wine-grape varieties by their dark green, hedgelike, bushy appearance. In late summer, roll down your car window and inhale the aroma of delicious ripening fruit.

A short drive through **Sunnyside** yields a new perspective on a well-organized farm community. Neat, tree-lined streets, shady parks, and tidy businesses speak volumes about the economic success that agriculture has brought to the Yakima Valley. Another successful valley enterprise, the Yakima Valley Cheese Company (100 Alexander Road, Sunnyside; (509)837-6005), is where authentic Yakima Valley Gouda is made. Here you can observe the cheese-aging process and hear a little about the history of this unique valley product.

The Taquería La Fogata (1204 Yakima Valley Highway, Sunnyside; (509)839-9019) can relieve a longing for real Mexican food, with esoteric specialties (tripe and cow's-foot stew) for the more adventurous, traditional taco and burrito fare for the cautious, and great prices for everyone. Farmers in the valley since the '20s, the Tuckers of Sunnyside have now joined the wine boom with their own winery, Tucker Cellars. Their selection of varietal wines is complemented by the area's freshest in-season produce, at Tucker Farms Fruit Stand (70 Ray Road, Sunnyside; (509)837-8701).

Founded in the 1930s, **Chateau Ste. Michelle** (205 W 5th Avenue, Grandview; (509)882-3928) is the oldest continuing winery operation in the state. The best time to visit this facility is in early October, when guided tours reveal the remarkable production techniques

Time Out from Wine

For some quick exercise before or after a day of wine-sampling, try the Greenway Bike Path, which winds easily along the Yakima River for 4½ miles. Look for great blue herons and bald eagles; stop to fish if that's your pleasure. Start in Sherman Park in Yakima, and go to Selah Gap.

involved in making red wines. The wine flows through epoxied concrete troughs and back up over the fermenting grapes. The process can be seen at other times but lacks the intoxicating aroma of fermenting cabernet and merlot.

Prosser is the birthplace of the Yakima Valley winemaking renaissance. It was here that Washington State University researcher Walter Clore predicted the suitability of wine grapes for the area's climate. And here too is the cinderblock garage where Mike Wallace founded Hinzerling Vineyard and Winery (1520 Sheridan Road, Prosser; (509)786-2163) and brought recognition to the valley after he was profiled in *Time* in the late 1970s. Chinook Wines (Wine Country Road, Prosser; (509)786-2725) is a small operation dedicated to handcrafting limited bottlings of a few varietals. Drop in for a unique, homey visit with Kay Simon and Clay Mackey—owners, winemakers, gardeners, and everything-elsers. Don't miss the merlot. Down the road, the successful Hogue Cellars (at the corner of Lee and Wine Country roads, Prosser; (509)786-4557) produces hundreds of thousands of gallons of premium wine for every palate; look especially for the "reserve" wines. The Hogue family has been vastly successful in other farming endeavors, including asparagus (look for jars of their delicious pickled asparagus at specialty food stores throughout the state), mint, and hops.

While in Prosser, have some pasta at Pastas (1206 Meade Avenue, Prosser; (509)786-1130) or head to the Blue Goose (306 7th Street, Prosser; (509)786-1774) for breakfasts and dinners (try the teriyaki chicken). The Chukar Cherry Company (306 Wine Country Road, Prosser; (509)786-2055) has become regionally famous for its tart, dried cherries and other specialty foods. Their chocolate-covered cherries give candy a good name.

Columbia Crest Winery (Highway 221, Paterson; (509)875-2061) is a 30-mile diversion south of Prosser, just above the Columbia River. (It's an easy stretch of straight, flat road, but watch your speed here; an unmarked state patrol car may be watching *you*.) The beautiful building and grounds are exceptional, and the winemaking facility is the largest north of California.

Benton City boasts a number of interesting wineries: Oakwood Cellars (Demoss Road, Benton City; (509)588-5332), one of the newest additions to the growing number of wineries near Red Mountain; Kiona Vineyards (Sunset Road, Benton City; (509)588-6716), the first Red Mountain winery, producing remarkable cabernet, lemberger, and a dry, sweet riesling; Blackwood Canyon (Sunset Road, Benton City; (509)588-6249), a no-frills facility making controversial but distinctive wines (particularly notable are the late-harvest ones); and Seth Ryan

Winery (Sunset Road, Benton City; (509)588-6780), named for the sons of the owners, with a selection of fine whites and a pleasant picnic area.

The neat rows of homes and local businesses in **Richland** owe their prosperity to nuclear power. This is undeniably a historic place no matter what your political leanings. The **Hanford Science Center** (825 Jadwin Avenue, Richland; (509)376-6374) presents a remarkable look at the subject. All-day free tours of the Hanford site (bring lunch) leave from the Science Center and hit the highlights of the 560-square-mile nuclear reservation, including the World War II plutonium separation and Purex plants, the now-decommissioned reactors, and the areas that have been or are in the process of being cleaned up. Tours run on selected weekends from early April through October; if you're interested, call (509)376-0557 for information and reservations.

Just across the river in north **Pasco**, Quarry Lake Vintners (2520 Commercial Avenue, Pasco; (509)547-7307) welcomes visitors and produces fine cabernets, chardonnays, merlots, and sauvignon blancs. Preston Premium Wines (502 E Vineyard Drive, Pasco; (509)545-1990), off Highway 395, has a big tasting room and park; and Gordon Brothers Cellars (531 Levey Road, Pasco; (509)547-6224) promises a beautiful vista and a fine merlot.

From here, bop down to Levey Park and take a dip in the Snake River. Between Pasco and Othello to the north, a small country restaurant called the Goose and Gander (11760 N Glade Road, Eltopia; (509)297-4458), serves a highly recommended lemon pie, along with soups and salads. Prices are low (even for here).

A little farther south, just off I-182 near Burbank, is Chateau Gallant (S 1355 Gallant Road, Pasco; (509)545-9570). The winery specializes in white wines and has a view of the **McNary Wildlife Refuge**, whose majestic flocks of waterfowl create a pastoral backdrop to your wine-tasting. In Kennewick proper, try the Spaghetti Establishment (2107 4th Avenue, Kennewick; (509)586-6622) for pasta dinners (which include dessert) in the $5–$11 range. Kids are entranced by the model trains

Ellensburg Rodeo

The biggest rodeo in these parts brings riders from far and wide for four days of Wild West events over Labor Day weekend. Admission to the colorful event is $8.00–$17.00, depending on your seat, and a family ticket (two kids and two adults for $29.95) is a good deal; (509)962-7831 or (800)637-2444.

running on overhead tracks. Near Kennewick, the Alkali Flats Cafe (Highway 12, Touchet; (509)394-2310) serves bountiful breakfasts, noble lunches, and a home-style dinner once a month, all in a doublewide.

CHEAP SLEEPS

Rio Mirada Motor Inn

1603 Terrace Heights Drive, Yakima, WA 98901 • (509)457-4444

From the parking lot this looks like many Best Westerns (and indeed, it is one). So what's the attraction? There's a pool, but even better, the Yakima River is right out back, and you can fall asleep to the murmur of nature flowing past your room. In the morning, take a stroll along the Yakima Greenway or through the Yakima Arboretum (which has a playground for kids).

Sunnyside Inn Bed and Breakfast

800 E Edison Avenue, Sunnyside, WA 98944 • (509)839-5557

The Sunnyside Inn offers the best of B&B accommodations with the advantages of a hotel and a great price. Ten cheery, individually decorated rooms provide a cozy touch, with amenities such as color TVs, phones, air conditioning, and huge private baths; all but two have Jacuzzis. Jim and Geri Graves, resident managers and chefs for the past five seasons, bought the Sunnyside Inn in 1994. They also own and operate the Country Steak House and Bakery 7 miles away in Mabton.

Apple Valley Motel

903 Wine Country Road, Grandview, WA 98930 • (509)882-3003

On the west end of downtown Grandview, this little gem offers the perfect spot to spend the night in a clean, quiet, simple room. A small pool offers a chance for a spring or summer dip, although the attraction here is being right smack in the middle of wine country with a bargain place ($30!) to hit the rack when the sun goes down. Kitchenettes are available.

Wine Country Inn

1106 Wine Country Road, Prosser, WA 99350 • (509)786-2855

Perched on the bank of the Yakima River, this 100-year-old home has been converted to a charming B&B with four rooms for rent and an attached restaurant (which serves dinner Wednesday through Sunday). Relax under the huge oak tree by the river or admire the crafts and art in the gallery.

Nendels

615 Jadwin Avenue, Richland, WA 99352 • (509)943-4611 or
(800)547-0106

There's nothing fancy about Nendels, but you can get a clean room for a fair price with a moderate amount of style. Standard motel–chain amenities are available here, but you can find them at a dozen other places along George Washington Way as well. What makes this motel special is its location—it's convenient to Giacci's restaurant and shops, and it's just a hop off the freeway to the Tri–Cities wineries.

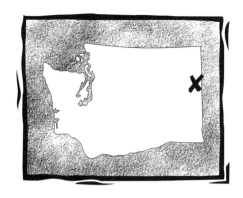

Spokane & the Palouse

Long before the Nez Percé, Cayuse, Umatilla, and Coeur d'Alene Indian tribes roamed the region, thousands of years of near-constant winds deposited rich dust on rounded volcanic mounds, creating the rolling hills of southeast Washington. French fur trappers named the area Palouse, a French word meaning "waves of blowing grass." These days, it's not grass but wheat that the wind moves. Dust from plowed fields yields stunning sunsets of deep orange throughout the summer and fall.

Spring comes quickly to the Palouse. Warm April winds blow across the rolling hills, sweeping away the last of the snow and revealing a carpet of green winter wheat. Mallards paddle about in shallow ponds, grazing on tender wheat shoots; red-winged blackbirds sing from cattails and fence posts.

North is Spokane, the biggest city in Washington east of the Cascades. It has all the trappings of a city while retaining the feel of a small town. A second-floor enclosed skywalk system connects all the major department stores and office buildings in the downtown shopping district. Well-kept neighborhoods radiate from the city's core, which features the handsome Riverfront Park.

ON THE ROAD

Spokane has a reputation as a sort of sleepy place, but locals know it's an ideal location for those who like to play outside. There's a plethora of lakes near Spokane, most of which have public beaches. The spacious sandy beach at the edge of **Coeur d'Alene City Park** in Idaho on Coeur d'Alene Lake, just a 30-minute drive east of Spokane, is a favorite. The Spokane County Parks Department also maintains Bear Lake, 20 miles north of Spokane on Highway 2. No motorized boats are allowed on this small lake, which draws mostly swimmers, picnickers, and those who paddle about in rubber rafts. A small vehicle fee is charged at the gate.

Riverfront Park is the pleasant green heart of Spokane's downtown core. It was developed from old railroad yards by Expo '74, a world environmental exposition staged by the city. The park is now an airy place full of meandering paved paths and ice skating in winter (weekdays at the Ice Palace; $4.25 adults, $3.25 children). During the

Birding

North of the city limits and straddling the Little Spokane River is the **Little Spokane River Natural Area**, (509)456-3964, part of Riverside State Park. There are two canoe launches and trails where walkers can watch great blue herons, an occasional bald eagle, and waterfowl among the clumps of yellow iris.

The **Dishman Hills Natural Area** is a 400-acre preserve in the Spokane Valley with a network of trails through mixed habitats. Nearly 400 plant species and 100 species of birds have been spotted here. It's wise to pick up a detailed topographic map at Northwest Map Service (525 W Sprague Avenue, Spokane; (509)455-6981), since it's easy to get lost on the preserve. Take I-90 east from Spokane to the Sprague Avenue exit, go east 1½ miles to Sargent Road, turn right, and continue for a half mile.

Forty-five minutes south of Spokane, the **Turnbull National Wildlife Refuge** is a 15,000-acre area dotted with pothole lakes and ponds that attract migrating waterfowl in the spring and fall; (509)235-4723. There's a small admission fee for vehicles. The 5-mile auto route takes you near several large ponds where the waterfowl viewing is excellent.

summer the ice rink is converted to minigolf and rides for small children. There's also an IMAX theater and a restored 1909 carousel; (509)625-6600 or (800)336-PARK. Free concerts in the outdoor amphitheater provide some of the best entertainment. The annual Fourth of July fireworks show features live music and draws thousands. The Spokane Symphony Orchestra can be heard at a free Labor Day evening concert held each year in Comstock Park on W 29th Avenue.

Cyclists, joggers, walkers, and roller bladers use the paved **Centennial Trail**, which stretches from Riverfront Park to the Washington-Idaho state line. Spokane's annual Bloomsday Run, held during the lilac season on the first Sunday in May, is the second-largest road race in the country, drawing about 60,000 runners.

The city plays **golf** with a passion, and 12 courses are often open from late March through late November. Two of the most beautiful public courses in the nation are Indian Canyon, (509)747-5353, where greens fees run about $21 for 18 holes and $16 for 9 holes, and Hangman Valley, (509)448-1212, where you can play 18 holes for $17 and 9 holes for less than 10 bucks. Both courses offer discounts to Spokane residents.

It's not rare to have snow in the city from November to March, and cross-country skiers can ski trails, groomed by the parks department, at city golf courses—Downriver, Esmeralda, Hangman, and the more challenging Indian Canyon. When the snow melts in the city, Nordic skiers head for the nearby **Mount Spokane Nordic Area**, where gliding the 17 kilometers of groomed trails is free but driving vehicles requires a state Sno-Park pass. There are also separate groomed snowmobile trails. Just up the road from the Nordic area is the **Mount Spokane Ski Area** (31 miles north on Highway 206, Spokane; (509)238-6281), which has fair facilities and some challenging runs. Several of the main runs are lit for night skiing.

If you get hungry while in Spokane's Browne's Addition neighborhood, stop at Cannon Street Grill (144 Cannon Street, Spokane; (509) 456-8660) for a caesar salad or Reuben sandwich. Hale's Ales (5634 E Commerce Street, Spokane; (509)534-7553), a microbrewery that welcomes visitors when the day's brewing work is done, offers brewery tours and an opportunity to taste their pale ale, bitter, porter, Moss Bay ale, and seasonal specialties. For beverages without a kick, the Elk (1931 W Pacific Avenue, Spokane; (509)456-0454), a former drugstore with a soda fountain, serves milkshakes and sodas and a half-dozen daily specials. Dick's Drive-In (10 E 3rd Avenue, Spokane; (509)747-2481) has the best deals on burgers and fries.

Auntie's Bookstore and Cafe (402 W Main Avenue, Spokane;

 *Rodeo*

The annual Cheney Rodeo offers roping, bronco riding, barrel racing, and bull riding. The bleachers are close to the action, and for munching there is corn on the cob as well as hot dogs and burgers. Expect a parade, community breakfasts, and a barbecue. The rodeo usually takes place the second weekend in July. Call for a schedule of events and ticket prices; (509)235-4848.

(509)838-0206) serves pastries, desserts, and beverages, making it a great place to settle in with a cup of coffee and a good read. The magazine rack has a respectable selection of literary journals and hard-to-find publications. Locals who aren't picky about ambience head to the industrial area on E Trent Avenue for a bite at the Town & Country Restaurant (5615 E Trent Avenue, Spokane; (509)534-3868), where a basic meal of steak, baked potato, roll, and salad is delivered to your table for less than $10. The city's best bargain restaurant view can be had while lunching at Viewpoint, the cafeteria on the 17th floor of the Farm Credit Bank Building (601 W 1st Avenue, Spokane; (509)838-9219). Dinners are quite pricey.

Cultural entertainment includes amateur performances at the Spokane Civic Theatre (1020 N Howard Street, Spokane; (509)325-2507) and professional theater at Interplayers Ensemble (174 S Howard Street, Spokane; (509)455-PLAY). Attend a matinee and you save a few dollars. Second-run movies are shown at the Fox Theatre (1005 W Sprague Avenue, Spokane; (509)624-0105) and the Garland Dollar Theater (924 W Garland Avenue, Spokane; (509)327-1050), where you can see a flick for only a buck. Foreign and art films are screened at the Magic Lantern Theatre (123 S Wall Street, Spokane; (509)838-4919).

Bing Crosby's memorabilia is housed at Gonzaga University's Crosby Library (502 E Boone Avenue, Spokane; (509)484-2831), the crooner's gift to his alma mater. There's no charge to see lots of gold records, an Oscar, and more. Bing grew up at 508 E Sharp Avenue, a block away. Cheney Cowles Museum (2316 W 1st Avenue, Spokane; (509)456-3931) has an art gallery and an exhibit focusing on the area's early history. Admission is free on Wednesday evening and half price earlier in the day.

You can take in one of the most commanding views of the rolling farmlands of the Palouse from the top of Steptoe Butte, 47 miles south of Spokane. Sunrise and sunset are especially good times to go. This spot is

 *Autumn Picks*

It's an annual ritual for locals to make an autumn visit to Green Bluff, a small farming community north of Spokane (take Highway 2 to Day-Mount Spokane Road, and then turn east). Harvest is celebrated with great zest, and the abundant produce includes apples, squash, potatoes, onions, carrots, and pumpkins. Many of the orchardists help spice up the occasion with freshly squeezed apple cider and homemade specialty foods such as jams, preserves, and honey. Those in the know go to Walter's Fruit Ranch (9807 E Day Road, Mead; (509)238-4709), where a tractor-drawn wagon takes U-pickers deep into the orchard to pluck Delicious apples; those who prefer ready-picked fruit gather from big bins in a barnlike store. The bonus is the chance to relax with a piece of homemade apple pie, pungent with cinnamon, and hot apple cider, enjoyed on a second-story deck overlooking the orchard (in less cooperative weather, you can sit at one of the cafe tables inside). In July, Green Bluff growers sell raspberries, cherries, and peaches.

a favorite of amateur astronomers, and it can get downright crowded on clear nights.

Palouse Falls gushes over a basalt cliff higher than Niagara Falls and drops 198 feet into a steep-walled basin. **Palouse Falls State Park** has 105 acres of camping and picnicking areas and hiking trails. The falls are most full from late winter to early summer. Near the falls, at the confluence of the Palouse and Snake rivers, is the **Marmes Rock Shelter**, where remains of the earliest known inhabitants of the Western Hemisphere were first excavated by archaeologists in 1962. The Marmes area is now underwater, however, and the cliff walls adjacent to the site can be viewed only from the water.

Founded in 1890 as a land-grant university, **Washington State University** made Pullman (75 miles south of Spokane) more of a lively college town than a gathering place for wheat farmers. Activities naturally center on the campus. Visitors can arrange all sorts of free tours—one is through the university creamery, which produces Cougar Gold cheese. Call WSU Information at (509)335-3936.

Or you can pick up a campus map and visit the Museum of Art in the Fine Arts Center; the Museum of Anthropology and Maurice T. James Entomological Collection in Johnson Hall; the Marion Ownbey Herbarium in Herald Hall; the Beef, Dairy, and Swine centers (call

185

(509)335-2280 for a tour); and the Jewett Observatory (which is not always open to the public, so call ahead; (509)335-8518).

The university hosts a full slate of athletic events, theater performances, and other entertainment at the 12,000-seat Beasley Performing Arts Coliseum. For tickets and an events calendar, call G&B Select-a-Seat; (800)325-SEAT.

During the week, Ferdinand's, in WSU's Food Quality Building (behind the new Food Science and Health Nutrition Building), serves thick milkshakes and ice cream made with milk from WSU's own dairy herd. For more substantial sustenance, try Swilly's (NE 200 Kamiekan, Pullman; (509)334-3395), a small brick cafe in downtown Pullman. The sandwiches are more inventive than standard deli fare, and you can linger over a latte and dessert. If cafeteria food fits the bill, stop by Compton Union Building (the CUB, on campus) and eat burgers, salads, and sandwiches cafeteria-style.

Walla Walla, best known as the home of the Washington State Penitentiary and the sweet onion, was named after a native phrase meaning "many waters." And Main Street was built on the Nez Percé Indian Trail, another indication of the city's ties to the past. The thousands of artifacts at Fort Walla Walla (Myra Road and Rose Street, Walla Walla; (509)525-7703) also point to the past, in this case to life on a pioneer farm. It's closed in winter; admission is $2.50 for adults and half that for kids. Learn about pioneers Marcus and Narcissa Whitman, who

Juniper Dunes

At the southwest corner of the Palouse, the Juniper Dunes Wilderness is all that remains of an ecosystem that once stretched over nearly 400 square miles south to the Snake and Columbia rivers. Protected under the 1984 Washington Wilderness Act, the 7,140-acre wilderness includes some of the biggest sand dunes (up to 130 feet high and a quarter mile wide) and largest natural groves of western juniper (some 150 years old) in the state. Expect to see the same wildlife and birds you would encounter in a true desert region. No camping or fires are allowed in the wilderness. The most scenic portion is a 2-mile hike northeast from the parking area toward the junipers and the largest dunes (bring drinking water). For directions to the parking area, contact the Bureau of Land Management (1103 N Fancher Street, Spokane, WA 99212; (509)353-2570).

attempted to bring Christianity to the Native Americans, at the Whitman Mission National Historic Site; (509)529-2761. Visitors can also tour the well-maintained mission grounds. Admission is $2 (free for seniors and those under 17). Another local attraction is the leafy campus of **Whitman College**, a private liberal arts school.

In good weather, the community of 26,000 can best be seen by bicycle. Pick up a free bicycle map at the Chamber of Commerce (29 E Sumac, Walla Walla, WA 99362; (509)525-0850). For art, the town boasts the oldest continuing symphony west of the Mississippi River—the Walla Walla Symphony—and a host of cultural events at Whitman College. For sheer entertainment and gluttony, this town throws a free onion festival each year in late July. And last but not least, bird lovers can visit a collection of exotic and colorful birds in the Pioneer Park Aviary.

Although the area's wine country is not as extensive as that near the Tri-Cities, Walla Walla has its own version of a **winery tour**, with stops at Woodward Canyon Winery (Highway 12, Lowden; (509)525-4129), Waterbrook (just south of Lowden off McDonald Road; (509)522-1918), L'Ecole No. 41 (in Lowden; (509)525-0940), Leonetti Cellar (1321 School Avenue, Walla Walla; (509)525-1428), and Biscuit Ridge Winery (11 miles east of Walla Walla on Highway 12 in Dixie; (509)529-4986). Call ahead, as these small wineries do not always keep regular hours.

CHEAP SLEEPS

Cavanaugh's Value Inn
1203 W 5th Avenue, Spokane, WA 99201 • (509)624-4142

This motel has easy access to downtown, and even though it's just south of I-90, it's not so near the freeway as to make guests feel they are still driving. You can stroll through one of Spokane's oldest residential areas, with deciduous trees lining the streets. The rooms offer all the standard motel amenities, and rates start at $52 for two ($39 off season). Pay a bit more and you can get a larger room with a kitchenette.

Waverly Place
709 W Waverly Place, Spokane, WA 99205 • (509)328-1856

Across the street from what was, in Spokane's early days, a racetrack, Waverly Place retains the elegance of the Victorian era. The track is now Corbin Park, a lovely oval with a couple of tennis courts, a tree canopy, and plenty of places to walk. Guests can cool off in the swimming pool or sit on the broad porch overlooking the park and sip lemonade.

CUB Hotel

Compton Union Building (CUB), Washington State University, Pullman, WA 99163 • (509)335-9444

The university operates 30 simple rooms as a small hotel. Some rooms have tubs and showers; others have only a shower ($55). Parking's no problem for guests; a permit comes with the room. Don't expect to find rooms available when the football team's playing a home game. Open during the regular school session.

Paradise Creek Quality Inn

SE Bishop Boulevard, Pullman, WA 99163 • (509)332-0500

This Quality Inn gives you proximity to the university yet allows you a bit of distance from the fray of college life. The least expensive rooms have walk-in showers only and two queen-size beds. During the summer you can swim in an outside pool; otherwise guests can use the indoor Jacuzzi and sauna. A nearby physical therapy office makes its exercise equipment available to guests. A continental breakfast comes with your room, as do cookies and milk in the evening.

BRITISH COLUMBIA

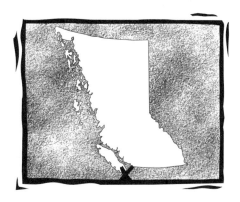

Victoria & Beyond

Victoria may be far from England geographically, but no place on the North American continent is more reminiscent of the Old Country than this impressive Canadian city. The imposing stone architecture of the Parliament buildings and the Empress Hotel are your first hint. The link becomes even more apparent as you walk the streets: shop windows display Waterford crystal, English toffee, and Scottish tartans, and cafes serve cups of Earl Grey tea or fish 'n' chips wrapped in newspaper. Victoria's 250,000 citizens also have a spirit of their own, exemplified in spring and summer by the colorful flower baskets that line every downtown street. This is a bright and friendly garden city, with none of the dourness sometimes associated with Britain.

The city now called Victoria had its beginnings in 1843, when the Hudson's Bay Company built Fort Camosun as its western headquarters. The settlement was later renamed in honor of Queen Victoria and subsequently became the provincial capital of British Columbia. Timber, shipbuilding, and other industries brought considerable wealth to Victoria in the late 19th and early 20th centuries. The beautiful homes and impressive gardens that grace the city today are the legacy of this turn-of-the-century pride and prosperity. Its climate, sunnier and milder than that of either

Vancouver or Seattle, soon brought steamers across the water, drawing vacationers from these cities to Victoria's refined streets and old-world airs.

ON THE ROAD

One of Victoria's most impressive sights is not in the city but 21 kilometers north, on an arm of the Saanich Inlet—the renowned **Butchart Gardens** (800 Benvenuto Avenue, Brentwood Bay; (604) 652-4422). This miracle of modern horticulture, spread across 50 acres of a private estate, began as the creation of Jenny Butchart, wife of cement manufacturer Robert Butchart, who took it upon herself to re-landscape her husband's limestone quarry. Over the years, the Butcharts added Japanese and Italian gardens and an English rose garden, and populated them with ducks, peacocks, and trained pigeons.

Today, the place is a mecca for gardening enthusiasts from every corner of the globe (as touring maps in 12 languages will attest). Consider visiting in the evening during the summer months, when the gardens are lit with thousands of colored lights, crowds are thinner (though not by much), and entertainers give free performances. Spectacular fireworks displays (set to music!) are held on Saturday nights in July and August. Bring a sweater and something to sit on.

The city's other leading attraction is the **Royal British Columbia Museum** (675 Belleville Street, Victoria; (604)387-3014), located between the Empress Hotel and the Parliament buildings. Exhibits depict the province's natural and human history through lifelike dioramas, including forests and seascapes, a re-created turn-of-the-century townscape (complete with sounds and smells), and life-sized working models of industries. The gallery of tribal art and customs deserves a careful look. Coin-operated lockers are available to store bags and backpacks while

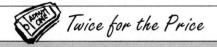

Twice for the Price

Why make a day of it when you can make two? Your admission tickets at Butchart Gardens ($11) and the Royal British Columbia Museum ($5) are good for 24 hours, so if you go after noon, you can come back at no charge the next morning.

Harbouring Visitors

It's not the *QE II*, but then you're no Prince Charles. Victoria Harbour Ferry Company's miniature ferryboats (each seats 12) squire passengers to and from shore points all along Victoria Harbour. You can get on at any stop and take a round-trip, 40-minute cruise while viewing waterfront activity, floatplanes, seabirds, seals, and otters, among other attractions ($10). For a truly inexpensive outing, hop the ferry to Fisherman's Wharf ($2.50), eat your fill of fish 'n' chips at Barb's Place, and then walk back downtown.

you explore. Admission is $5 except on Mondays from November through February, when it's free.

Even though rooms at the Francis Rattenburg-designed 1908 **Empress Hotel** (721 Government Street, Victoria; (604)384-8111) are well beyond the price range of budget travelers, make a reservation for an opulent and filling afternoon tea; otherwise, stiffen your upper lip and sashay among the restored Victorian antique furnishings in the public areas.

Behind the Empress is the **Crystal Garden** (713 Douglas Street, Victoria; (604)381-1213). Once the site of the largest saltwater swimming pool in the British Empire, this building now holds a tropical garden with dozens of species of exotic birds and rare flowers. Although admission is $6, afternoon tea here has a much smaller price tag than at the Empress.

The **Parliament** buildings (501 Belleville Street, Victoria; (604)387-3046) are especially stunning at night, when they're outlined with thousands of lights. Built in 1897, they still serve as the legislative center for the province. Free tours are offered weekdays by reservation, except when Parliament is in session.

As hokey as it may seem, a $10 tour on one of the **Tallyho horse-drawn carriages** offers an insightful lesson in the history of the city—one that shouldn't be missed. Two Belgian draft horses clop along to the cadence of the driver's hourlong, narrated tour (complete with humorous historical anecdotes) starting at the Parliament Building (just across from the Wax Museum), winding through 155-acre Beacon Hill Park to the waterfront, and trotting through the residential community of James Bay.

No visitor with an interest in architecture or history should miss the

Beacon Hill Children's Farm

Kids of every age will get a kick out of (though hopefully not *from*) the baby goats, sheep, Vietnamese potbelly pigs, and other animals that call Beacon Hill Children's Farm home. A dollar donation is a small price to pay to visit this kid-friendly minizoo and its turtle house, aviary, duck pond, chicken yard, and petting corral. Closed in winter. In Beacon Hill Park; (604)381-2532.

1889 **Craigdarroch Castle** (1050 Joan Crescent, Victoria; (604)592-5323), a short distance from downtown. Built by a wealthy industrialist, this remarkable mansion with 39 rooms and 18 fireplaces is notable for its fine woodwork and leaded-glass windows, arches, turrets, and soaring stone walls. Not far from Craigdarroch, the Art Gallery of Greater Victoria (1040 Moss Street, Victoria; (604)384-4101) contains works by leading Canadian contemporary artists, important American and European painters of recent centuries, and an extensive collection of Asian art, including a complete Shinto shrine from Japan.

Chinatown, marked by the Gate of Harmonious Interest (at Fisgard and Government streets), offers an odd mix of Chinese restaurants and groceries that are slowly being encroached upon by a growing number of upscale boutiques and decidedly non-Chinese coffee bars and bistros. Walk through Fan Tan Alley, Canada's narrowest thoroughfare, and stop in at La Paz Raku Studio Gallery (16 Fan Tan Alley, Victoria; (604)383-5223) to see the raku work of owner Larry Sims and the colorful oils of local artist Luis Merlino. Enjoy an espresso at the beautifully appointed Grace Bistro (533 Fisgard Street, Victoria; (604)385-5677) or an unpretentious Chinese dinner at Wah Lai Yuen (560 Fisgard Street, Victoria; (604)381-5355).

Inexpensive eats in Victoria include Cafe Mexico (1425 Market Street, Victoria; (604)386-5454), offering creative south-of-the-U.S.-border fare; Fogg 'n' Suds (1630 Store Street, Victoria; (604)383-BEER), with international finger food and a menu of 200 beers; Beacon Drive-In (corner of Beacon and Douglas streets, Victoria; (604)385-7521), where locals go for a burger and the best soft-serve ice cream in British Columbia; the James Bay Tea Room (332 Menzies Street, Victoria; (604)382-8282), serving traditional British cuisine (and delicious breakfasts); and Barb's Place (at Fisherman's Wharf, Victoria; 384-6515), for great fish 'n' chips.

East of downtown, the Red Mango (1725 Quadra Street, Victoria; (604)385-2827) is both a corner store and a restaurant serving big portions of good-for-you foods and lots of exotic drinks. In Victoria's Fernwood neighborhood, Fiddleheads (1284-D Gladstone Avenue, Victoria; (604)386-1199), a funky little vegetarian cafe, is the place for coffee and dessert. George & Dragon (1302 Gladstone Avenue, Victoria; (604)388-4458) is a lively pub that dishes up a great onion soup and caesar salad combo. There's live music almost every night (no cover) and plenty of outdoor seating.

West of downtown, across the harbor on the Esquimalt Peninsula, the Old England Inn (429 Lampson Street, Victoria; (604)388-4353) is a replica of Anne Hathaway's 16th-century cottage. There's good pub fare in Esquimalt at Spinnakers Brew Pub (308 Catherine Street, Victoria; (604)386-BREW).

Beacon Hill Park stretches south from the Royal British Columbia Museum along the Strait of Juan de Fuca, and is a popular destination for walkers, remote-control airplane flyers, kite flyers, sunset watchers, and bikers. A 2½-kilometer path skirts the shoreline. Rent bikes from Budget Cycle Time (727 Courtney Street, Victoria; (604)388-7874) or Harbour Scooter Rentals (843 Douglas Street, Victoria; (604)384-2133. Also popular are Fort Rodd Hill National Historic Park and Fisgard Lighthouse National Historic Site (603 Fort Rodd Hill Road, Victoria; (604)363-4662). **Fort Rodd**, built at the end of the 19th century on the west side of Esquimalt Harbor, has three separate batteries with gun emplacements; locals find inviting places for picnics on the grassy point. The lighthouse, the first permanent light on Canada's Pacific coast, was built in 1860 and is still in operation. Sample the pub grub out this way at the Six-Mile Pub (494 Island Highway, Victoria; (604)478-3121).

Horticulture Centre of the Pacific

505 Quayle Road, Victoria, BC V8X 3X1
(604)479-6162

This delightful volunteer-run botanical garden and horticultural school might be considered a poor relation when compared to the better-known and more grandly maintained Butchart Gardens. But you'll never have to fight a crowd as you walk among the flower-lined paths, examine the herb garden or fuchsia arbors, rest on a multitude of comfortable benches, and enjoy the bounty of peace and quiet available on this 100-acre preserve. Admission is $1. Take Quadra Street and head northwest to West Saanich Road, then go left onto Beaver Lake Road. Watch for signs.

Sooke, a half-hour drive west from Victoria, is still relatively undiscovered. There's wilderness for all tastes nearby. For peace and serenity visit East Sooke Park, an enormous (3,400 acres) semiwilderness park with great day hiking and beach walking. Only hardy and experienced backpackers are advised to try the West Coast Trail, an hour's drive west at the end of the road. The Sooke Region Museum (2070 Phillips Road, Sooke; (604)642-6351) displays Indian artifacts and old logging equipment as well as an historic cottage detailing the way of life at the turn of the century. You can nosh on soup and housemade bread at the Good Life Bookstore and Cafe (2113 Otter Point Road, Sooke; (604)642-6821), a converted old house filled with eclectic furnishings.

CHEAP SLEEPS

Backpacker's Hostel
1418 Fernwood Road, Victoria, BC V8V 4P7 • (604)386-4471

This hostel-type lodging is close to but not in downtown—a nice compromise. Two floors of this big house are male and female dorms, and the top floor is a coed loft. A couple of double rooms top out at $30, as does a honeymoon suite with private bath and queen-sized bed. There's usually a barbecue on Wednesday nights.

Battery Street Guest House
670 Battery Street, Victoria, BC V8V 1E5 • (604)385-4632

Pamela Verduyn, a gracious (and charmingly eccentric) Dutch woman, lives in the attic of her 1898 bed-and-breakfast home in Victoria's James Bay neighborhood. Her personality carries throughout this quiet, reasonably priced guest house, located just around the corner from Beacon Hill Park. The six spacious rooms (some with ocean views) are quite homey. Two rooms have a sink and toilet (but no bath), and there are two shared bathrooms.

Cherry Bank Hotel
825 Burdett Street, Victoria, BC V8W 1B3 • (604)385-5380

The Cherry Bank is a congenial kind of place that caters to a working-class crowd. Every table in the games room of this 26-room Victorian has a built-in trivia game, and there's a sing-along piano bar in the pub. The old-fashioned, saloonlike atmosphere in the Cherry Bank Spare Rib House restaurant is fun, too. Guest rooms lack TVs and telephones (and there are no nonsmoking rooms, which might explain why the units smell of air freshener), but they're clean and comfortable (and surprisingly quiet, considering there are a pub and restaurant below). Off season, the rooms with private bath are quite decently priced, and rooms with kitchenettes are available, although breakfast—served downstairs in the restaurant—is included in the room rate.

Christine's Place

1408 Taunton Street, Victoria, BC V8R 1W9 • (604)595-4774

This elegant 1910 heritage home was completely gutted and remodeled in 1994—which accounts for its cheerfully bright, modern, townhouse-like interior. The comfortable living area with TV, handsome book-lined dining room, and high-tech kitchen have a "model home" look about them, as do the two small guest rooms (which share a bath) and the larger suite with private bath. Interestingly, this ever-so-much-fussier B&B is affiliated with the nearby Renouf House (see below); owner Christine Rougeau is the sister of Renouf's inexhaustible Caroline Cooper (who handles reservations—and baking duties—for both houses).

Craigmyle Guest House

1037 Craigdarroch Road, Victoria, BC V8S 2A5 • (604)595-5411

Owner Jim Pace has honed his dry humor over the course of nearly 20 years spent running Victoria's first B&B. Built as a guest house in 1913 by famed architect Sam McClure, the Craigmyle boasts wood wainscoting and stained-glass windows—much like the Craigdarroch Castle (which happens to be across the street). All rooms have private baths. Breakfast is a feast including cereal, fresh-fruit compote, eggs, bacon, toast with housemade preserves, and Pace's special blend of coffee.

Crystal Court Motel

701 Belleville Street, Victoria, BC V8W 1A2 • (604)384-0551

The first motel built in downtown Victoria (1950) is still one of its best bargains. Centrally located a block from the Crystal Gardens, the Royal British Columbia Museum, and the Inner Harbour, the Crystal Court is ideal for folks who want to be close to the sights but don't want to dine out every night. Every other room has a fully equipped kitchen (for an additional $2) stocked with everything but a casserole dish and roasting pan. All the rooms have either refrigerators or old-fashioned iceboxes, private bathrooms, color TVs, radios, and phones.

Hotel Douglas

1450 Douglas Street, Victoria, BC V8W 2G1 • (604)383-4157

Opposite City Hall in the hectic heart of the city, the old Hotel Douglas can't promise quiet, modern rooms—but it can (and does) offer spacious, clean, well-maintained accommodations, all with TVs, telephones, and oversized closets and bathrooms. This very basic hotel has a small cafe and a cocktail lounge with musical entertainment (ranging from jazz to karaoke sing-along).

The James Bay Inn
270 Government Street, Victoria, BC V8V 2L2 • (604)384-7151

This longtime budget favorite underwent a facelift in 1992 and, with it, an upgrade that *almost* lifts it off our list of cheap sleeps. The interior of this 1907 Edwardian manor, the last home of famed painter Emily Carr, has been completely made over. A turn-of-the-century Victorian look, with reproduction antique furnishings, now extends from the lobby to the guest rooms. Fortunately, rooms without private baths remain affordable. Be sure to ask for any special rates the inn may be offering. The Colonial Cafe serves budget-priced meals, and the James Bay Inn Pub serves up ales for those in need of a nightcap.

Lilac House
252 Memorial Crescent, Victoria, BC V85 3J2 • (604)389-0252

The best thing about this authentically restored Victorian house is its location—on a quiet street opposite beautiful, historic Ross Bay Cemetery, where the dearest of Victoria's dearly departed (including coal baron Robert Dunsmuir and painter Emily Carr) are buried. You will rest in peace in one of Lilac House's three guest rooms, which are artfully and carefully dressed in lilac hues that offset the plethora of tasteful antiques. A single shared bathroom (with tub but no shower) makes for a bit of inconvenience come morning. Owner Gail Harris is a writer whose imagined history of the 1892 house and its inhabitants is the basis for a book of poetry and a locally produced play.

Renouf House Bed & Breakfast
2010 Stanley Avenue, Victoria, BC V8R 3X6 • (604)595-4774

What do you get when you cross Mother Jones with Martha Stewart? Why, Caroline Cooper, of course. When the surprisingly young owner of this stately 1912 heritage home isn't cooking, cleaning, or booking custom-guided tours for Intertidal Explorations (a sea kayaking company owned by Cooper and her partner, Shaen Chambers), she'll be happy to share her recipe for homemade muesli, her opinions on clear-cutting and sewage disposal, and her grand store of knowledge about traversing Vancouver Island's backcountry. The Renouf, in Victoria's Fernwood neighborhood, has four simply but prettily appointed guest rooms sharing two baths, and a common room that doubles as an office/gallery. And while the B&B rooms are among the cheapest in town (less than $50— scrumptious breakfast included), the Renouf *Bunk* and Breakfast, down in the basement, costs a measly $18 per person (same great breakfast). Two rooms with four railcar style bunks each share a modern bathroom and a fully equipped kitchen—perfect for a group of bosom buddies on a budget.

Scotsman Motel

490 Gorge Road E, Victoria, BC V8T 2W4 • (604)388-7358

Friendly service and a near-ideal location (away from yet accessible to the downtown core) has set this family-style hotel apart from similar properties. Coffee and pastries are served each morning in the office, beneath the shadow of traditional Scottish battle-axes. The clean, pet-friendly guest rooms all have queen-sized beds, cable TV, and standard furnishings; adjoining rooms, suites, and kitchen units are available.

Victoria International Hostel

516 Yates Street, Victoria, BC V8W 1K8 • (604)385-4511

Victoria's youth hostel is housed in a wonderful building (a renovated heritage property dating from the late 19th century) in a wonderful location (just a few steps off waterfront Wharf Street, in the heart of downtown). There are 109 beds available in the men's and women's dormitory rooms, with toilets and hot showers down the halls. A pair of fully equipped kitchens, a dining room, a TV lounge, a library, a games room, and a laundry round out the place. There's lots of info available for those seeking cheap eats, travel-adventure trips, and rides (or riders) to points beyond. A stay here will set you back only $14.00 ($12.50 for hostel members), and family rooms are available for a few bucks more per person. Beds fill up fast during the summer months, so be sure to reserve in advance.

University of Victoria

Housing and Conference Services (PO Box 1700), Victoria, BC V8W 2Y2
(604)721-8395

From May to August, when university students are on holiday, their campus dormitory rooms are made available to Victoria visitors. It's wise to book ahead for the single or twin-bedded rooms ($46), although some drop-in units may be available. There are toilets and showers, pay phones, and a TV lounge on every floor; there's also a coin-op laundry in each residence building, and full towel and linen service. A full breakfast is included. Guests have access to campus services.

YM-YWCA of Victoria

880 Courtney Street, Victoria, BC V8W 1C4 • (604)386-7511

This adult women's residence, a few blocks east of downtown, has 31 small college-style rooms with twin beds, a dresser and closet, and little else. They're clean but basic, with shared toilets and showers, and available only on a nightly basis from May through September (rooms are rented by the month the rest of the year). The building has a TV lounge, pay phones, laundry facilities, and a budget-priced cafeteria; guests are invited to use the Y's swimming pool and other athletic facilities.

ACCESS

BC Ferries cross the Strait of Georgia between Tsawwassen and Swartz Bay, about 28 kilometers north of Victoria on the Saanich Peninsula, eight or more times daily all year (schedules vary seasonally); (604)669-1211. Washington State Ferries link Anacortes with Sidney, 24 kilometers north of Victoria, twice daily in summer and once a day in winter; (206)464-6400. Black Ball Transport's *Coho* ferry shuttles between Port Angeles and Victoria's Inner Harbour between one and four times daily, again depending upon the season; (360)457-4491. The *Royal Victorian*, the Victoria Line's cushy British Columbia ferry, offers the only car-ferry service between Victoria and Seattle, with one round trip daily from mid-May to mid-September, leaving Victoria at 7:30am daily for the 4½-hour trip to Seattle, then departing from Seattle at 1pm and arriving in Victoria at 5:30pm; (604)480-5544 in Victoria or (206)625-1880 in Seattle. The *Victoria Clipper*, a waterjet-propelled catamaran, carries foot passengers only between Seattle and Victoria's Belleville Street four times a day from mid-May to mid-September, and once or twice a day (depending on the season) the rest of the year; (604)382-8100 in Victoria or (206)448-5000 in Seattle.

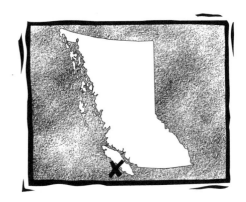

Vancouver Island's West Coast

Only two paved roads briefly touch Vancouver Island's western edge. But where these roads end, a natural path to adventure begins: long, sandy beaches and thriving tide pools in Pacific Rim National Park, nature trails through cedar groves on remote islands, a rain forest with natural hot springs, colonies of sea lions, and—perhaps the biggest attraction of all—migrating gray whales, whose vapor spouts trail across breathtaking, if often moody, skies twice each year (in March and September).

At the very end of Highway 4 is Tofino, a small town built by loggers and fishermen and populated by a number of watchful environmentalists. En route to Pacific Rim National Park and Tofino, you'll view the only blotch on the paradisiacal landscape: tree-shorn escarpments that stick out like rude stains amid a carpet of green. But loggers aren't the only disrupters of the pristine peninsula, where a stubborn sense of serenity has always encouraged a more laid-back lifestyle among the locals. Though Pacific Rim National Park has an average of 148 inches of rainfall a year (compared to Seattle's 39 inches) and only two remaining groves of old-growth forest, the park's challenging terrain is becoming a popular destination for adventurous travelers. (Even in the slack season, the area's ever-changing canvas attracts *curious onlookers who are fascinated by the winter storms.) Too many tourists can be as hard on the environment as too much logging. Trouble is, the local economy needs both. Despite philosophical tensions in recent times, this is one of the few areas on Vancouver Island where the residents recognize the importance of maintaining a delicate balance between the economy and the environment. As such, they've been working hard to welcome tourism but not encourage it, to regulate logging but not end it, and to limit development but not stop it.*

ON THE ROAD

Pacific Rim National Park, the first national marine park in Canada, encompasses three separate areas—West Coast Trail, Broken Islands, and Long Beach—from which visitors can experience the beauty of the Pacific Ocean.

The **West Coast Trail**, a rugged 72-kilometer path, stretches along the southernmost portion of the park. It can be traveled only on foot (from Port Renfrew to Bamfield), and is a strenuous but spectacular five- to seven-day hike for hardy and experienced backpackers; call (800)663-6000 for information. At the trail's northern end is the tiny fishing village of Bamfield. Return by the *Lady Rose* from Port Alberni rather than via the bumpy dirt road—which has some frightening logging traffic. (See box for more information on catching the *Lady Rose*.) In Bamfield you can rent boats for fishing or exploring the islands.

The **Broken Islands**—more than 100 islands in all, at the entrance to Barkley Sound—are accessible only by boat (take the *Lady Rose* from Port Alberni). This area is famous for sea lions, seals, and whales, and is very popular with fishermen, skin divers, and kayakers. Arrange island drop-offs and pickups through the *Lady Rose*.

Long Beach, on the Himwista Peninsula, is a 30-kilometer expanse of sand and rock outcrops backed by forest and mountains. There are lots of places for beach walks and shorter coastal hikes here that can be tailor-made for short, family-oriented jaunts or slightly more challenging treks. If chasing around a little dimpled white ball is your idea of exercise, you can take advantage of a great deal at the Long Beach Golf Course; (604)725-3332. Twenty-five dollars buys one round of golf and includes club rental, pull cart, and green fees.

Barkley Sound

If Ucluelet or Bamfield (at the northern end of the West Coast Trail) is your destination, leave the car in Port Alberni and hop on the *Lady Rose*, (604)723-8313, which carries mail, cargo, and passengers. This stout packet freighter departs from the Harbour Quay at Argyle Street Dock in Port Alberni and voyages through the Broken Islands in Barkley Sound to Bamfield on Tuesdays, Thursdays, and Saturdays, with special Sunday trips during July and August. Round-trip fare is $30. From June 1 to September 23, she sails for Ucluelet on Mondays, Wednesdays, and Fridays. Besides being a better way to reach these remote towns than navigating the area's rough roads, the five-hour cruise down Alberni Inlet and through the Broken Islands is breathtaking. Kayakers can make arrangements to be dropped off or picked up at Sechart Island. Breakfast and lunch are available, and the galley food is actually good.

For more information on Pacific Rim National Park, go to the information center at the park entrance on Highway 4, or call (604)726-4212. Or you can visit the Wickaninnish Interpretive Center (10 kilometers north of Ucluelet off Highway 4; (604)726-4701), which has park information and interesting oceanic exhibits, including displays and films that tell the story of the great whales. The expansive view is enhanced by telescopes on the observation decks.

At the very tip of Himwista Peninsula sits the small town of **Tofino**. You can easily spend an entire day in town wandering through the two fine native art galleries (the Eagle Aerie Gallery, owned by celebrated native artist Roy Vickers, and the House of Himwista). Treat yourself to the cheese loaf at the Common Loaf Bake Shop (180 First Street, Tofino; (604)725-3915), and you'll be rewarded with some of the best bread you've ever eaten—if you can wait out the laid-back service. In the mood for a vegetarian burrito? Drop by Christina Delano-Stephens's Alley Way Cafe (305 Campbell Street, Tofino; (604)725-3105). You can order a pound-and-a-half crab, a caesar salad, and some sourdough bread for around $16 at the Crab Bar, (604)725-3733, or you can do as the locals do: buy the crab live, steam it elsewhere, and have a sunset picnic on the beach. And though dinner prices are a bit high at the Wickaninnish Inn, you can still enjoy the marvelous view for the price of a drink.

~ Whale Watching

You can save a considerable amount of money by combining a whale-watching trip with a trip to the hot springs. Another money saver is traveling in groups of eight. (If you're a few friends shy of a group, consider buddying up with the other clients for a group discount.)

Zodiac excursions are the most exciting because you're closest to the water. (This also means you get wet, but rain gear is usually provided. Be forewarned: the ride can be a little rough, especially for those with back problems.) Call Remote Passages, (604)725-3163, for information on Zodiacs. Joe and Carl Martin, craftsmen who are active in educational and cultural affairs in Tofino, run Clayoquot Sound Charters; (604)725-3195. Their boat is specifically designed for whale-watching tours. Other companies include: Ocean Pacific Whale Charters Ltd., (604)725-3919, and Sea Forth, (604)723-4252, which uses a Boston Whaler and also charters fishing and diving excursions with advance notice.

Although everything north of Tofino is accessible only by water or air, you don't need to bring your own boat. **Water taxis** are as ubiquitous here as taxicabs are in Manhattan. They all charge roughly the same fare (about $20 for a drop-off and pickup to nearby Meares Island, and $55 round trip to the hot springs, about a half hour up the coast). **Whale-watching trips** run about $35 for 2½-hour tours. Cheaper tours spend less time on the water, diminishing your chances of seeing the whales. The best months for catching a glimpse of these magnificent mammals are March and April. (See box for more information.)

At other times of the year, one of the best ways to decide what to do is to pull out a map of the area, pick an island or an inlet, and ask one of the water taxis to drop you off there. Camp as long as you like, and the taxi will pick you up at a prearranged time.

More adventurous travelers will want to explore Clayoquot Sound by **sea kayak**. Neophyte paddlers should contact the Tofino Sea-Kayaking Company, (604)725-4222, for guided day trips with experienced boaters and naturalists in single or double kayaks. The intimidated can double up with an instructor. Rentals are available for experienced paddlers, although no more than eight people go out at a time. Trips range from a 2½-hour sunset paddle ($36) to full-day trips to Meares Island. A four-hour trip is also available for about $50.

Like water taxis, Tofino Air Lines (1st Street Dock, Tofino; (604)725-4454) will drop you off on the island or cove of your choice and pick you up at a prearranged time. There are four **floatplanes**: three hold up to three passengers and charge $102 per 20 minutes; the other accommodates up to seven passengers and costs $160 per 20 minutes. Therefore, the bigger plane, if full, is cheaper. You can cut costs by being flexible; airpool with other parties, or arrange the drop-off with someone who is being picked up at the same place.

CHEAP SLEEPS

Bed and Breakfast at Burley's
1078 Helen Road and Marine Drive (PO Box 550),
Ucluelet, BC V0R 3A0 • (604)726-4444

This wonderfully scenic B&B is located on the inlet of Hi-Focus Island, linked by causeway to Ucluelet proper. The nonsmoking household has six bedrooms and a large living room. Hosts Micheline and Ron Burley (he used to be the mayor of Ucluelet; now he's the coroner) fix simple morning meals and stay out of your way. A rowboat and a canoe are available free to guests to take out in the inlet. And, for those who prefer a cue stick to an oar, a pool table is on the premises. No children under age 10. Closed November 1 through the end of April.

Middle Beach Lodge
200 McKenzie Road (PO Box 413), Tofino, BC V0R 2Z0
(604)725-2900

Tofino is always overbooked in peak (summer) season, so bargains are tough to find. But the West Coast really comes into its own during the rest of the year, when tourists blow out, storms blow in, and peaceful relaxation reigns. This beautifully designed adult retreat, which opened in 1993, offers bargain rates Monday through Thursday from mid-October to the end of April. During peak season, rooms 2 and 3, with four single beds, rent for $64 (two people), $80 (three), or $96 (four), including continental breakfast. The lodge has a wonderful lounge with rock fireplace (good thing, because the guest rooms are too small for lounging). In the works: a 50-unit family-oriented lodge with cabins nearby.

Vargas Island Inn
PO Box 267, Tofino, BC V0R 2Z0 • (604)725-3309

Perhaps the Vargas Island Inn is not all up to code, but it's only a couple of hours by kayak or a half hour by skiff from Tofino (you can either paddle or pay). There are a few sacrifices, however, such as no showers (except in summer) or chefs. But you can turn your back on the notoriously damp weather and face a fireplace, or sip tea in the wood-furnace kitchen. You have to start the fire in the wood-burning sauna on the beach by yourself, but the wood's already chopped. Six rooms are in the main house; a hobbitlike A-frame, known as a "beach studio," is nearby. The owners make a pickup every day at the Crab Dock just south of town ($20 round trip—the water taxis won't give you as good a deal).

ACCESS

There's no easy, cheap, or quick way to get to the west coast of Vancouver Island, because it is not on the road to anywhere. And first you have to get to Vancouver Island. Catch a ferry to Nanaimo from Horseshoe Bay or Tsawwassen; (604)943-9331. The sailing from Tsawwassen is about a half hour longer. The trip from Horseshoe Bay runs about every other hour until 9pm. Both cost $27.50 for the car and driver, and $6.00 for all other passengers. Discounts are available to British Columbia students and seniors, and groups of 15 or more.

Vancouver Island's Inside Passage

Half a million cruise ship passengers can't be wrong. The natural setting for Vancouver Island's eastern coast, plied daily by the 20-plus Alaska-bound cruise ships whose summer homeport is Vancouver, is unabashedly spectacular: idyllic islands ringed with serene waters, snow-capped mountains rising above luxuriously forested hills, and the sparkling lights of Vancouver across the water to the east. Unfortunately, the heady mixture of fishing, industry, and the oddly crafted dose of tourism hasn't always succeeded in creating welcoming—or even interesting—towns. Still, there is much to be gleaned from the eastern shores of the island if you look in the right places. If you're driving (rather than cruising) the Inside Passage, you'll be traveling the Malahat Highway to Nanaimo and then taking the renowned Island Highway (aka Highway 19), much of it only two-lane, from Nanaimo. And so will everyone else. A good look at a map shows how amazingly few roads there are on Vancouver Island. Caught in the summer crawl up-island, just try to think of yourselves as part of a wagons-north convoy.

ON THE ROAD

North of Victoria lies **Cowichan**, meaning "land warmed by the sun," an area that includes Mill Bay, Shawnigan Lake, Cowichan Bay, Duncan, Chemainus, Ladysmith, Yellow Point, and Lake Cowichan. Keep an eye out for signs to small farm wineries with shops (such as Cherry Point Vineyards, near Cobble Hill, and Venturi-Schulze, a new winery south of Duncan, whose sparkling wine was chosen for Queen Elizabeth II's visit during the 1994 Commonwealth Games).

Duncan is a town known mainly for its large Cowichan Indian population. The artistic Cowichans carve the totem poles that line the highway and appear throughout the town, and knit the namesake hand-crafted sweaters familiar throughout the Northwest. (Beware: British Columbia is loaded with pseudo-Cowichan sweaters. Chances of finding the real thing are greater here at the source.) Be sure to stop at the much-lauded **Native Heritage Center** (200 Cowichan Way, Duncan; (604)746-8119) for a chance to try traditional food, watch carvers at work on poles or jewelry, and view the "Great Deeds" multimedia theater presentation. Admission $6, or $15 for families. On a summer evening, you might want to take in the memorable four-hour program "Feast & Legends" ($35). East on Cowichan Bay Road toward the water, the gracefully winding road takes you past quiet inlets and startling cliffs. Back in town, locals like the Arbutus Cafe (195 Kenneth Street, Duncan; (604)746-5443) for sandwiches, burgers, and good conversation.

One of the best things about driving the Island Highway is driving off it whenever you can—detouring inland or to an island. Head west from Duncan to the large **Cowichan Lake** and the Honeymoon Bay Wildflower Reserve (something of a summer resort area in itself). Lake Cowichan is a resort community on Cowichan Lake with an excellent provincial campground. It's also the launching point for trips out to the West Coast's now-famous old-growth forests of Carmanagh Valley, site

Nootka Sound Day Trip

The *M.V. Uchuck III*, a nifty converted 1943 minesweeper, now chugs the West Coast inlets, carrying freight, passengers, and mail to isolated communities along Nootka Sound. The one-day round trip to Tahsis—with a one-hour stopover and sometimes a guided bus tour—is a bargain at $45 (Government Wharf, Gold River; (604)283-2325).

of much controversy between loggers and environmentalists. Check out Beach Drive B&B (6918 Beach Drive, Honeymoon Bay; (604)749-6114) or Sturgess Place Lodge (68 Stanley Road, Lake Cowichan; (604)749-4464), a former police barracks, newly refurbished with a "bachelor" room for $64.

When MacMillan Bloedel closed its sawmill in the town of **Chemainus**, the residents of the community (known as "the little town that could") saved it from becoming a ghost town by covering it with historical murals. The murals are more enticing than you might think, and they make for a fun wander (especially if your legs need stretching). Grab an ice cream from Billy's Delight Ice Cream Parlour (9752 Willow Street, Chemainus; (604)246-4131) and follow the yellow footsteps on the sidewalk to the murals. Continue down Oak Street to the ferry terminal, where more murals grace the walls of Old Town.

On the way through Ladysmith, stop at the Crow and Gate Neighborhood Pub (2313 Yellow Point Road, Ladysmith; (604)722-3731) for some soul-warming English country food: flaky pasties, steak and kidney pie, and Yorkshire pudding.

You'll know you're close to **Nanaimo** when you spot signs telling you that 11 kilometers south is the Bungy Zone (call (604)753-JUMP or (800)668-7771 from the western United States). More than 35,000 adrenaline seekers have jumped off the Zone's 140-foot bridge—tied by the feet to a stretchy umbilical cord—and lived to take home the video. A jump is definitely not cheap—$95, not including videotaping—but watching is free. Stand on the bridge and look down into the rippling Nanaimo River below; watch jumpers-to-be shiver on the waiting block.

If Victoria's history is genteel, Nanaimo's is working-class, but its coal mines are long gone. With the help of bungee jumping, bathtub races (an annual, internationally known event offering big prizes), and Nanaimo Bars (an addictive chocolate and butter confection), the island's second-largest city has put itself on the tourist map. Recently, it has even acquired some charm, with boutiques in the old city's **Heritage Mews** and intriguing restaurants such as Filthy McNasty (corner of Commercial and Terminal streets, Nanaimo; (604)753-7011), for live jazz, lattes, and wunder-muffins, and the Olde Fire Hall Coffee Roasterie (#2-34 Nicol, Island Highway, Nanaimo; (604)754-7733), where 37 types of coffees, 27 teas, and housemade sandwiches and treats (try the Iced Chocolate if you dare) are served among hand-painted church pews, brick walls, and fire-hall memorabilia; board games and newspapers are provided. Upstairs, Pagliacci's offers popular and reasonably priced build-your-own pasta; (604)754-3443.

Parking will drive you crazy here: ask at the helpful **Tourism**

Free Tours

Tours around Nanaimo span the natural and industrial facets of the city. Try the Morrell Wildlife Sanctuary (1050 Nanaimo Lakes Road, Nanaimo; (604)753-5811) or one of a slew of self-guided tours at Malaspina University College—arboretum nature trails, Tamagawa Gardens, the art gallery and exhibition center, bee yard, aquaculture, and the Museum of Natural History (900 Fifth Street, Nanaimo; (604)753-3245). There's also St. Jean's Custom Cannery (242 Southside Drive, Nanaimo; (604)754-2185), the MacMillan Bloedel Harmac pulp mill (980 MacMillan Road, Nanaimo; (604)722-3211), Pacific Biological Station (Hammond Bay Road, Nanaimo; (604)756-7049 or (604)756-7000), and any of the area's salmon hatcheries (call Tourism Nanaimo, (604)754-8474, for more information).

Nanaimo (266 Bryden Street, Nanaimo, BC V9S 1A8; (604)754-8474) how to get onto Old Victoria Street behind the Olde Fire Hall, where parking is available. Other fun shops in the retail core include the venerable Bookstore on Bastion Street (76 Bastion Street, Nanaimo; (604)753-3011) and the Scotch Bakery (87 Commercial Street, Nanaimo; (604)753-3521), where you can sink your teeth into a true Nanaimo Bar, if you haven't already sampled a free one at Tourism Nanaimo. Ask there for the "ultimate" recipe and discount coupons for everything from golf courses to restaurants and museums.

Pipers Lagoon, northeast of downtown, includes a spit that extends into the Georgia Strait and is backed by sheer bluffs great for bird watching. **Newcastle Island**, (604)753-5811, is an autoless wilderness island reached by ferries that leave hourly from behind the civic arena; it has a long shoreline trail, a trail for the handicapped, and some fine old-growth timber.

The trick in Nanaimo is to escape the frightening sprawl of roads you'll hit on arrival at the ferry terminal and both ends of the island. Your best bet is to get into the heart of Nanaimo, park your car, and explore on foot, bike, or ferry. The **waterfront walk**—from Maffeo-Sutton Park along Swy-A-Lana Marine Park (a human-made lagoon) to the Bastion (an 1853 fort)—is a pleasant diversion. The Nanaimo District Museum (100 Cameron Road, Nanaimo; (604)753-1821) explores early coastal geology and offers dioramas of native life and a life-sized replica of part of a coal mine. Admission is $2.

When hunger hits, try the hearty, ample Mexican food at brightly colored Gina's (47 Skinner Street, Nanaimo; (604)753-5411), "a tacky but friendly place" that's a favorite with locals, families, and visitors in the know. Lunch on the open deck is $4–$7; dinner is $6–$9. For a no-nonsense bowl of chowder or plate of fish 'n' chips, the Bluenose (1340 Stewart Avenue, Nanaimo; (604)754-6611), on the way to the ferry dock, is practically an institution.

Just north of the city center, the younger, boom-box-toting set hangs out on the rocky beach of **Departure Bay** in the summer; the quieter crowd, and those with young children, head farther north to **Rathtrevor Provincial Park**, where sandy shores invite sunbathers and tide pools encourage exploring. The park has a great campground, but car space is booked three days ahead in summer (try walking or bicycling in instead). Departure Bay is the place for reasonable water-sports rentals. North Island Water-Sports (2755 Departure Bay Road, Nanaimo; (604) 758-2488) rents kayaks at $40 per day for a single or $75 for a double.

Parksville and **Qualicum Beach** are beach towns with a difference. Both have broad sweeping beaches. Parksville (with its fairy-tale miniature golf course and "imported" sandy beaches) is rather commercial, but it's a better choice if you're traveling with the kids. The much more low-key Qualicum (British royalty have stayed with "friends" in the area) has huge sandbars and an interesting, walkable village worth a detour, but the beach is pebbly when the tide's in. Resorts and hotels crowd the shore, and golf courses fill all other available space.

Consider a side trip along Highway 4 toward the paper-mill town of **Port Alberni**. The combination of oddities and natural wonders on the way make the trip worthwhile: Englishman River Falls, a provincial park with pretty hiking trails and some swimming holes; the quite interesting Butterfly World (1080 Winchester Road, Coombs; (604)248-7026), where butterflies fly free in an oversized greenhouse (open mid-March through October); Coombs Old Country Market, where goats live on the grass roof in summer (Highway 4, Coombs; (604)248-6272); and Cathedral Grove, a truly wondrous slice of old-growth forest 11 kilometers west of Coombs. Be sure to walk, not drive, through. For information on Port Alberni's *Lady Rose* and Pacific Rim National Park, see the Vancouver Island's West Coast chapter.

Keep an eye peeled on the left side of the road for **Big Qualicum Fish Hatchery**, where you can get a firsthand look at the life cycles of salmon and trout. A little farther down the road, also on the left, is the Crown and Anchor Pub (6120 Island Highway, Qualicum Bay (*not* Beach); (604)757-9444), where you can grab a tasty, inexpensive lunch or dinner. Show up on a Saturday and take advantage of the pub's $1.49

Day (a draft costs just $1.49, as does a burger or chicken wings). Before you reach Comox Valley, you round the bend in **Fanny Bay**. Look for the bright blue Fanny Bay Inn (7480 Island Highway, Fanny Bay; (604)335-2323)—it's hard to miss. Known to locals as the FBI, this is the spot for general (and generally good) pub fare, such as creamy chowder with buttery garlic bread, accompanied by a good pint of something or other. Down the road a bit farther, you can catch a ferry for Denman and Hornby, two islands where life is reminiscent of the '60s.

Comox is the pretty valley that tourism forgot. Most people mentally jump from Qualicum to Campbell River, and admittedly, from the highway, Comox and Courtenay look like mill towns. But real estate is booming here in the province's fastest-growing region; it's also the launch point for **good skiing** at Mount Washington; (604)338-1387. In summer you can ride the ski lift to a mile above sea level for a weekend brunch, then mountain-bike down. Few people know that this ski area gets more snow than any other in British Columbia and has 35 kilometers of cross-country skiing trails as well. Lift tickets are $32 all week long. On Getaway Tuesday, a lift ticket, lesson, and lunch set you back a mere $38; call (604)338-1386 for information.

The towns of Comox, Courtenay, and Cumberland claim to be year-round recreational spots; in milder weather, try kayaking in the harbor with Comox Valley Kayaks (1595 Comox Road, Courtenay; (604)334-BOAT). Of the three towns, Comox is the most pleasant. Drive out to Goose Spit for wide-open views of Comox Harbor and the snow-crested mountains sitting back on their haunches; then pass back through Comox for a beer and seafood at the Leeward Pub (649 Anderton Road, Comox; (604)339-5400) or, better yet, have tea at the delightful Filberg Lodge (61 Filberg Road, Comox; (604)339-2715), a lumberman's home built of local woods in the early '30s, now home to the annual four-day Filberg Festival of BC Arts and Crafts in early August. Nine acres of meadows, orchards, lawns, and specimen trees slope down to the ocean.

Campbell River, only halfway up the island but as far north as some ever go, is primarily a town for fisherfolk, as is evident in the amenities offered by most of its hotels: smoking, canning, and cleaning (of fish, that is), but not too many Jacuzzis. It has something of the boomtown feel that Victoria must have had when Klondike-bound gold seekers arrived there to provision in the 1890s. The best reason to venture this far north is either to fish or to strike out east and west—to Strathcona Provincial Park, a hub for hiking and water sports galore, or to the lovely, remote islands of Quadra and Cortes. Golfers can try their luck at Storey Creek Golf Club, (604)923-3673, which made the

Quadra Island

The coves and channels of Quadra Island are lovely from every side. Hike up Chinese Mountain for a full view of the island—and then some. In Cape Mudge Village you'll find the Kwakiuth Museum and Cultural Center, (604)285-3733, which has a display of returned potlatch artifacts. Ask about making a rubbing of ancient petroglyphs. Lunch on fresh shrimp at Tsa-Kwa-Luten Lodge, run by the Kwagiutl; (604)285-2042 or (800)665-7745 (reservations). Some find April Point Lodge, (604)285-2222 or (800)663-5555, a luxury fishing resort for the rich and famous— including General Norman Schwarzkopf, Julie Andrews, and John Wayne—snooty and pricey, but stop in for a drink anyway. The 12-minute ferry ride back to Campbell River is a treat in itself; wait for the boat at the Landing Neighbourhood Pub (at the ferry landing; (604)285-3713), a rather nice place with airy ceilings, stained-glass windows, pub food, and friendly folks.

Financial Post magazine's list of British Columbia's top 18 courses based on degree of difficulty, memorability, and conditioning.

Not fishing in Campbell River is like not skiing at Whistler. Unfortunately, chartering a boat can be prohibitively expensive. We found only one inexpensive way to fish—cast off from **Discovery Pier** in downtown Campbell River. It costs only $1 (summer rate) to spend the day under one of the pier's glass enclosures; you can rent equipment at the concession stand for $2 an hour. Kid stuff, you say? Resort guests were gnashing their teeth when someone at the pier hooked a 50-pounder during his lunch hour!

Grab some grub at Piccadilly Fish and Chips, housed in the abandoned-looking double-decker bus across the street from Discovery Pier. For breakfast, try the Beehive (921 Island Highway, Campbell River; (604)286-6812), where most tables have a view of the fishing boats docked in the marina, Discovery Passage, and the islands. Its French toast is several inches thick. Del's Drive-In (1423 Island Highway, Campbell River; (604)287-3661) is home to some great burgers.

On **Cortes Island**, two ferry rides away, the soul is free to expand (and does, at Hollyhock Seminar Centre). Many of the island's 800 residents earn their keep by farming and exporting oysters and clams around the world. (Quadra Island, between ferries, is lovely, too—and only 12 minutes from Campbell River.) On Cortes, make reservations for dinner at the excellent Old Floathouse Restaurant (transplanted from Kingcombe Inlet and now landlocked at the Gorge Marina Resort on Hunt Road; (604)935-6631), where you can rent scooters ($12 per hour) or boats (from $17). The Cortes Cafe, on Manson's Landing, operates on mail days (Monday, Wednesday, and Friday), when it offers espresso and the best soup on the island. Smelt Bay and Sutil Point are great spots to watch the sun set.

CHEAP SLEEPS

Deer Lodge Motel
2529 Trans Canada Highway, Mill Bay, BC V0R 2P0
(604)743-2423 or (800)668-5011

This 30-room motel, with a great view overlooking Georgia Strait and the Gulf Islands, has three different wings. Each room or mini-housekeeping suite is different. For the budget-conscious, B&B rooms can be had for $51 (or $10 less without breakfast). A large suite has pretty linens on its king-size bed, a fireplace flanked by easy chairs, and a fully outfitted kitchen.

Chemainus Hostel
9694 Chemainus Road, Chemainus, BC V0R 1K0 • (604)246-2809

Given Chemainus's history of logging, it's especially appealing to stay in this onetime company house that has been renovated with the budget traveler in mind ($15 for nonmembers; towels and linens extra). It's an easy walk from the Chemainus murals, the bus, and the E&N Railway, which runs between Victoria and Nanaimo. The place is clean and bright, with separate dormitories for men and women. The kitchen's well equipped, and the front porch provides a relaxing place to sit on a warm evening.

Horseshoe Bay Inn
9576 Chemainus Road, Chemainus, BC V0R 1K0 • (604)246-3425

This is your best bet for decent (and inexpensive) lodging between Duncan and Nanaimo. Just down the road from the murals and overlooking a golf course, the Horseshoe Bay Inn is the kind of cozy, family-run place where the owners' grandchildren shyly examine the guests, and the pub downstairs attracts a lively local crowd. Some of the rooms have a private bath; others share a bathroom with a large, old bathtub. Food at the restaurant (next to the pub) is reasonably priced.

Dorm Stay

You can stay in a single room at Malaspina University College (750 4th Street, Nanaimo; (604)754-6338) for $15–$20 per night, depending on how much "hotel" service you want (bring your own linens and save a few bucks).

Buccaneer Motel
1577 Stewart Avenue, Nanaimo, BC V9S 4E3 • (604)753-1246

Just three blocks from the BC Ferries terminal at Departure Bay, the Buccaneer doesn't have the waterside setting of the Moby Dick Motel, five blocks down the street, but it does have ocean views. We like the cheerful, bright rooms, fully stocked kitchenettes (BBQs and picnic tables, too), and helpful management—not to mention the two-story-high mural of a swashbuckling buccaneer.

Carey House Bed and Breakfast
750 Arbutus Avenue, Nanaimo, BC V9S 5E5 • (604)753-3601

Motherly Catherine Molnar dishes up Scottish-style hospitality, complete with marmalade, in a quiet residential area not far from Tourism Nanaimo. The inexpensive rooms ($45–$50, or $35 for a single lodger) are of the bathroom-down-the-hall variety, but the lack of private bath is a small price to pay in exchange for reasonable rates and the opportunity to enjoy the Carey House's award-winning garden.

Nicol St. Hostel
65 Nicol Street (Island Highway 1), Nanaimo, BC V9R 4S7
(604)753-1188

Open year-round in the heart of Nanaimo, this hostel has rooms for families and is only a five-minute walk from the Newcastle Island ferry. Ask about special hosteler discounts at nearby businesses. Nicol St. welcomes Canadians, too—unlike the nearby Thomson's Hostel, (604)722-2251, which offers the quiet benefits of a country setting (and free use of a canoe or kayak) but has an "international guests only" policy.

St. Andrews Lodge and Glen Cottages
3319 W Island Highway, Qualicum Beach, BC V9K 2B3 • (604)752-6652

This seaside flashback in time, sandwiched between beach and highway, is spotlessly clean and a true bargain. The proprietor, Miss Elizabeth Little, has been here since 1938, when the house-sized "Lodge" was established and her family began adding the cottages (named Glen

Morag, Glengarry, and so on). There is a distinctive smell from the oil stoves (full of roasting turkeys come Christmas), but all the basics are here, and the cottages look out to the sea. (Unlike neighboring Parksville, Qualicum has a beach with decent swimming—even when the tide's out.) A grocery store and a handful of restaurants are within walking distance. The lodge has small rooms with private baths, but we prefer the tiny one- and two-bedroom cottages, complete with cable TV ($45 in summer, $38 off season).

The Beach House
3614 S Island Highway, Courtenay, BC V9N 8H9 • (604)338-8990

This private, comfortable cedar home is just right after a day of skiing or summer rambling. The open kitchen and casual sitting room are heated by two wood stoves; the Strait of Georgia is in plain view just beyond the sliding doors. Owner Anke Burkhardt and her son Carlin welcome children (but not smokers) and are full of information about the area. Breakfast is included with each of the four rooms (one has a bath).

Economy Inn
2605 Island Highway, Courtenay, BC V9N 2L8 • (604)334-4491

Courtenay's hotels offer tempting ski packages by making their room rates low, low, low and tacking on a lift ticket to Mount Washington (about 45 minutes away). This chain's lack of any particular charm is balanced by its remodeled units with kitchens (from $49 for a double) and its helpful staff. For local color (and lots of secondhand smoke), check out Courtenay's Arbutus Hotel and Pub, one of British Columbia's six TBC Race Centres, with betting and live horse racing via satellite.

Strathcona Park Lodge

To enjoy breathtaking views of upper Campbell Lake and the peaks that surround it, and to take advantage of all the area's boating, rock climbing, and hiking opportunities, stay at the Strathcona Park Lodge in Campbell River; (604)286-8206. Generally, it's expensive for what you get, but you can avoid much of the expense by requesting the lodge's hostel accommodations. If they're available (call first), you'll pay just $20. You might end up sharing a deluxe cabin with a group of people you have never met—but that's part of the fun.

The Log Cabin
DeeKayTee Ranch
6301 Headquarters Road, Courtenay, BC V9N 7J3 • (604)337-5553

This little beauty is a real find! We love the fact that this cozy, new, light-colored log cabin, nestled in the trees on an 80-acre farm, has wood heat and comfortably sleeps up to four. You can play tennis on the ranch's own court or lend a hand with the farm animals or the haying. For more solitary pleasures, owners Dan and Maggie Thran can point you toward the Tsolum River swimming hole or the area's peaceful walking trails. The $75 rate for one night drops to $50 if you stay for two. And who wouldn't?

Passage View Motel
517 Island Highway, Campbell River, BC V9W 2B9 • (604)286-1156

Tucked unobtrusively among a string of expensive resorts on the high-way at the south end of town, the Passage View offers pleasant, colorful rooms with a view of Discovery Passage and Quadra Island. For an extra $5, you may rent a housekeeping unit. A small yard in the back allows access to the beach.

Roberts Lake Resort
RR 1, Sayward, BC V0P 1R0 • (604)287-9421

With Campbell River and Sayward 28 kilometers away on either side, this little resort in Sayward Forest really is in the middle of nowhere. The five rustic cabins are $38 per night, while a room in the bunkhouse is decidedly less. Enjoy the wildlife, rent a rowboat (you're the only folks on Roberts Lake), or visit the small museum with its old logging equipment.

Joha Eagle View
Quathiaski Cove (Box 668), Quadra Island, BC V0P 1N0 • (604)285-2247

Joyce and Harold Johnson's low-lying house is in a residential area just minutes from the ferry dock (a savings if you come over as a foot passen-ger for a night). It sits right on the cove overlooking Discovery Passage (the backyard steps lead to their own dock), and you can watch the cruise ships and tugs with barge loads heading farther north. Guests in the two bed-and-breakfast rooms ($55; $60 for ocean view), which feature antique quilts, brass beds, and stained-glass windows, share an inviting living room with rock fireplace, as well as a broad, shade-dappled verandah over-looking the sea. Guests share a bathroom too, but there's an extra half-bath just downstairs. The self-contained lower unit (minimum three-night stay) is a good family or group deal at $75. If you're lucky, Joyce will be cooking up oven pancakes with sautéed apples and offering a wealth of suggestions for making your stay on the island a memorable one. **217**

Blue Heron Bed and Breakfast

Potlatch Road, Cortes Island, BC V0P 1K0 • (604)935-6584

We don't know what we liked most: the deck chairs overlooking the sunset, Emilia's oatmeal pancakes with blackberry sauce, or the blissfully peaceful setting within earshot of the waves in the waterfront home of the low-key but charming Hansens. Danes understand real coffee, too. Three rooms are in a separate wing with private entrance. The room with ocean view and private bath is a splurge, but worth it. A short walk around the B&B's beach to the left (facing the ocean) takes you to a sandier beach.

The Gulf Islands

The Gulf Islands, a 240-kilometer chain of small islands in the Strait of Georgia, are British Columbia's more remote version of Washington's San Juans. Similar in geography and character to their southern neighbors, the Gulf Islands also enjoy the same temperate weather and offer wonderful boating and cycling opportunities. Six main islands snug against the southeast coast of Vancouver Island; smaller ones speckle nearby waters. Eagles soar above the forests, deer graze on roadsides, and seals swim under kayaks and canoes. Mountainous terrain, clear water, quiet glens, and pebble-and-shell beaches are nature's other gifts to this enchanting archipelago.

Native culture, present at Montague Harbour on Galiano Island as long as 6,000 years ago, is still intricately woven into the mystique of the Gulf Islands. Farmers have always been an integral part of local lore too. The oldest farm in British Columbia is on Saltspring (the largest and most populated island). Unfortunately, Gulf Island farmers are now barely holding their own. Still, fields of sheep, well-kept properties, and huge, weather-worn barns lend a pastoral element to all of the islands.

Islanders are a diverse lot. Artists are drawn to the stunning physical beauty of the area, and an active artist community *enriches everyone: painters (world-famous wildlife artist Robert Bateman lives here); singers (Canadian folk institution Valdy calls Saltspring home); authors (where do we start?). Even the silversmith who makes the intricate trophies for the Queen's Plate, Canada's top horse race, plies his trade here.*

ON THE ROAD

Galiano Island is a secluded, narrow strip of lushly forested hills, 30 kilometers long. Services (clustered on the southern end) are not abundant. There are one gas station, a couple of grocery stores, and no bank.

No wonder, then, that **hiking and biking** are the main pastimes on Galiano. Mount Galiano and Mount Sutil provide hiking on logging roads and trails that lead to the summits of each, where views take in Active Pass, Saltspring Island, Mayne Island, the Pender Islands, and Vancouver Island. At the north end of the island, the 900-foot-high Narrow Bodega Ridge provides hikers with a breathtaking walk. One can easily spend hours on these trails, so pack a lunch and potables. Ask at the tourist information booth by the ferry terminal for detailed directions to any of the island's trails.

Montague Marine Park is one of the most popular marine parks in British Columbia, and for good reason. White shells, driftwood, and sunbathers line the beaches at Montague in summer months. Hiking trails weave throughout the park. The interpretive center offers periodic lectures on Galiano flora, fauna, and natural history. An underwater archaeological dig during the summer of 1991 found evidence of ancient native civilizations here.

The first Saturday in August brings the much-anticipated **Galiano Fiesta**. Games of chance, Barterin' Bob, local arts, crafts, cooking, and a salmon barbecue make this the event to introduce neophytes to the pulse of the island. It's a guaranteed traditional good time for everyone.

Public **tennis courts** can be found on the larger islands (there are especially good ones on Saltspring), but test your game on the *wood* tennis court at Galiano Golf and Country Club; (604)539-5533. The club's golf course is as good as it is hazardous. The fourth hole is a chip shot over the third hole's green, and the second hole is a short iron that crosses the fairway of the first. Green fees for a nine-hole round are a pricey $16.50, but you can play all day.

Head to the Hummingbird Inn (47 Sturdies Bay Road, Galiano

Lamb Bake

Every year on July 1, Saturna Islanders put on a community fund raiser at Winter Cove Park. Those who want to join in the free festivities (or indulge in the lamb feed, for a nominal fee) are encouraged to come by boat but are welcomed even on wheels. For information, call the Saltspring Tourist Information Centre; (604)537-5252.

Island; (604)539-5472) for pub food in a West Coast atmosphere. Along with the hearty food and reasonable prices, you get billiard tables, darts, and occasional live music.

On Saturna, the least populated of the islands serviced by ferry, **Winter Cove Marine Park** is the place to visit. Trails meander deep through the forest and along the exposed north edge of the island. Windswept trees hug the shale rock formations. Herons, seagulls, ducks, and seals are easily spotted; beachcombers will have a heyday. Picnic tables and fire pits are provided. And there's great swimming off the helicopter pad at high tide.

When the stomach rumbles, head for the Light House Pub, beside the ferry terminal, for lunch and hearty dinner specials; (604)539-5725. Your entertainment options include pool tables, TV, and views of Lyle Harbour, home to an abundance of seals.

Green, rural **North and South Pender islands** are separated by a canal and united by a bridge. These islands have retained public access to many of their beaches so anyone can enjoy them. Mount Norman, the **highest point** on the Penders, is a wonderful hike. Old logging roads lead the way up, with a short but steep bit at the end of the 30-minute climb. A remarkable view of Bedwell Harbour and the San Juan Islands awaits you at the summit. Near Magic Lake, practice your skills at a wilderness Frisbee park. Frisbee enthusiasts and novice tossers alike will enjoy the free course.

For a glimpse of the old days, visit quaint **Port Washington**, with a general store, a public wharf, and a crafts center. Cottages, orchards, fences, and dense shrubbery add an Old English atmosphere. Even islanders think a visit is a must.

Mayne Island is only 11 square kilometers, perfect for a day trip. Sink your teeth into a burger on the deck of the Springwater Lodge (400 Fernhill Road, Mayne Island; (604)539-5521), hike out to the grassy point of the Indian reservation, drop by the lighthouse, or stroll to the top of Mayne's mountain for a view of the Strait of Georgia, and you'll begin to discover what tiny Mayne is all about. Spend a day at the tranquil beach at Dinner Bay Park, with views of Navy Channel and Active Pass. All the amenities for an enjoyable picnic are here, including picnic tables, a cook house, barbecues, running water, and toilets.

The **Mayne Museum**, at one time the local jail, gives visitors a taste of Gulf Island culture and history. Galleries display Indian artifacts documenting aboriginal life on the Gulf Islands, a collection of tools and utensils used by white settlers, and relics from a local 1872 shipwreck.

If you have time for only one Gulf Island, visit **Saltspring**. It is certainly the most developed, yet it manages to maintain much of its rural character. Sheep here barely outnumber artists and their flock of galleries. The best way to take in the island's art scene is to stop by ArtCraft, a summerlong art exhibition on display at Mahon Hall in Ganges. Saltspring holds a Festival of the Performing Arts, usually in July, where jazz, classical, bluegrass, country, and folk music is presented by local and international artists. Theater, dance, and comedy shows add to the festive atmosphere. For information, call the Saltspring Tourist Information Centre; (604)537-5252.

Every Saturday morning from April through October, on the waterfront in the center of Ganges at Centennial Park, a **farmers market** sells everything under the blazing sun: island-grown fresh produce, shell earrings, tie-dyed T-shirts, secondhand goods and not-so-goods, pottery, tacos, paintings, and carvings. (The market vendors association is attempting to regulate sales to ensure that only locally grown or produced goods are sold. The results so far have been mixed, but the effort is being made to minimize the schlock factor and the flea-market element.)

Getting Around

Saltspring Island has a bus service that, for a very reasonable $3, will get you just about anywhere you want to go on the island. The buses, which take the scenic route, run from Ruckle Park at the south end to North Beach Road at the north end, with convenient stops along the way, including one at the entrance to the Cusheon Creek Hostel. The buses meet all ferries except the late-evening one at Long Harbour, which is frequently late and therefore is impossible to fit into a transit schedule. Cyclists and backpackers can stash their gear in the buses' capacious trunks.

Shower and Swim

Those camping on Saltspring may be able to grab a swim and shower at the local summer pool at Portlock Park, (604)537-4448. Lakes scattered throughout the island provide superior swimming. Motorboats are not allowed on any lakes.

Ruckle Park, at the south end of the island, encompasses a farmhouse dating from the 1870s, complete with barns and sheds containing farm implements and knickknacks. Sheep still graze in the fields, and visitors are able to wander at will. Ten kilometers of hiking trails join Ruckle's farmland to the rocky seashore and beaches. Picnic tables and fire pits are provided.

Saltspring has lots of good eats. Rodrigos (2921 Fulford-Ganges Road, Ganges; (604)653-9222) is a Mexican greasy spoon popular with islanders because of the eclectic atmosphere, decently priced food, and scenic location adjoining the Fulford ferry terminal. Two other popular island eateries are Pomodori (170 Fulford-Ganges Road, Ganges; (604)537-2247), with its funky, Greek-village atmosphere and creative Mediterranean-vegetarian menu, and Moby's (120 Upper Ganges Road, Ganges; (604)537-5559), which serves up hearty pub-style food, lots of local color, and great views of Ganges Harbour. Stella's Boardwalk Cafe (Dockside, Mouat's Mall, Ganges; (604)537-1436) is a favorite stop for housemade soup, pastries, cappuccino, and people-watching.

Gabriola Island (20 minutes by ferry from Nanaimo; contact the ferry at (604)537-9921) has become a bedroom community for the nearby city. Even though it's easily accessible from Vancouver Island, it manages to remain fairly rustic. **Gabriola Sands Provincial Park** has picnic tables, a play area, a large sports field, and twin sandy beaches in Pilot and Taylor bays with views of the mainland. The highlight of the fine beach walks is the Malaspina Gallery, with its weird rock formations and caves carved by the sea. To get there, go to the end of Malaspina Drive, look for the beach access, turn left at the beach, and walk around the point.

White Hart Pub (South Road, Gabriola; (604)247-8588), on the doorstep of the ferry landing, is a convenient place to grab a bite—either outdoors, on the spacious deck, or inside, amid the dark, English-pub atmosphere. There's a pool table and a vast choice of beer.

CHEAP SLEEPS

The Tides Inn

132 Lower Ganges Road, Ganges, BC V0S 1E0 • (604)537-1470

Located in the center of Ganges, above one of the town's nicer restaurants, the Tides Inn is one of the better finds on Saltspring. Except for glimpses of the harbor, there's not much of a view from the bedroom windows, but the rooms are charming and immaculate—with enough character to inspire rumors of a ghost. The Tides is within walking distance of Moby's Pub and several restaurants, galleries, and shops. While the village bustles during the day, nightlife is nonexistent, ensuring a peaceful night's rest. Bathrooms are shared, and a full breakfast is complimentary. Though rates may break the cheap-sleep limit during the warmer months ($59–$69), rooms rent for less than $50 from January through April.

Cusheon Creek Hostel

604 Cusheon Lake Road, Saltspring Island, BC V8K 2C2 • (604)537-4149

For the adventurous and socially inclined traveler on a budget, the hostel rents very basic, clean, and comfortable accommodations for $16 a night. A member of the International Hostel Association, Cusheon Creek is the only official hostel in the Gulf Islands, offering two dorms, a family room, and three tepees (sleeping platforms and mattresses included). There is no outdoor cooking allowed, but there is a well-equipped

Free Service

Canadian Gulf Islands B&B Reservation Service
Southwind Drive, Montague Harbour, Galiano Island, BC V0N 1P0 • (604)539-5390

Tom and Ann Hennessy, who own Galiano Island's Sutil Lodge, provide a booking service for B&Bs, inns, resorts, lodges, and cottages throughout the Gulf Islands. The service is free to the customer, and using it will save you 10 percent of your room bill. Here's how it works: if you book your room through the service, the proprietor will deduct 10 percent from your costs and remit that money to the registry. The Hennessys personally check out all of their listings during the off season and make recommendations in all price ranges. They also organize kayaking, cycling, and sailing excursions.

kitchen and a living room with a wood-burning stove. From this secluded wooded setting, you're only a short hike from Cusheon Lake and Beddis Beach for a choice of fresh- or saltwater swimming. For rustic simplicity, with only a few neighboring sheep and goats and a nearby bagpipe enthusiast to disturb the tranquillity, the hostel is a genuine bargain.

The Pink House

c/o Victor Campbell, 4323 Hope Bay Road, Pender Island, BC V0N 2M0
(604)629-6485

At $15 a night, negotiable, the Pink House probably offers the cheapest (and most colorful) sleep in the Gulf Islands. Something of a local legend, it's a favorite stopping point for the under-25 set, who frequently barter work in exchange for discounted accommodations in the sleeping loft. The ever-present music tends to be loud and alternative, and the meals are vegetarian, generous, and cheap at $5 (though that's negotiable, too). Older backpackers who are nostalgic for the lost nation of Woodstock might enjoy this experience for a night or two.

Cliff Pagoda Bed and Breakfast

2851 Montague Harbour Road, Galiano Island, BC V0N 1P0
(604)539-2260

The Oriental-style Cliff Pagoda, which looks as if it was plucked from Beijing's Forbidden City, stands out for its design, amenities, and breathtaking view of Montague Harbour and Park Island. Bicyclists may struggle up the long dirt driveway, but they're rewarded with bicycle racks. Rooms are small and bathrooms are shared, but with the large porch and hot tub, why stay in your room?

Hummingbird Inn

47 Sturdies Bay Road, Galiano Island, BC V0N 1P0 • (604)539-5472

Not the most relaxing accommodation on Galiano, but quite possibly the cheapest, and certainly the most gregarious. Located over one of the prettiest pubs anywhere, the three rooms offer basic but perfectly acceptable lodgings. One room, with private bath, costs $38 a night; the other two, which share the facilities, go for $28 each. No meals are included, but the pub serves decent food at reasonable prices.

Sutil Lodge

Southwind Drive, Montague Harbour, Galiano Island, BC V0N 1P0
(604)539-5390

Sutil Lodge boasts an ocean view, woodland seclusion, and a heritage island home. Throw in a sumptuous breakfast and use of a canoe to explore the beaches of Montague Harbour, and the chance to book a

---

Island Camping

Provincial Parks; (604)387-4363

Provincial campgrounds are probably the best deals going on the islands. Most have water, firewood, and separate areas for tent campers. To avoid the summer crunch, arrive early; only some of the campgrounds have spillover areas. No reservations are accepted, except for large groups. Fees run between $6 and $10 per site.

• **Galiano** Montague Harbour Marine Provincial Park, (604)539-2115: Along with the beaches, hiking, and educational opportunities, Montague has 32 wooded campsites just off the beach. Nearby is a marina with a seasonal store where you can purchase groceries and supplies. Dionisio Park has free camping but little in the way of amenities.

• **Pender Islands** Prior Centennial Provincial Park; (604)387-4363: For those who do not mind camping but do not want to cook, the campground is convenient to the pub. There are 17 campsites.

• **Saltspring Island** Ruckle Park, (604)653-4209: Ruckle offers 70 tent sites with picnic tables (the best are the waterfront sites). On weekends things can get tight, and on long weekends the place is crammed. It's far from a restaurant so bring provisions. Mouat Park, (604)653-4209, is not far from Ganges. Its 15 wooded camping spots are great if you want access to the town's restaurants and nightlife or want to get an early start on the Saturday farmers market. Unfortunately, you also have to watch out for thieves here.

---

four-hour sailing trip, complete with picnic lunch, aboard the host's 56-foot catamaran, and you have a naturalist's dream vacation. For $65 a night, you can book a small but charming room overlooking the old orchard. An extra $10 buys a larger room with an ocean view.

Springwater Lodge
400 Fernhill Road, Mayne Island, BC V0N 4J0 • (604)539-5521

Established in 1892, the Springwater is reportedly the oldest continually operated hotel in British Columbia. And it's also among the cheapest island lodging options ($35), aside from sleeping under the stars (which merits consideration on warm summer nights). The charmingly dilapidated lodge has six bedrooms. The bathrooms are old, but for character, price, and friendly people, it's a fine spot indeed. There are two duplex cabins, each with two bedrooms, kitchen, and bath. At night, local folksingers sometimes drop by and entertain the guests and island residents.

Breezy Bay Bed and Breakfast
131 Payne Road (PO Box 40), Saturna Island, BC V0N 2Y0
(604)539-2937

For pure, funky island character, Breezy Bay is hard to beat. Just down the road from Poppy Hill Farm, this is a house set aside for guests in a communal farm setting. Nothing fancy, though a sense of history permeates the century-old building. A comfortable library with ancient furniture is open to guests, as is the spacious deck overlooking the lovely farmland.

Poppy Hill Farm Bed and Breakfast
104 Payne Road (PO Box 44), Saturna Island, BC V0N 2Y0
(604)539-5002

Two can stay in the top room of this archetypal bed and breakfast, with its view of Boot Cove just beyond the orchard, for $65. Host Janet Comstock is always ready to sit and socialize over a cup of tea and, on request, will cheerfully mix up a batch of the best biscuits and gravy west of the Rockies.

Surf Lodge
RR 1, Site 1, C17, Gabriola Island, BC V0R 1X0 • (604)247-9231

This rustic wood and stone lodge is across from the beach on the northwest shore of Gabriola. You'll find a very relaxed, comfortable atmosphere,

 *Traveler's Tip*

Ferries charge the car owner plenty, and if you are inclined to visit three or four islands, the bill for your car alone could easily set you back $65. Many people opt to just bike or walk onto the ferries (hitchhiking is safe and quite accepted on the islands). Biking is a great way to get around, although hills and cracked roads demand that bikers be alert and in at least fair shape if they are to enjoy their travels to the fullest. Narrow roads and hairpin turns make for hazardous biking, so wear a helmet. Regardless of the mode you choose, access to the Gulf Islands is via BC Ferries. Ferries travel to the southern Gulf Islands from Tsawwassen, 20 minutes south of Vancouver, or from Swartz Bay, north of Victoria on Vancouver Island. Call BC Ferries for rates; (604)669-1211.

with a great stone fireplace in the lodge's sitting room, a saltwater pool, and outdoor recreational facilities. Accommodations include either rooms or cabins, some with kitchens. The lodge has a restaurant and a cocktail lounge.

Romney House

430 Berry Point Road (Box 21), Gabriola Island, BC V0R 1X0
(604)247-9422

This is a real, English-style B&B, with huge English-style breakfasts designed to fuel you for a full day. The pretty, Tudor-style house on Twin Beaches has two double rooms and one single, and is a great accommodation for a group of four (the proprietor's preferred number of guests for maximum sociability and hospitality). The double rooms have ocean views and private baths, and the guests have use of an outdoor deck overlooking the ocean.

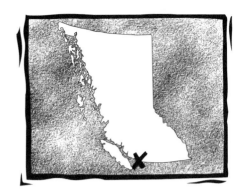

Vancouver

In the international pageant of urban beauty, cities like San Francisco, Hong Kong, and Rio de Janeiro are habitual contestants. Yet many world travelers regard Vancouver as the most irresistible of them all. Surrounded by water and set against a stunning high-mountain backdrop, Canada's third-largest metropolis stirs the senses. Downtown Vancouver thrusts into the blue of English Bay, with the green fist of Stanley Park at its head. The park is a symbol of the city's pride—in its environment, its heritage, its cosmopolitanism—and most of all, perhaps, in its future as Canada's progressive window on the Pacific Rim.

In the mid-1860s, Vancouver was only a small coal-and-timber port on Burrard Inlet. Today, the city is the center of a metropolitan area of 1.6 million people. Canada's British Commonwealth ties have always encouraged immigrants from Asia, but the influx has multiplied in recent years as well-to-do Chinese from Hong Kong have moved their assets and families out of the Crown Colony. While there are also large and highly visible communities of Indo-Pakistanis and Southern Europeans in this international city, a quarter of Vancouver's population is of Far Eastern descent.

ON THE ROAD

Canada Place, which extends into Burrard Inlet at the north end of Howe Street, has become Vancouver's landmark in much the same way the Sydney Opera House is emblematic of the Australian city. Built for Expo 86 as the Canada Pavilion, it now does multiple duty as a luxury hotel, a trade and convention center, and the Vancouver cruise-ship terminal. The structure's 80-foot fiberglass "sails" make it look vaguely like a clipper ship about to leave port.

East of Canada Place along Water Street is historic Gastown. Its cobbled streets, shaded by trees and lined with imitation gas lamps, make it one of Vancouver's most charming neighborhoods. Amid the art galleries and souvenir shops, restaurants and nightclubs, keep your eyes open for the Gastown Steam Clock (at the corner of Water and Cambie streets), the only one of its kind in the world. You can get good cheap eats in Gastown at Al Forno, a pizzeria (103 Columbia Street, Vancouver; (604)684-2838); Sitar Indian Restaurant (8 Powell Street, Vancouver; (604)687-0049), serving mild curries (look for coupons in the local weekly *Georgia Straight*); and the Only Fish & Oyster Cafe (20 E Hastings Street, Vancouver; (604)681-6546), a tiny seafood institution.

The financial district is south of Canada Place between Hastings and Georgia streets. After a free tour of the Vancouver Stock Exchange (609 Granville Street, Vancouver; (604)689-3334), eat a ploughman's lunch at the Elephant & Castle (700 W Dunsmuir Street, Vancouver; (604)685-4545) or an open-faced Scandinavian *smorrebrod* at the Tivoli (750 W Pender Street, Vancouver; (604)683-6219).

The heart of the city's downtown shopping district interconnects underground shopping malls anchored by such department stores as the

Lights! Camera! Action!

Vancouver has acquired a reputation as Hollywood North. You can pick up the BC Film Commission's Film List of projects currently in production at the BC Business Info Centre (601 W Cordova Street, main floor, Vancouver) on weekdays between 8:30am and 4:30pm. Or call their hotline, (604)660-3569, for film-listing updates. Failing the above, just drive around the city; you're bound to bump into a movie being shot somewhere—just look for the big white trailers and trucks parked along the street and lots of busy folks running around wearing baseball caps and sneakers.

Bay and Eaton's. A 4-block stretch on Granville Street between Robson and Dunsmuir streets is a pedestrian shopping and entertainment mall; the venerable 1927 Orpheum Theatre (884 Granville Street, Vancouver; (604)684-2787), home of the Vancouver Symphony, offers free tours by reservation.

The heart of **Robson Square** (800 Robson Street, Vancouver; (604)660-2830) is a conference center that offers free films and concerts, an ice-skating rink, restaurants, and government offices. The nearby **Vancouver Art Gallery** (750 Hornby Street, Vancouver; (604)682-5621) is housed in the imposing former law courts. Its permanent collection includes works by Picasso, Chagall, Goya, Gainsborough, and other European and North American masters. The museum's Emily Carr Gallery has collected some 200 paintings and drawings by the Vancouver Island native renowned for her depictions of indigenous West Coast cultures. Admission is by donation every Thursday evening.

The West End, located west of Bute Street between downtown and Stanley Park, is a residential area liberally sprinkled with restaurants and shops. Two of the most bustling areas are on Robson and Davie streets.

Stretching along fashionable **Robson Street** from Burrard to Denman are buskers, boutiques, and restaurants. Even here, however, there's hope for the slender wallet: grab a seat at the rear of the Olympia Fish Market & Oyster Co. (1094 Robson Street, Vancouver; (604)685-0716) for fresh no-frills fish 'n' chips; try Settebello (1133 Robson Street, Vancouver; (604)681-7377), serving salads, pastas, and individual brick-oven pizzas on a rooftop patio; or squeeze into the Ezogiku Noodle Cafe (1684 Robson Street, Vancouver; (604)687-7565), a 14-seat ramen shop. A second Ezogiku recently opened (1329 Robson Street, Vancouver; (604)685-8606).

Davie Street, which parallels Robson 6 blocks to the south, has become a center for Vancouver's counterculture and for good cheap eateries. For those in cholesterol denial, hit the healthiest juice bar in town, O-Tooz The Energie Bar (1055 W Georgia Street, Vancouver; (604)689-0208) for a basmati wrap and beet juice. The good Greek food is worth the wait at Stepho's Souvlakia (1124 Davie Street, Vancouver; (604)683-2555). Or try the Fresgo Inn (1138 Davie Street, Vancouver; (604)689-1332), a garden-style cafeteria open until 3am (except Sunday, when it closes at midnight), or A Taste of Jamaica (941 Davie Street, Vancouver; (604)683-3464), a tiny Rasta-style diner that serves foods like *ackee* and goat curry. On Denman Street, look for the Original Souvlaki Place (1181 Denman Street, Vancouver; (604)689-3064), which dishes up skewered Greek delights, or order the roast chicken and gravy at Piccata's (1080 Denman Street, Vancouver; (604)683-5766).

The West End is the gateway to spectacular **Stanley Park**. A heavily forested, 1,000-acre promontory surrounded by a 10-kilometer seawall, this natural sanctuary was set aside by city fathers in 1889. Cycling and walking trails weave through groves of fir, cedar, and hemlock, connecting inland lakes and ocean beaches, restaurants and picnic grounds, a variety of sports facilities (from tennis courts to a par-3 golf course to a cricket oval), rose gardens and an outdoor amphitheater, and two small zoos. Don't miss the world-renowned **Vancouver Aquarium** (Stanley Park, Vancouver; (604)682-1118 or (604)685-3364), which has a marine-mammal center and galleries of north Pacific and tropical sea life.

At the east end of downtown Vancouver, just beyond Gastown and adjacent to the former Expo 86 site on the north shore of False Creek, is Vancouver's **Chinatown**, the second largest in North America after San Francisco's. Wander the open-air markets around Pender and Main streets, duck into one of the many bakeries for moon cakes, or visit an herbalist to discover uses you'd never have considered for dried sea horse. Almost every restaurant is good and reasonably priced; try Julia Child's favorite Asian restaurant, the Phnom Penh (244 E Georgia Street, Vancouver; (604)682-5777), or the New Diamond Restaurant (555 Gore Avenue, Vancouver; (604)685-0727), a dim sum parlor.

There are free public exhibitions at the **Chinese Cultural Centre** (50 E Pender Street, Vancouver; (604)687-0729). Just behind the center is the **Dr. Sun Yat-sen Classical Chinese Park and Garden** (578 Carrall Street, Vancouver; (604)662-3207). The first full-scale classical Chinese garden ever built outside of China, it charges admission, but the adjoining park is free. On summer evenings, the garden offers Enchanted Fridays, when the grounds are illuminated with lanterns, providing a soft glow for music and dancing.

Other ethnic communities in Vancouver, each fascinating in its own way, include the **Punjabi Market** (Little India), along Main Street between E 49th and E 51st avenues, where you'll find *Gujarati* (vegetarian) food at Surat Sweet (6665 Fraser Street, Vancouver; (604)322-9544) that would be cheap at twice the price. In **Little Italy**, on Commercial Drive between Venables Street and E Broadway, stop at Nick's Spaghetti House (631 Commercial Drive, Vancouver; (604)254-5633) for homey pasta and no-nonsense meatballs. Drop into Tio Pepe (1134 Commercial Drive, Vancouver; (604)254-8999) for margaritas and chicken flautas. Or try Nazarre BBQ Chicken (1859 Commercial Drive, Vancouver; (604)251-1844) for rum-spiced chicken with hot garlic sauce. In **Greektown**, on W Broadway between MacDonald and Alma streets, grab a pita at Pita Plus Bakery and Deli (2967 W Broadway, Vancouver; (604)733-9900); the hot-from-the-oven pockets are filled with your choice from two dozen mostly vegetarian salads. For bargain-priced lunch specials, stop at Tang's Noodle House (2805-2807 W Broadway, Vancouver; (604)737-1278).

Granville Island, a 38-acre island of reclaimed warehouses, is now many things to many people: an artists' community, a market center with food stalls, a dining and entertainment district, an industrial site, and even a self-contained community. Wander the **Granville Island Public Market**, open daily (except Mondays in winter) and stop for a sampling at the Granville Island Brewery (1441 Cartwright Street, Granville Island; (604)687-2739) every day at 3pm. Both you and the kids will enjoy Isadora's (1540 Bridge Street, Granville Island; (604)681-8816), where the pizzas come with faces and the wholesome menu caters not only to vegetarians but also to vegans. Granville Island has an in-house play area and an outdoor water park in the summer, too.

The **Vancouver Museum** complex (1100 Chestnut Street, Vancouver; (604)736-4431) in Vanier Park traces Vancouver's history from pre-European cultures to the late 20th century. A planetarium and observatory share the site. Rest your feet in the Vanier Cafe, a budget cafeteria with a multimillion-dollar view. A few steps away are the Vancouver Maritime Museum (1905 Ogden Avenue, Vancouver; (604)737-2211), documenting the city's growth as an international port, and in the same building, St. Roch National Historic Site (1905 Ogden Avenue, Vancouver; (604)666-3201), offering tours of the first sailing vessel to navigate the Northwest Passage (in 1944).

Lovers of the **performing arts** find Vancouver one of the most exciting cities on the West Coast. For information on current happenings, consult the **Arts Hotline**, (604)684-ARTS; the weekly *Georgia Straight*; or the two daily newspapers (see Thursday's calendar section of *The Vancouver Sun* or Friday's Preview section of *The Province*). Tickets are often discounted for midweek performances and matinees, and there are occasional two-for-one previews (check with individual theaters).

Major touring shows—from Broadway musicals to symphony and dance, as well as productions by the Vancouver Opera and Ballet British Columbia—take place at the beautiful, 2,800-seat Queen Elizabeth Theatre (600 Hamilton Street, Vancouver; (604)665-3050). The adjoining 650-seat Vancouver Playhouse (600 Hamilton Street, Vancouver; (604)665-3050) is home to the city's leading resident theater troupe. The two share a box office (543 W 7th Avenue, Vancouver; (604)873-3311).

The acoustically acclaimed Orpheum Theatre (884 Granville Street, Vancouver; (604)684-2787) is the home of the Vancouver Symphony Orchestra and the Vancouver Chamber Choir, and it frequently hosts touring acts as well. The Vancouver Little Theatre (3102 Main Street,

⋆ *Pacific National Exhibition*

Better known to locals as simply PNE, the fifth-largest fair on the North American continent runs annually for 17 days from the third week of August through the first Monday of September. The PNE grounds are just east of downtown, at Exhibition Park (E Hastings and Renfrew streets, Vancouver; (604)253-2311). If you want to see any of PNE's big-name concert acts, reserve ahead. Accommodations—especially the budget variety—are often hard to come by in Vancouver during the PNE, so be sure to reserve a room well in advance. And don't miss the Food Building.

Vancouver; (604)876-4165) presents new dramas, while the Firehall Arts Centre (280 E Cordova Street, Vancouver; (604)689-0926) features experimental theater. The Vancouver East Cultural Centre (1895 Venables Street, Vancouver; (604)254-9578), a converted church, hosts a variety of fringe performances, from folk and jazz concerts to ethnic dance and light theater. Fans of contemporary dance should try to catch a performance by the Anna Wyman Dance Theatre, a local troupe with a worldwide following. The company often has free outdoor shows at Granville Island or Robson Square in the summer; (604)662-8846.

After the Vancouver Playhouse, the city's best-known stage venue is the Arts Club Theatre (1585 Johnson Street, Granville Island; (604)687-1644), in a former industrial warehouse. Major dramas, comedies, and musicals are presented on its Mainstage, and small improvisational productions and offbeat musicals are performed on its Revue Stage. Also on Granville Island, the Waterfront Theatre (1410 Cartwright Street, Granville Island; (604)685-6217) features original works by British Columbian playwrights as well as entertainment suitable for children.

For **rock music**, check out Richard's on Richards (1036 Richards Street, Vancouver; (604)687-6794) or the Town Pump (66 Water Street, Vancouver; (604)683-6695); for blues, the Yale Hotel (1300 Granville Street, Vancouver; (604)681-9253); and for country, Boone County (801 Brunette Avenue, Coquitlam; (604)525-3144), in the 'burbs. The hottest spot for major cabaret-style performances is the Commodore Ballroom (870 Granville Street, Vancouver; (604)681-7838).

For **jazz**, try Carnegie's (1619 W Broadway, Vancouver; (604)733-4141) or the Glass Slipper (2714 Prince Edward Street, Vancouver; (604)877-0066). Hipsters can also call (604)682-0706 for information about upcoming jazz concerts and the annual du Maurier International

Jazz Festival, which occurs in late June and early July and offers many free performances on both weekends of the two-week fest.

The newest **sports bar** in town is the Shark Club, in the Sandman Inn (180 W Georgia Street, Vancouver; (604)687-4275), with 25 screens, pool tables, and a dance floor with a DJ playing Top 40 and classic rock. For **comedy**, stop by Punchline's (15 Water Street, Vancouver; (604)684-3015).

A string of **beaches** extends west from Vanier Park along the southern shore of English Bay. They include Kitsilano Beach, on Cornwall Avenue; Jericho Beach, on Point Grey Road; and Locarno Beach and Spanish Banks, on NW Marine Drive. Budget restaurants in the area include the Japanese Bistro (1815 W 1st Avenue, Vancouver; (604)734-5858), for all-you-can-eat sushi; and Woodlands Natural Foods Restaurant (2582 W Broadway, Vancouver; (604)733-5411), for filling vegetarian meals. Have a stick-to-the-ribs breakfast at Sophie's Cosmic Cafe (2095 W 4th Avenue, Vancouver; (604)732-6810) or a slice of Deep Purple Pizza till 3am at the Flying Wedge (1937 Cornwall Avenue, Vancouver; (604)732-8840).

Atop a bluff at the tip of Point Grey, Vancouver's westernmost point, is the sprawling campus of the 40,000-student University of British Columbia. The main public attraction here is the **Museum of Anthropology** (6393 NW Marine Drive, Vancouver; (604)822-5087), with the world's finest collection of West Coast Indian art and artifacts, including totem poles, house posts, and longhouses. Admission is free on Tuesdays.

The suburb of North Vancouver is connected to downtown by the Lion's Gate Bridge from Stanley Park. **Capilano Canyon Regional Park** (3735 Capilano Road, North Vancouver; (604)985-7474) has a famous wood-and-wire suspension bridge that traverses the canyon amid

Salmon Spawning at Capilano Salmon Hatchery

Observe one of the great life-cycle stories in nature free of charge at this federal government fish hatchery (Capilano Park, 4500 Capilano Park Road, North Vancouver; (604)666-1790). The self-guiding facility offers information panels describing the life cycles of salmon. Then watch the juvenile Pacific salmon in the ponds, and see the returning adult salmon jump up a series of steps. The hatchery also houses some of the oldest and tallest fir trees still standing on the Lower Mainland.

a dense rain forest. The park is free, but teetering across the bridge will cost you $6.95. For a less scary but equally dramatic experience, board the Royal Hudson Steam Train (1311 W 1st Street, North Vancouver; (604)688-7246 or (800)663-1500) for a round trip up the rugged Howe Sound coastline to the logging town of Squamish, 56 kilometers north. Or ride the rails one way and sail on the *M.V. Britannia* (Harbour Ferries, north foot of Denman Street, Vancouver; (604)688-7246) on the way back.

CHEAP SLEEPS

Backpackers Youth Hostel
927 Main Street, Vancouver, BC V6A 2V8 • (604)682-2441

This isn't really a hostel in the traditional sense; 15 of the rooms are private, and even the 18 dorm rooms contain only three or four beds apiece. But everything else (bathrooms, kitchen, dining room, TV room, laundry) in this former guest house, located on the edge of Chinatown, is shared. Don't worry about curfew here; everyone gets a front-door key. Many travelers still refer to the hostel as Vincent's Guest House.

City Centre Motor Inn
2111 Main Street, Vancouver, BC V5T 3C6 • (604)876-7166

The City Centre is a good option for folks who want to avoid downtown traffic. Located near the east end of the Expo 86 site, beneath the geodesic shadow of the Science World kids' museum, this modern motel is an easy walk from the Main Street SkyTrain station and a short stroll south of Chinatown. The most expensive room is $60. Parking is free, as is the coffee served in the lobby each morning.

Hostelling International Vancouver
1515 Discovery Street, Vancouver, BC V6R 4K5
(604)224-3208 or (604)224-7177

Beautifully situated on Jericho Beach off Point Grey Road, this hostel is Canada's largest, and the second largest in North America. Youth hostelers accustomed to cooking in communal kitchens can do that here too, but they'll be delighted to find a cheap cafeteria as well. There's also a TV lounge with a big-screen, satellite-fed television. Formerly the barracks of the Canadian Air Force, the hostel has 260 dormitory bunks and nine private rooms for families and couples (these must be booked two weeks in advance). There's lots of free parking.

Hotel California

1176 Granville Street, Vancouver, BC V6Z 1L8 • (604)688-8701

The hard-rock club that once occupied the ground floor has moved to Gastown; the guest rooms have been completely renovated; and this six-story hotel, just south of the Granville Street Mall, has discovered new life. Though the place may look marginally seedy on the outside (and it rents rooms by the *hour*), its 132 guest rooms are quite pleasant (most have their own bath) and feature new carpeting, cable TV, direct-dial phones, and even an automatic wake-up service. A pub featuring live music is on the lower level.

The Hotel at the YWCA

580 Burrard Street, Vancouver, BC V6C 2K9 • (604)662-8188

Although its name suggests it's for young women only, this Y (smack in the middle of bustling downtown) welcomes everyone else too—couples, families, groups, and men. There are 169 tidy rooms (all very reasonably priced) on 13 floors. The units vary in size from simple single rooms, with shared baths down the hall, to family suites that sleep four or more and have private baths. The rooms are interspersed with TV lounges. Five community kitchens are located throughout the hotel; all are equipped with stoves, refrigerators, toasters, and teakettles, but you have to bring your own utensils. A cafeteria serves filling meals for about $5. Only the swimming pool, weight room, and sauna are restricted to women's use.

Kingston Hotel

757 Richards Street, Vancouver, BC V6B 3A6 • (604)684-9024

Newly renovated with a European facade of cut granite and heavy wood windows, this three-story bed and breakfast continues to be one of downtown Vancouver's best values. The 60 cozy rooms (some with bath) have recently been upgraded with new furniture, carpeting, quilts, and other touches. A few have color TVs, and all have phones. A continental breakfast is served each morning in a small downstairs lounge. Facilities include a sauna and a coin-op laundry. There's no parking available, so management reimburses guests for the overnight rate at downtown parkades (up to $3).

The New Backpackers Hostel

347 W Pender Street, Vancouver, BC V6B 1T3
(604)688-0112 or (604)687-9837

This hostel is more upscale than the Backpackers Youth Hostel (listed earlier) and has larger rooms (some have full kitchens). The location near Gastown makes it a prime choice.

Sylvia Hotel
1154 Gilford Street, Vancouver, BC V6G 2P6 • (604)681-9321

For the location and the ambience, it would be hard to find a lower-priced hotel in Vancouver than this gem. Built in 1912 as an apartment building, the Sylvia has gracefully accepted its role as one of Vancouver's leading senior citizens. Its ivy-cloaked stone walls, facing English Bay across Beach Avenue, only hint at the friendly warmth within. Every room is a little different, though true budget watchers might have to accept a small unit in the rear. If the continental restaurant here is priced too high, sate yourself with light snacks in the adjacent bistro lounge.

University of British Columbia (UBC)
Walter Gage Residence, 5961 Student Union Boulevard,
Vancouver, BC V6T 2C9 • (604)822-1010

When UBC students are off campus during the summer months, the university opens student residences to the traveling public—3,600 rooms in all. You can choose from three types of rooms: simple dormitory rooms (as low as $20) with a bathroom down the hall; bedrooms with a washroom, kitchen, and living room shared among six units; studios for one or two people (the best value here), with a small private washroom and kitchenette; and one-bedroom apartments (never more than $72). The latter, some four dozen of which are also available during the regular school year at a lower price ($69), have two twin beds, a Murphy bed, a full kitchen, a television and a telephone. Dine in the UBC cafeteria across the street. For a small fee, you can use the university's athletic facilities.

YMCA
955 Burrard Street, Vancouver, BC V6Z 1Y2 • (604)681-0221

The college dorm-style rooms here are spartan, to say the least (with a bed, night table, desk, lamp, and closet), but they're impeccably clean. The corridors access washrooms, showers, pay phones, and a coin-op laundry. The central location (in the heart of downtown) is one good reason to stay here; free use of all Y facilities, including swimming pool, weight room, and gymnasium, is another. The building houses a small cafe serving breakfast and lunch. Women as well as men are welcome here (seniors and students get a 10 percent discount), but liquor is verboten.

Capilano RV Park
295 Tomahawk Avenue, North Vancouver, BC V7P 1C5 • (604)987-4722

If you've brought your recreational vehicle or tent to Vancouver, this is the place to park it. The Squamish Nation owns much of the North Shore waterfront and operates this first-class, 280-site camping facility on the north end of the Lion's Gate Bridge, just minutes from down-town. Campsites are $18–$28 (full hookup). There are showers and laundry facilities.

Simon Fraser University
Room 212, McTaggart-Cowan Hall, Burnaby, BC V5A 1S6
(604)291-4201

What a deal! And what a view on top of Burnaby Mountain. From late April until August 31, Simon Fraser rents student accommodations to visitors. Furnished single rooms cost $19 per night if you bring your sleeping bag, $26 per night if you want linen and maid service. Twin rooms are available at $37. Families or groups can rent four-bedroom townhouses complete with bath and kitchen for $89 per night.

ACCESS

Vancouver International Airport, (604)276-6101, is 15 minutes south of downtown. Rail excursions begin at the Vancouver Depot (1150 Station Street, Vancouver; (604)669-3050), just south of Chinatown. There is no rail service from Seattle to Vancouver. The bus terminal for both Greyhound and Pacific lines is at the Pacific Central Station (1150 Station Street, Vancouver; (604)662-8074). By ferry, you arrive from Sidney on Vancouver Island at Tsawwassen, then pick up Highway 99 north to Vancouver. Other routes go from Tsawwassen or Horseshoe Bay to Nanaimo, the Gulf Islands, and the Sunshine Coast.

Once you're in the city, you'll encounter Vancouver traffic, one of the city's few negatives. The light-rail system installed for Expo 86 has provided a partial solution, with tracks from downtown Vancouver to Surrey via Burnaby and New Westminster. Additional legs are planned. Or you can cross Burrard Inlet via the speedy SeaBus, a 400-passenger catamaran that travels from Vancouver's Waterfront Station (at Granville and Cordova streets) to West Vancouver's Lonsdale Quay every 15 minutes; (604)261-5100.

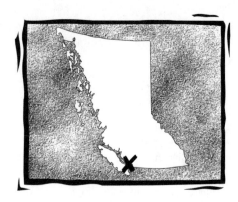

The Sunshine Coast

Lying in the rain shadow of Vancouver Island and its mountains, the Sunshine Coast has become a minor mecca for vacationing Vancouver denizens in search of the sun. Bordered by Howe Sound in the south and remote Desolation Sound in the north, the coast is dotted with lakes, and water sports abound. The modest towns of the Sunshine Coast are hardly attractions in themselves, but Powell River, with its warm, protected waters and shipwreck remains, calls itself the diving capital of Canada. Canoes and kayaks are perfect alternatives to exploring on foot (or by motorboat), and the fishing is good nearly all year long. The area abounds with wildlife, from orcas slicing through the waters of Pender Harbour to eagles circling above the islands. Trails and logging roads offer adventures on terra firma.

The towns are perfectly good hubs for a series of day trips—perhaps to view the Skookumchuck Narrows, do some telemark skiing at Mount Elphinstone, or visit one of the many accessible provincial or marine parks. A drive between the seaside fishing villages winds along the forests and bays of the pretty Sunshine Coast Highway.

ON THE ROAD 🚗

As you progress north along the coast from Horseshoe Bay, the first town on the map is the fishing village of **Gibsons**, whose population swells in the summer. Stroll along the Gibsons Seawalk; visit the set of Molly's Reach Cafe, where "The Beachcombers," a popular television show, was shot for many years. You can also visit the Elphinstone Pioneer Museum, (604)886-8232, or the spot on Gower Point where Captain George Vancouver landed in 1792. Stop by Ernie and Gwen's Drive-In (Highway 101, Gibsons; (604)886-7813) for real milkshakes and burgers with all the fixings.

Farther north lies **Sechelt**, an artists' community where work is displayed at the Sechelt Arts Centre and various galleries around town. Before crossing from Earls Cove over to Saltery Bay, take a short hike (via a brief detour to Egmont) to see the tides of three bodies of water rip through the **Skookumchuck Narrows**.

Powell River is notable as the location of one of the world's largest pulp and paper mills—MacMillan Bloedel's Powell River Division, which employs around 2,000 people and offers free mill tours in the summer; (604)483-3722. It's a town where you really sense the power of industry, past and present: flagpoles were hewn from the surrounding tall trees at the turn of the century, fishing boats clang at the docks, and limestone is mined on Texada Island. You can get a glimpse of the town's past at the historical museum; admission is $1.50 (4800 Marine Avenue, Powell River; (604)485-2222).

Over the years, this good-sized mill town has achieved destination status on the Sunshine Coast. Although it's unassuming on land, underwater it's a diver's dream. Powell River attracts hundreds of **scuba divers** to explore its miles of shoreline and view Mermaid, reportedly the world's first underwater sculpture. Interestingly enough, in this diving capital of Canada there is only one outfit that provides guided dives and arranges charters: Emerald Sea Diving Adventures (4675 Marine Avenue, Powell River; (604)485-7637), which will arrange the whole affair. It isn't cheap, but in the winter (when the smaller number of plankton increases underwater visibility), Emerald Sea offers two-day packages at more affordable rates.

Consider renting a canoe and spending a few days exploring the **Powell Forest Canoe Route**, a great trip for families, with its 72 kilometers of paddling and 8 kilometers of portage on 12 lakes. We like Mitchell Canoe Rentals (9537 Nassichuk Road, Powell River; (604)487-4448), where you can rent (or buy) a canoe and any canoeing accessories you may need. Depending on the canoe's size, rentals run $22–$30 a day (less, if you keep the canoe for an extended trip).

There are fish to be caught all along the coast and in the freshwater lakes. Charters are pricey, so try your luck at the eastern shore of Sechelt Inlet or the public docks on Powell River. Gather oysters and clams from Porpoise Bay near Sechelt, on the beaches at Saltery Bay, or at Okeover, just south of Lund. The fishing wharves as well as the 18-kilometer hiking trail at Inland Lake (25 minutes northwest of Powell River) are wheelchair-accessible. Highway 101 ends—literally—in the water at Lund, and Desolation Sound is a mere boat ride away.

CHEAP SLEEPS

Bonniebrook Lodge
1532 Ocean Beach Esplanade, Gibsons, BC V0N 1V0 • (604)886-2887

We like this old yellow clapboard lodge at Gower Point, even if a water-view room (plus all those Canadian taxes) stretches our financial limit a bit. This 1922 house has undergone a recent remodel since new owners Karen and Philippe Lacoste bought the place. The four rooms (there used to be six) are a bit more spacious, and the views of the Strait of Georgia are still lovely. Breakfast is served at Chez Philippe, which offers French-influenced West Coast cuisine and is open to nonguests at dinnertime only.

Cattanach Bed and Breakfast
F18 C7 RR2, Roberts Creek, BC V0N 1V0 • (604)885-5444

Barb and Ian Cattanach run a cozy two-room bed and breakfast with rock fireplace, wood stove, and antiques throughout. The log home (which the Cattanachs built themselves) sits on 5 acres and has one twin room and one double as well as a sitting room for guests. Barb's breakfasts might feature Fraser Valley blueberry pancakes.

The Old Courthouse Manor Bed and Breakfast and Vault Cafe
6243 Walnut Street, Powell River, BC V8A 4K4 • (604)483-4000

In 1986, Wendy Boniface and Arvine Norgren converted Powell River's 50-year-old historic courthouse into an inviting and inexpensive lodging. Trans-Canada cyclists and older folks alike come to stay in the 18 rooms, which top out at $40 for two. All but two have shared baths, and some have views (beyond the pulp and paper mill) of the strait. The small Vault Cafe serves home-style food for breakfast and lunch, and the pie selection is legendary.

Lund Breakwater Inn
9737 Lund Highway, Lund, BC V0N 2G0 • (604)483-3187

This motel/restaurant/pub/antique shop/post office/general store is pretty much the entire town of Lund, but it makes a comfortable berth for those drawn to Desolation Sound (or those who just have a hankering to go to the end of the road). The original part of the Breakwater was built at the turn of the century, and those rooms are rented out by the month. Travelers stay in the adjacent motel's 20 rooms, from which it's possible to catch a sunset. Lund personifies remoteness—even isolation—and you'll need a boat to go any farther north.

 *Getting There and Back*

The pleasant 119-kilometer drive up the Sunshine Coast is interrupted by two spectacular ferry rides. First there's the 40-minute ferry from Horseshoe Bay (just west of West Vancouver) to Langdale. Later, you board the Earls Cove ferry for a 50-minute ride from Sechelt Peninsula to Saltery Bay. A ferry ticket is good for two rides—either a round trip on one or one way on both. The ferries run about eight times per day. Call BC Ferries for schedules; (604)669-1211.

Instead of driving out to Powell River and back, you might want to make a loop. At Powell River. cross over to Comox, on Vancouver Island, via the *Queen of Sidney*; (604)339-3310. Drive down the eastern coast of the island and return to the mainland via BC Ferries from Nanaimo or Sidney.

Whistler & the Fraser River Canyon

Highway 99, running north from Vancouver to Whistler, is an adventure in itself. The aptly named Sea-to-Sky Highway hugs fir-covered mountains that tumble sharply into island-filled Howe Sound. The views are breathtaking. But don't get carried away—the curves of the road are often demanding (watch out for occasional delays caused by rock slides). As you climb beyond Howe Sound, you enter spectacular Garibaldi Provincial Park, crowned by the toothed Black Tusk Peak.

Two hours north of Vancouver, the Whistler-Blackcomb Ski Area offers some of the finest skiing in North America. (Whistler has been ranked the number one ski resort in North America for three years, and it's a favored destination for some Japanese and Europeans as well.) The village (actually two cheek-by-jowl communities—Whistler Village and Blackcomb Resort) boasts a world-class reputation (and two world-class mountains). Here you'll find swank resorts, fine art galleries, and designer stores (Ralph Lauren is here, though Armani is not—yet). During the winter, the area is often booked to capacity, and in the summer it becomes a popular destination for anybody in search of mountain *air and an après-play Jacuzzi. As usual, the best does not come cheap, but prices are drastically reduced come summer, and they drop even more in the "shoulder" seasons. Trust us, you can stay—and play—at Whistler even if the only car you own is a Volkswagen Rabbit.*

ON THE ROAD

Just north of Horseshoe Bay, as you head up Highway 99, turn right to **Furry Creek Golf & Country Club**; (604)896-2216. It's a spectacular and brutally tough new Robert Muir Graves-designed course that was forced to go public when it couldn't sell enough memberships (original fee: $36,000). Lucky you. A superb clubhouse overlooking the mountains is a big bonus for pay-as-you-play golfers.

Also on the way to Whistler, at **Britannia Beach**, there's a funky roadside collection of former mining-company buildings that are now a museum. Vancouver skiers stop for dinner at the 99er Restaurant (on Highway 99; (604)896-2497), where you can still get change from a dollar for coffee and a cookie to go.

An hour north of Vancouver, you'll find the logging-and-rock-climbing town of **Squamish**. About four kilometers south of Squamish is the mammoth granite Stawamus Chief, reportedly one of the top 10 climbs in North America (there's a viewing pullout nearby) and the second-largest granite monolith in the British Commonwealth. You'll find more climbers on the Smoke Bluffs, right at the entrance to downtown. Squamish is lobbying to get these cliffs (now on private property) classified as the first Canadian national park designated strictly for climbers.

Nearby **Shannon Falls**, the fifth-largest waterfall in the world, plummets 335 meters past granite and air (six times the elevation of Niagara). Wind surfers set sail at Squamish Spit, where geography and climate combine to create the effect of air rushing through a wind tunnel. About 14 kilometers north of Squamish at Brackendale, the **Sunwolf Outdoor Centre**, (604)898-1537, fronts on the Cheakamus River at an ideal spot for rafting, kayaking, and fishing. In the winter, thousands of bald eagles hunt the shorelines of the Cheakamus.

Garibaldi Provincial Park's 400,000 acres of glacier-fed lakes, towering evergreens, and volcanic peaks stretch from Squamish to Pemberton, interrupted briefly by the village of Whistler. The park is cherished by avid hikers and skiers. Picnic shelters (and a few rudimentary

Free Tennis

You can play tennis at no charge (in snowless months) on one of the 18 public tennis courts scattered throughout the village communities. The courts are marked on the Whistler Valley Directory map.

overnight quarters) are sprinkled throughout the area. Call Garibaldi/ Squamish BC Parks for maps or trail suggestions; (604)898-3678.

Whistler's citizens have done a tremendous job of making the resort fun even when there's no more white stuff on the slopes. (If you're a determined skier who just can't give up the downhill, though, you *can* ski all summer long on Blackcomb's Horstman Glacier.) The area's summertime offerings are so daunting, in fact, that Whistler Mountain hosts free **mountain orientation tours** twice daily.

Hikers and mountain bikers can self-power up to mile-high Seventh Heaven. Or save your energy for the ultimate descent by taking Whistler's gondola (up to five kids under 15 years of age ride free with an adult) or Blackcomb's chairs to the top. **Mountain biking** in Whistler today is as new and adventurous as skiing was 20 years ago. (An off-road trail from Squamish to Whistler is being built.) Stop by tiny Armchair Books (4205 Village Square, Whistler; (604)932-5557) and buy a detailed local trail guide. Or bike (or hike) the trails to Lost Lake— which start directly from the village.

In-line skaters (the only wheels allowed in the Town Centre), joggers, cyclists, pedestrians, and walkers somehow share the **Valley Trail**. Whistler's mostly paved foot-freeway runs from one end of the valley to the other—past all the lakes and golf courses. Whistler Blades in Delta Whistler Resort, (604)932-9669, rents in-line skates and offers group lessons.

There are plenty of **water sports** at the five lakes in the surrounding valley. Fishing and swimming are best in the clear, not-too-cold Lost Lake. Others might opt for volleyball at Rainbow Lake, board-sailing at Alta Lake, or canoeing, sailing, or waterskiing (rentals available from Whistler Outdoor Experience Company, Whistler; (604)932-3389). The Alpha Lake free-form tree house will capture kids' imaginations.

The area's best easy canoe trip is the meandering River of Golden Dreams, especially if you arrange for someone to pick you up at the other end (most rental companies will). Families might try Meadow Park, home to a skating rink and swimming pool. Golfers can tee off at the scenic Arnold Palmer-designed Whistler Golf Club or the rugged, link-style Robert F. Trent Jones-designed Chateau Whistler golf course.

Concerts occur daily in the village from June through September, with free music festivals featuring everything from classical and jazz to country and blues. In mid-August, catch the Vancouver Symphony on top of Whistler Mountain. A $39 ticket buys a lift up (and down), admission to the concert, and a bale of hay to sit on. (BYO picnic.) The year always ends with Whistler First Night, an outdoor, nonalcoholic family New Year's Eve celebration with entertainment ($5 per person). Call or drop by the Whistler Activity and Information Centre in the Town Centre for more event information; (604)932-2394.

For those who'd rather rough it, stream-side campsites at the Calcheak trailhead, 12 kilometers south of Whistler, are free. From here it's a pleasant 1½-hour hike to Brandywine Falls. Another good hike is up to **Rainbow Lake**, about an 18-kilometer round trip through glorious ancient cedar groves. The Whistler Activity Centre can provide maps and directions.

There are three **horse outfitters** near Whistler: Whistler Trails Layton Bryson Outfitters, (604)932-6623; Whistler Outdoor Experience Company near Pemberton, (604)932-3389; and the W-D Bar Ranch in Mount Currie, (604)894-5669. It seems that the farther you get from Whistler, the more saddle time you get for your money. Locals say the best real riding is in the Pemberton Valley (Mount Currie).

Of course, winter is Whistler time, with an average snowfall of 11-plus meters (450 inches) a year, a vertical drop of over 5,000 feet at each area, and 25 lifts (including a gondola, seven quads, and eight triples) to cover 200 runs. Lift tickets will set you back $42 any day of the week, unless you plan ahead. Here's how: call the ticket number at Whistler, (604)932-3434, or Blackcomb, (604)932-3141, for specific information on where they may be offering **discounts on ski tickets**. You'll find the

Groceries

With IGA in Village North and Nester's Shop Easy just north of the village (Nester's has everything from raclette grills for rent to dozens of exotic mustards), there's not much point in shopping before you come. Besides, every Sunday from summer to early October, you can get provisions at the farmers market (at the base of Blackcomb in Upper Village) attended by Pemberton Valley, Okanagan, and Gulf Island farmers.

best prices on rental skis at either of the Whistler Mountain Sports shops (Whistler Creek, (604)932-5422, or Carleton Lodge, (604)932-6712).

Cross-country ski trails begin at the village edge and wind through the adjacent residential communities. A favorite trail leads out to Lost Lake. There's a warming hut at the trailhead ($6) and lights for evening skiing, free after 4pm; (604)932-6436. You can usually have a beer-and-burger meal at the Chateau Whistler golf course's clubhouse for under $10; (604)938-8000. The ski trails are free on the other golf course (across Highway 99 from Whistler).

Other **winter activities** in Whistler include snow-boarding (rentals and lessons are available), dogsledding, snowmobiling, sleigh rides, and heli-skiing. One favorite cold-snap sport that won't cost you a thing (if you have your own skates) is skating on Alta Lake (check first to make sure the ice is safe). You don't need to be a guest to use hotel health clubs. For a small daily fee, nonguests can use Delta's health club (pool, indoor tennis, and gym); (604)932-7336.

You can purchase baked goods at a number of places in the village, or you can save a few cents and get them at the wholesale outlet of Little Mountain Bakery (#7 1212 Alpha Lake Road, Whistler; (604)932-4220) in Function Junction, Whistler's industrial park just south of the village. While there, check out the discounted outdoor gear at Katmandu Consignment, (604)932-6381, and drink a round of Whistler's own premium lager or Black Tusk Ale with the brew master at Whistler Brewing Company (1209 Alpha Lake Road, Whistler; (604)932-6185). Tours available Tuesday through Saturday.

If you need to dine out but don't want to spend a fortune, rest easy. The diner-style Southside Deli (1202 Lake Placid Road, Whistler Creek; (604)932-3368) makes great breakfasts and at night turns into Flipside, with pasta under $10. In Whistler Village, stop in at Chalet Deli, (604)932-8345, or the local vegetarian fave, Ingrid's Cork and Cheddar, (604)932-7000. For hearty fare at reasonable prices, but definitely a louder, more local atmosphere, try Tapley's Pub, (604)932-4011; Jimmy D's, (604)932-4451; or Peter's Underground, (604)932-4811. Lunch is a deal at Misty Mountain Pizza's, (604)932-2825; pick up a pizza card for a free slice. Thai One On, (604)932-4822—tricky to find in Le Chamois

Hotel—is new, busy, and a good place to share a few affordable dishes that aren't pasta.

For dinner, many locals dine outside of the village at Hoz's Pub and Cafe (2129 Lake Placid Road, Whistler; (604)932-4424 or (604)932-5940), just around the corner from the train station in Whistler Creek. It's comfortable without being too fancy. The fireplace is a nice addition, and families are welcome. Or try the cheesy enchiladas and the cilantro-laced salsa at the Border Cantina in Shoestring Lodge, (604)932-3373, in the White Gold Estates subdivision.

North of Whistler is the no-glitz town of **Pemberton**, home to the Lil'wat people and the annual May (and sometimes September) Lillooet Lake Rodeo; (604)894-6507. Just outside of Pemberton, take a pleasant, flat half-hour walk into dramatic Nairn Falls. During May through October you can four-wheel it to the natural Meager Creek Hot Springs (ask at Pemberton's Petro-Can gas station for directions and a map). Pemberton Valley Golf & Country Club, (604)894-5122, and the new Big Sky course, (604)894-6106, are a deal at $25 per round.

For good, reasonably priced food in Pemberton, try the new, organic Pony Espresso, (604)932-4424; lively Willy G's, (604)894-6411; or the Roadside Cafe, 10 minutes down Highway 99 toward Mount Currie, (604)894-6622. Stop for herb tea or a home-style meal at Deanna Pilling's Spirit Circle Art, Craft and Tea Company, (604)894-6336, in Mount Currie.

If you've got time on your hands, tour the circle route via Lillooet and the **Fraser River Canyon**. It's one of the most scenic loops in British Columbia, winding past fields of cultivated ginseng and ranch mesas. The Fraser and Thompson rivers descend from Lillooet and Ashcroft, respectively, to converge in Lytton, where they squeeze through the narrow walls of the Fraser River Canyon. British Columbia's mightiest river rushes through the canyon for 85 kilometers. You can get a good sense of the whirling rapids from the many roadside pullouts.

It's far more fun on a hot summer day, when you can buy some wet thrills on a **raft trip**. The biggest fleet on the river is Kumsheen Raft Adventures Ltd. (Main Street, Lytton; (604)455-2296). Other companies include Fraser River Raft Expeditions (PO Box 10, Yale, BC V0K 2S0; (604)863-2336 or (800)363-RAFT) and River Rogues (Spences Bridge; (604)452-2252). Downriver, from mid-April to mid-October, the popular **Hell's Gate Airtram** (Boston Bar; (604)867-9277) takes you across the boiling waters of the Fraser at the narrowest part of the gorge.

The river turns sharply west and calms at **Hope**, 140 kilometers east of Vancouver. Keep your eyes to the sky while passing through Hope; many hang gliders have been enticed to the area by consistent mountain updrafts in nearby hills. Stop 3 kilometers north of Hope at Lake of the Woods Resort, (604)869-9211, for some German sausage before returning to the big city (the restaurant closes at Christmas and reopens on Good Friday, before Easter).

CHEAP SLEEPS

Garibaldi Inn
38012 3rd Avenue, Squamish, BC V0N 3G0 • (604)892-5204

Squamish is not Whistler, but getting to Whistler is quite easy from here. It's a half-hour drive, bus trip (Maverick Coach Lines; (604)255-1177), or train ride (BC Rail; (604)984-5246). And unlike Whistler, there are a number of reasonably priced lodgings here. The Garibaldi is the smaller of the motels (25 rooms). Nine rooms have kitchenettes (from $49).

Sunwolf Outdoor Centre
70002 Government Road (PO Box 244), Brackendale, BC V0N 1H0
(604)898-1537

These 10 rustic, riverside guest cabins and 5 acres of campsites along the Cheakamus River double as the base camp for Rivers and Oceans Unlimited's rafting and kayaking expeditions, but anyone is welcome. All of the cabins have a shower or bath and minimal cooking equipment. Cabins are operated on a first-come, first-served basis. Summer only.

Brio Haus
3005 Brio Entrance (Brio), Whistler, BC V0N 1B3 • (604)932-3313

You get a lot here for not too much money. Four people can rent the family room (a king-sized bed and two bunks), lounge in the deep

The Eleventh Hour

Sometimes it pays to make last-minute reservations. Of course, you risk not getting one at all. But you also might luck into a bargain room in the village, thanks to cancellations or a slow day. Ask Central Reservations, (800)944-7853, for their special deals; they change daily. If that doesn't work, call the Whistler Activity and Information Centre, (604)932-2394, and request their list of private homes, condominiums, and more inexpensive private studios and dormitories.

Jacuzzi, sweat in the large sauna, cook dinner in the guest kitchen, watch a video on the VCR in the living room, and dry their wet ski clothes. Room rates jump from $55 in summer to $80 in winter; the family room costs $110–$135.

Chalet Beau Sejour

7414 Ambassador Crescent, Box 472 (White Gold Estates), Whistler, BC V0N 1B0 • (604)938-4966

After skiing, congenial Sue and Hal Stangel like to have a snack and a glass of *Glühwein*—and that's what they provide for their guests around the big rock fireplace in their contemporary home in White Gold Estates. Sue can suggest lots of good, reasonably priced restaurants, but you're welcome to order in a pizza or buy deli fare and prepare your own lunch.

Fireside Lodge

2117 Nordic Drive (Nordic Estates), Whistler, BC V0N 1B2 (604)932-4545

Don't be fooled by the boxy exterior or the tough-eyed manager, Marj Currie. We suspect she's the reason this big, comfortable lodge owned by the Power Mountain Ski Club (which opens it on a limited basis to non-members) is run so well and looks so great. Lots of families flock to this place. It has 12 private rooms, a dormitory that sleeps 31, and a large stone fireplace in an impressive living room. It's run on a cooperative basis: bring your own groceries, bedding, and towels, and cook and clean for yourselves. Club members have priority when it comes to making reservations. Nonmembers can't book until 30 days before their stay.

Golden Dreams Bed and Breakfast

6412 Easy Street (Whistler Cay), Whistler, BC V4L 4L2 (604)932-2667 or (800)668-7055

Ann Myette-Spence's three-room B&B in the Whistler Cay subdivision is set up in such a way that guests seem to have their own separate apartment, away from Myette-Spence's own busy family. The owner has prettied the rooms with three different themes: Oriental, Victorian, and Aztecan (the only one with its own bath). There's a Jacuzzi in the extra bathroom. Ski conditions are discussed around the breakfast table (Terry Spence is a Canadian National Ski Team coach with tales of the World Cup circuit).

Rainbow Creek Bed and Breakfast

8243 Alpine Way, Box 1142 (Alpine Meadows), Whistler, BC V0N 1B0 (604)932-7001

Almost taller than it is wide, this three-story log home reminds us of the ultimate tree house. Inside, Heidi Lieberherr's house evokes warmth (and not just from the fireplace) with its purposeful combination of privacy and sociability. The B&B has three rooms (each with bath) and a spare fridge for extra food. Enjoy a steaming cup of tea in the afternoon, or stroll over to the new ice rink and swimming pool at Meadow Park.

Southside Lodge

2101 Lake Placid Road (Whistler Creek), Whistler, BC V0N 1B0
(604)932-2554

Kitty-corner from the Whistler Creek quad, across from Union Station, and two floors above the Southside Deli (which has been known to crank up the music), the "lodge" is more like a back entrance to six low-key rooms with baths. It's primarily for the young at heart. The longer you stay, the lower the rates; a bunk room sleeps four for $80. The best part is the location: you can walk to the Whistler Creek quad and to the train station. Who needs a car?

Stancliff House

3333 Panorama Ridge (Brio), Whistler, BC V0N 1B0 • (604)932-2393

If you want to know everything about Whistler, Shirley and Stan Langtry should be your hosts. They're two informed, involved locals who make anyone's stay in Whistler a good one. They know where to direct families looking for an inexpensive meal, couples in search of romance, or two guys heading out for a beer. The three rooms are simple (they all share the facilities and a large indoor hot tub), but the knit slippers provided are as warm as the fireplace upstairs.

Swiss Cottage Bed & Breakfast

7321 Fitzsimmons Drive, Box 1209 (White Gold Estates), Whistler, BC
V0N 1B0 • (604)932-6062

White Gold Estates is turning into B&B heaven, and where better to stay than in this cottage in a quiet cul-de-sac, with Lost Lake trails out the door, a tennis court just beyond the lawn, and an easy walk to

 *Free Bus*

The Whistler Transit System runs buses throughout Whistler; (604)938-1BUS. Pick up a map (one of the clearest of the valley) and schedule at the Chamber of Commerce or the Whistler Conference Centre. The bus is free between the village, White Gold Estates, Tapleys, and Whistler Cay; the fare is $1.25 elsewhere (be ready with exact coin fare).

 *Cheap Hot Soaks*

The Whistler Campground & RV Park just north of Whistler Village, (604)932-5181, is a great setup: hot tub, sauna, and free hot showers, from $16.50 a night. Make reservations.

Blackcomb. While you're stepping out from underneath the duvet onto the heated floor, Willy and Louise Gerig are whipping up eggs Benny or waffles in their large kitchen.

UBC Lodge

2124 Nordic Drive (Nordic Estates), Whistler, BC V0N 1B0
(604)932-6604; (604)822-5851 in Vancouver

Another club lodge. What more can we say about them? They're great for what they are: a bargain ($12 for UBC students, $17 for others, $45 for three-night special). This 56-bed facility, managed by the University of British Columbia, definitely feels geared more toward students than families, but is open to all. Management is friendly; the rooms can be a bit frosty.

Whistler Hostel

5678 Alta Lake Road, Whistler, BC V0N 1B0 • (604)932-5492

Aside from being 15 minutes south of Whistler Village, this former fishing lodge has a great location on the west side of Alta Lake. If you arrive by train, you can get dropped off at the Whistler Hostel flag stop in the backyard, but if you're going to ski, you'll need a car or a big, friendly thumb. The no-shoes policy inside the hostel keeps the place clean and dry. There's a large living room with a wood stove, an upright piano, and well-used sauna, pingpong, and pool tables. Free use of canoes in summer. The eight bunk rooms (four bunks to a room) are upstairs, and one private double is available ($14–$20 a night). The kitchen is shared. The hostel makes a primo base for windsurfing Alta Lake.

The Log House B&B

1357 Elmwood, General Delivery, Pemberton, BC V0N 2L0
(604)894-6000 or (800)894-6002

This new, 5,000-square-foot log house looks slightly out of place on its residential street, but the space inside—and on the wraparound deck with wraparound view—is wonderful. Irish-born Margaret and husband Bill Scott have a flair for design and hospitality. Each of the three *very* large rooms—with sleigh or poster beds—has its own TV, Jacuzzi, private bath, guest robes, mini-fridges, and comfy reading chairs. There's an exercise area inside and a hot tub outside. The location alone (about 20 minutes from Whistler) keeps the place affordable; and daily buses make ski travel quite easy. If the Log House is full, there's always the Pemberton Hotel (7375 Frontier Street, Pemberton; (604)894-6313), where $50 buys a spare, clean room.

Steelhead Inn

Box 100, Spences Bridge, BC V0K 2L0 • (604)458-2398

Historic Steelhead Inn, on the Thompson River, is one of the few notable lodgings along the Coast Mountain route. Owner Jeremy Lewis is a superb chef and offers reasonably priced dinners in the restaurant. If you're feeling flush, spring the extra $15 for one of the five rooms with bath, so you won't have to fight over the common bath shared by the three without.

The Okanagan Valley

The arid Okanagan Valley, splashed with lakes from the Canadian border to Vernon, is a summer playground. Four lakes—Osoyoos (reportedly Canada's warmest freshwater lake), Skaha, Kalamalka, and the 112-kilometer-long Okanagan—cover three-quarters of the length of the valley itself. The climate is Canada's driest, with only 10 inches of rain a year. No wonder coastal British Columbians make a yearly pilgrimage to the sun-soaked shores.

Laden with orchards, the valley is especially appealing in spring, when the fruit trees are in full bloom. Autumn winemaking is a hot ticket, and vineyards climb the hills above the orchards. Then winter comes, and the valley is quiet. The local climate is a powdery compromise between the chill of the Rockies and the slush of the Coast Mountains, and challenging ski slopes ring the valley.

ON THE ROAD

The best time to pick up some of the valley's bounty is mid-August through early September; however, beginning as early as late June the **fruit** starts ripening: cherries (late June through mid-July), peaches

255

Cathedral Lakes

A half hour west of Osoyoos is Cathedral Lakes Provincial Park, where azure lakes are framed by jagged peaks. Unusual rock formations make the area a fascinating place to hike. Many trails begin from Quiniscoe Lake, the core of the park. Lakeview and Buckhorn are the only two vehicle campgrounds (no fee for overnight stays). Hikers must use specially designated backcountry campgrounds, and there's a $2 camping fee at Quiniscoe Lake. Vehicle access to the core of the park is prohibited, but hikers, campers, and anglers can reserve a spot and catch a ride on the Cathedral Lakes Lodge vehicle. Call (604)499-5848 for more information.

(mid-July through September), apricots (mid-July through mid-August), pears (August through September), apples (August through October), plums (September), and grapes (September through mid-October).

At the southernmost end of the valley, almost dipping into Washington, **Osoyoos** bills itself as "the Spanish capital of Canada." (No Spanish pioneers lived here, mind you.) In 1975 the city realized it needed a facelift, observed that the Bavarian motif had been pre-empted by cities elsewhere, and decided to "go Spanish" by tacking up some fake red-tile roofs and matador billboards. Just about everyone likes the Diamond Steak & Seafood House (Main Street, Osoyoos; (604)495-6223), which carries off the ersatz Spanish theme better than most (but which serves primarily steaks and pizza). A good short hike sends you up Mount Kobau, just west of Osoyoos, off Kobau Road. Take the 2-kilometer Kobau Lookout Trail to the fire lookout, or hike the 5-kilometer Testalinden Trail, with views of the Similkameen Valley.

Penticton takes full advantage of its dual lakefronts. The south end of town (essentially an unofficial summer amusement park, complete with go-cart tracks, amusement centers, miniature golf courses, water slides, and RV parks) touches the north shore of Skaha Lake. The north end of town sidles along the southern tip of Okanagan Lake. One of the most popular summer diversions is inner-tubing at a leisurely pace along the scenic river channel connecting the two lakes. Hydrophobics can cycle or in-line skate on an adjacent pathway. The ever-popular Theo's (687 Main Street, Penticton; (604)492-4019) sports a series of sun-dappled interior patios roofed with heavy rough-sawn beams, floored with red tile, and walled in white stucco. By all means, go in the late afternoon for an aperitif and a plate of excellent fried squid, or stop in late at night for moussaka.

Summerland is another theme town, only these residents chose Tudor. Old Summerland is down on the water, but most of the town's business now thrives up on the hill. Shaughnessy's Cove (12817 Lake Shore Drive, Summerland; (604)494-1212), built as close to the water as the law allows, features fare ranging from fish 'n' chips to chimichangas to a filling stew served in a hollowed-out loaf of bread.

Up the road a bit in **Peachland**, Chinese Laundry (5818 Beach Avenue, Peachland; (604)767-2722), a former laundromat, is now a good Chinese restaurant filled with laundry-related antiques. It's a popular place, especially on summer evenings. Swim at **Antlers Beach Provincial Park**, 5 kilometers south of Peachland, where you'll find a great beach. In mid-September, walk up the easy trail to watch the spawning kokanee leap the falls.

On the east side of Okanagan Lake, **Kelowna** is the largest and liveliest of the Okanagan cities, with some noisy nightlife, some culture (an art museum and summer theater), a growing range of continental and ethnic restaurants, a family regatta in July, and an interesting historical preserve at Father Pandosy's Mission; (604)860-8369. The town even has its own version of the Loch Ness monster: Ogopogo. Keep a look-out for him (or her) while supping on the festive paddle wheeler *Fintry Queen*, (604)763-2780. Younger customers might blanch at its kitschy appurtenances, but your grandparents will love it.

Families with kids too young to appreciate the Okanagan's oenolog-ical bounty can tour the Sun-Rype fruit juice facility (1165 Ethel Street, Kelowna; (604)860-7973). And of course, what would beach lounging be without a good book? Mosaic Books (1420 St. Paul Street, Kelowna; (604)763-4418) is the most impressive bookstore in the Okanagan, and if you're really lazy, they have plenty of books on cassette, too.

Serious amounts of lemon juice flavor the vegetables and grilled meats at Talos Greek Restaurant (1570 Water Street, Kelowna; (604)763-1656), and the prawns are excellent. The Okanagan's best alfresco dining (with a stunning view to boot) is on the porch at the Gatsby-esque Hotel Eldo-rado (500 Cook Road, just off Lakeside Drive, Kelowna; (604)763-7500). Go on Monday night for the inexpensive pasta-bar special. Wear white.

Wedged between Kelowna and Naramata, **Okanagan Mountain Provincial Park**, on the east side of Okanagan Lake, can be accessed only on foot, on horseback, or by boat. In this northern desert wilder-ness, the top of Okanagan Mountain affords views of the lake to the west and the Monashee Mountains to the east; for more information, call BC Parks at (604)494-0321.

Houseboating

Houseboating on 70-mile-long Lake Okanagan is a good three- to seven-day vacation alternative for the entire family—most houseboats sleep up to 10 and come complete with everything from a microwave oven to a water slide. No previous boating experience is necessary; contact Okanagan Boat Charters and Sailboats, Penticton; (604)492-5099.

You can also explore the approximately 1,000 miles of the spiderlike shoreline of Shuswap Lake at the northern end of the Okanagan Valley. A seven-day trip will cost you, but bring a bunch of friends and it won't be so painful; Waterway Houseboats, (604)836-2505.

At the Okanagan Valley's northern tip sits **Vernon**, the area's only city that isn't on a lake—though it's nestled between three of them. Kalamalka Lake boasts one of the Okanagan's prettiest beaches, at Jade Bay in nearby Coldstream. Its tropical hue is caused by the rich mineralization of the lake bed; for a better vantage point, hike to the summit of, um, Rattlesnake Hill. Back in town, cool down with iced coffee in summer or warm up with a steaming cappuccino in winter at Bean Scene (30th Avenue, Vernon; (604)558-1817). O'Keefe Historic Ranch, 11 kilometers north, is an original cattle ranch from the late 1800s. Now a museum, the compound contains most of the original buildings and equipment from the era. Tours run April through October; (604)542-7868.

Just like Rodney Dangerfield, British Columbian winemakers had become used to getting "no respect" from wine snobs and local folk alike. These days, however, they can hold their heads high; ever since British Columbia authorized estate and smaller "farm-gate" wineries, many **excellent small wineries** have sprung up. Some of the best estate offerings come out of Gray Monk, 5 kilometers west of Winfield off Highway 97, (604)766-3168; Cedar Creek, 14 kilometers south of Kelowna in the Mission, (604)764-8866; Sumac Ridge, off Highway 97, just north of Summerland, (604)494-0451; Hainle Vineyards, in Peachland, (604)767-2525; and Quail's Gate Vineyards, located between Westbank and Kelowna, (604)769-4451.

Other notable wineries worth a visit: Calona (1125 Richter Street, Kelowna; (604)762-3332); Mission Hill Vineyards, a recent award winner for one of the world's best chardonnays, located south of Kelowna, off Boucherie Road in Westbank, (604)768-5125; Gehringer Brothers,

4 kilometers south of Oliver, off Highway 97 on Road 8, (604)498-3537; Brights Wines, between Oliver and Okanagan Falls on Highway 97, (604)498-4981; St. Hubertus, on Lakeshore Road in Kelowna, (604)764-7888; and Divino, (604)498-2784, and Okanagan Vineyards, (604)498-6663, both 5 kilometers south of Oliver, off Highway 97. Most offer tastings and seasonal tours; call ahead for times and dates.

Skiers will appreciate Silver Star Mountain, east of Vernon, which has the Okanagan's largest vertical drop (2,500 feet) and the most extensive trail network for cross-country skiing. Its Klondike-style gaslight village has been favorably compared to larger (and more expensive) resorts like Whistler; (604)542-0224. East of Kelowna, Big White, (604)765-3101, features 51 runs descending 2,050 vertical feet; snowfall is so abundant that artificial snowmaking isn't necessary. You can do some cross-country skiing here, too. Apex Resort, located west of Penticton, has the Okanagan's best expert skiing. A new quad chairlift will complement its base-area facelift; a Western-style village will be constructed over the next three years; (604)492-2880. Their Nordic Centre has track-set trails, and more trails can be accessed at Nickel Plate Lake, about 5 kilometers south of Apex.

While on-mountain accommodations are available at each of these ski areas, we suggest staying in town and driving to the slopes each morning, since Okanagan hotels and motels are all but dormant during the winter months. All three resorts have toll-free reservation numbers: Apex, (800)387-APEX; Big White, (800)663-2772; and Silver Star, (800)663-4431. Southwest of Penticton on Highway 3A, the Twin Lakes Golf Club doubles as a cross-country course in winter; (604)497-8377. West of Osoyoos, there's more downhill skiing at Mount Baldy, usually one of the first mountains in the area to receive snow; (604)498-2262.

CHEAP SLEEPS

Avalon Motel
9106 76th Avenue (PO Box 92), Osoyoos, BC V0H 1V0 • (604)495-6334

The Avalon offers low rates ($35) and a central location just a walk up from Lion's Park and Legion beaches. Twelve rooms keep the motel manageable, and the new owner, Phil Elliott, likes his job.

Inkaneep Resort
RR 2, Osoyoos, BC V0H 1V0 • (604)495-6353

The best thing about this old resort is its location on its own miniature peninsula: all 10 beach-level rooms face directly south (getting maximum

There's no shortage of camping in the Okanagan Valley, since dozens of commercial sites have sprung up. The best choice is one of the two dozen provincial parks (most are open April through October). Be sure to bring your fishing rod and binoculars.

During the peak season of July and August, three parks employ a reservation system (which is, unfortunately, rather clumsy): if you arrive and the park is full, you are given a voucher that moves you to the head of the line for the next day. There are no phone reservations. "Campground full" signs appear before the turnoff to a park.

Listed below are some lakeside provincial parks that allow camping. For more information, contact BC Parks (101-1050 W Columbia Street, Kamloops, BC V2C 1L4; (604)494-0321). For a complete list of all area parks, pick up a copy of *Parks of British Columbia and the Yukon* by Maggie M. Paquet.

- **Bear Creek Provincial Park** (9 kilometers west of Kelowna): kokanee spawn in Bear Creek (mid-September), great hiking in a cool canyon, fishing for mountain whitefish in lake; ticket-reservation system during peak season.
- **Darke Lake Provincial Park** (18 kilometers northwest of Summerland): open year-round, ice-fishing and skating in winter, good fishing for rainbow and brook trout, only five sites.
- **Ellison Provincial Park** (northeastern shore of Okanagan Lake, southwest of Vernon): good fishing, six archaeological sites within park, underwater park for divers, watch for Ogopogo.
- **Haynes Point Provincial Park** (2 kilometers south of Osoyoos): good fishing for rainbow trout and bass, coveted lakefront campsites, ticket-reservation system during peak season.
- **Inkaneep Provincial Park** (6 kilometers north of Oliver): open all year, Okanagan River with good fishing and canoeing (if you don't mind carrying your canoe the short distance to the river), great bird-watching.
- **Mabel Lake Provincial Park** (76 kilometers northeast of Vernon): on the flanks of the Monashee Mountains, a mountain-cool respite from the desert heat of the Okanagan Valley.
- **Okanagan Falls Provincial Park** (in Okanagan Falls): sandy beaches and sagebrush, lots of little mammals to be spotted.
- **Okanagan Lake Provincial Park** (24 kilometers north of Penticton): open all year, the valley's biggest provincial park, sandy beaches, ponderosa pine and sagebrush, ticket-reservation system during peak season.
- **Vaseux Provincial Park** (25 kilometers south of Penticton): open year-round, excellent wildlife habitat, spring and winter range of Californian bighorn sheep, famous area for spying birds and waterfowl, winter conditions make for great ice fishing and skating.

sun) and are only minutes away from the water's edge. Families (some in their third generation of vacationing here) don't mind the fact that the accommodations are a bit campish, because what folks really come for is the sun. In summer you must rent by the week (and prices edge out of the cheap range), but winter rates ($55) are a bargain.

Chute Lake Resort

Mail: 797 Alexander Avenue, Penticton, BC V2A 1E6 • (604)493-3535

This rustic year-round basecamp for outdoorsmen offers ice fishing, cross-country skiing, snowmobiling, and apple pie by the fire in winter. In summer, the lake is clear, the trout are jumping, and the hiking is endless. Granted, it's a rickety old BYO-bedding kind of place; most cabins have wood stoves but only two have running water. The lodge houses eight rooms with slanted floors and plug-in electric heaters, shower facilities, and an informal dining room (meals are extra).

Club Paradise Motel

1000 Lakeshore Drive, Penticton, BC V2A 1C1 • (604)493-8400

Just across the street from Okanagan Lake's sandy beaches, this 11-room motel is a good bet. Some rooms have kitchenettes, and all have access to the indoor Jacuzzi. Picnic tables and barbecues make good summer's-eve fun. Ever-popular Salty's Seafood is right next door.

Penticton Youth Hostel

464 Ellis Street, Penticton, BC V2A 4M2 • (604)492-8775

Owner Rob Cooper's been in the accommodation business since he was 11 years old (his father owns major hotels in Prince George and Vernon). Now he manages the Penticton Youth Hostel, which sets standards that other local hostels can't hope to match. There are dorm rooms, family and couple rooms, communal dining facilities, a kitchen, a barbecue, a living room, and a coin operated laundry. In the summer months, if you haven't reserved a space, keep your fingers crossed and show up early. Hostel association members can save about 5 bucks a night, but no one will have to spend more than $20.

Blue Stream

4202 32nd Street, Vernon, BC V1T 5P4 • (604)545-2221

The smallest motel in town serves the biggest banana splits at its creekside ice cream parlor. The 11 sparkling rooms are located 6½ kilometers north of pretty Kalamalka Lake. Small pets okay. Rates start at $35.

Idabel Lake Resort

Site 13E, C2, RR 5, Kelowna, BC V1X 4K4 • (604)868-2722

During the summer, the Okanagan Valley can become stifling, and exhaust from jet skis and car traffic can be nauseating if there isn't a breeze to freshen the air. Heading for the mountains makes perfect sense, and Idabel Lake Resort offers great fishing and surprisingly warm water for a mountain lake. It's the perfect base camp for exploring the Kettle Valley Railway line at Myra Canyon. Although the "hot-tub suites" are luxurious but pricey, the outlying cottages sleep six and there's affordable camping as well. Horseback-riding trips and motorboat and canoe rentals are available, and there are horse-drawn sleigh rides and snowmobiling in the winter.

Lake View Motel

3377 Lakeshore Road, Kelowna, BC V1W 3S9 • (604)762-5300

Perfectly situated across from Boyce-Gyro Beach on Lake Okanagan, the Lake View's units are indeed a find, since rooms in most of the hotels along this popular strip cost almost twice as much. It's an easy cycle to the vineyards of Summerhill, St. Hubertus, and Cedar Creek, and there's good swimming at nearby Bertram Creek Regional Park.

The Kootenays

The sparkling waterways of the Columbia and Kootenay rivers divide the four dramatic mountain ranges of the Kootenays. The Columbia River widens into the glacial reserves of Upper and Lower Arrow lakes, carving along the eastern flanks of the remote and densely forested Monashees and the rugged Selkirks. Dividing the West and East Kootenays is the Kootenay River, which becomes the sparkling, 110-kilometer-long Kootenay Lake. The pinnacles of the Purcells rise from the eastern shore of the tranquil lake. Beyond, at the edge of Alberta, are the Rocky Mountains.

All in all, this is one of the most stirringly beautiful areas in British Columbia, with no fewer than 58 provincial parks, each graced with deep river valleys, shimmering alpine lakes, and noble granite peaks trimmed with spectacular glaciers that attract world-class mountaineers. Access to some of these natural wonders is quite a challenge in itself; adventurers must boat into the Valhallas, a spectacular wilderness on the virgin shoreline of Slocan Lake, hike into the peaks of the Purcell Wilderness Conservancy from the northeast shore of Kootenay Lake, or drive 45 kilometers on a gravel road to reach the edge of the massive sculpted peaks of the Bugaboos.

You don't necessarily need to climb the Kokanee Glacier to

263

enjoy the splendor of this area. Many of the jagged peaks, crevassed glaciers, and flowered meadows are visible from the roads that wind up and down Arrow, Slocan, and Kootenay lakes. And plenty of civilization fills such towns as tiny Rossland, historic Nelson, Bavarian Kimberley, and alpine Invermere.

ON THE ROAD

At the southwestern edge of the Kootenays, the 1890s Gold Rush town of **Rossland** is undergoing a second boom—this one fueled by snow. Red Mountain Resort Ski Area (6 kilometers southwest of Rossland; (604)362-7384) is one of the more challenging ski areas in British Columbia, with runs so steep that some carry a "triple black diamond" designation. Despair not, faint of heart, there's a whole mountain of **great intermediate skiing** on Red's Paradise lift; for snow conditions, call (604)362-7700, (604)362-5500, or (800)663-0105. For striders and skaters, Black Jack Cross-Country Ski Club, (604)362-9465, has cut over 40 kilometers of cross-country ski trails; about half are groomed on a regular basis. Backcountry skiers can buy a one-way ticket for the Granite Chairlift to access Record Ridge, Mount Kirkup, and Gray Mountain. Be sure to sign out with the ski patrol before you go. For local info, consult Val Ash at the Red Mountain Motel, (604) 362-9000.

In the summer, the colorful turn-of-the-century main street of Rossland bustles with hikers bound for alpine lakes, mountain bikers en route to numerous trails, and bored slackers sipping cappuccino. Many trailheads for **mountain biking** and hiking routes start on the fringe of downtown. Locals know many afternoon-length bike rides, such as the

Cheap(er) Tickets

Most accommodations in Rossland get ski lift tickets at a reduced rate. So purchase your ticket from your innkeeper before you get to the mountain and save about $5. Most of the locals have season passes, and if you're planning to ski at Red Mountain more than 12 days this year it might be worth your wallet to purchase one too. Or call Red Mountain Resort Ski Area, (604)362-7384, and ask if they're offering any special promotions.

🎵 Rock and Twang Festival

The Kootenays are truly a cultural oddity. In one valley you might find potters and poets sipping tea and singing "Don't Bogart That Joint, My Friend," while in the next valley, loggers, lead-smelter workers, and hard-rock miners might be working on the umpteenth verse of "A Hundred Bottles of Beer on the Wall." For the most part, they stay out of each other's way, but every August the Rock and Twang Festival attempts to bridge that gap. Still in its infancy, Rock and Twang bravely tries to please all musical tastes, presenting everything from hard-core country to something called "classical jazz." It's the kind of event that could become a seminal stop on the summer-music circuit for redneck and pinko alike. For information, call the Rossland Chamber of Commerce; (604)362-5666.

ones up Kootenay-Columbia, along the Smuggler's Loop (where boot-leggers used to cross the border), and over the Dewdney Trail. Find out about the area's trails from the Mountain Biking Society, which produces maps and information for people exploring the countryside (from mountain bikers, hikers, and cross-country skiers to horseback riders). Contact Rossland's extremely helpful Chamber of Commerce (PO Box 1725, Rossland, BC V0G 1Y0; (604)362-5666) for maps and information on the society. Or pick up maps at After the Gold Rush Espresso Bar and Bookstore (2063 Washington Street, Rossland; (604)362-5333).

With so much focus on the outdoors, it's no wonder that a number of **sports stores** have opened up in the area. You can rent mountain bikes and cross-country skis at most of the outdoor shops (although the only place to rent downhill equipment is up at Red Mountain; (604)362-7700). In Rossland, you can rent mountain bikes at Powder Hound Boutique (2040 Columbia Avenue, Rossland; (604)362-5311) in the summer ($18/day) and at High Country Sport (Red Mountain Motel, Highway 3B, Rossland; (604)362-9000). Rossland Bike and Board (1999 Second Avenue, Rossland; (604)362-7211) is run by "Bones" Bonnery, who offers great deals on used bikes and boards (his shop doubles as a snowboard store in winter). You can save a couple of bucks by renting down in Trail at Gerick Cycle and Sports (908 Rossland Avenue, Trail; (604)364-1661).

If you need a break from the outdoors, try going underground: tour Rossland's fascinating **Le Roi Gold Mine**, Canada's only hard-rock gold mine open to the public. With 109 kilometers of tunnels underneath Red Mountain, it's not just another roadside attraction. Open May through September; (604)362-7722.

After all this activity you'll be hungry, and Rossland offers plenty of places to sate yourself. The little Sunshine Cafe (2116 Columbia Avenue, Rossland; (604)362-7630) remains this small town's favorite. Breakfast, lunch, and dinner fare is nothing fancy—just good and filling. In summer, get comfortable at a rooftop table at Rockingham's (2061 Columbia Street, Rossland; (604)362-7373) while nibbling on a few of their 30 (!) different appetizers. The dining-room atmosphere is minimal at the Flying Steamshovel Inn (2003 2nd Avenue, Rossland; (604)362-7323), so we prefer to hang out in its pub, where the pool tables, pull tabs, and loud conversation make for a sociable evening, and the menu from the Roundhouse, the inn's restaurant, is available in addition to lighter (cheaper) pub fare. Hungry folk ought to drive down the road to Trail for dinner, where the LeRose family dishes up a spaghetti-and-chicken feed for less than $10 per person at the Colander (1475 Cedar Avenue, Trail; (604)364-1816), located in a spacious old Safeway building.

Nestled in a valley on the shore of Kootenay Lake, **Nelson** sprang up with a silver and gold mining boom in the late 1890s. About a decade ago, residents tore off the fake sheet-metal and plastic storefronts that proliferated in the '50s and '60s and restored the town's Victorian character. Over 350 heritage sites are listed in this small, picturesque city. In recent years, Nelson played a starring role in the films *Housekeeping* and *Roxanne*. Nelsonites are pleased with the attention these two movies have brought them, but they wearily remind recent visitors that their town is a lot more than just a pretty stage set.

From theatrical productions to wildlife lectures to nationally known folk-rock groups, there's almost always something going on at Nelson's Capitol Theatre; (604)352-6363. The most popular eatery in town is the Main Street Diner (616 Baker Street, Nelson; (604)354-4848), where locals congregate for steak and chips and moist souvlaki with warm pita

Nelson Artwalk

In June, July and August the entire town turns into an art gallery, with artists' work exhibited in almost 20 shops, restaurants, and galleries. Maps of **Artwalk Gallery Tours** can be picked up at the Tourist Information Bureau (225 Hall Street; (604)352-3433), or contact Artwalk, PO Box 422, Nelson, BC V1L 5R2; (604)352-2402.

bread. For a calendar of weekly events in town, pick up a free copy of *The Kootenay Weekly Express*.

If it's raining (and it often is in Nelson—the forest underbrush is nearly as dense as that of British Columbia's coastal regions), rock climbers descend from the hills to practice their craft on the synthetic climbing walls of the Gravity Club (719 Vernon Street, Nelson; (604)352-6125). Many mountain lakes are too cold for swimming, but Kootenay Lake's West Arm offers a refreshing dip. Located just before the bridge on Highway 3A, Lakeside Park has a great beach and beautifully landscaped gardens. There's even a Dairy Queen across the street.

It's worth the 45-kilometer drive to tiny **Winlaw** in the Slocan Valley to totally stuff yourself at the famous Duck Stop (Highway 6, Winlaw; (604)266-7355), which may by now have been renamed by its amiable new owner and chef, Bruce Jackson (just ask anybody in town to direct you to Jackson's great cheap eats). The eclectic menu ranges from an 8-ounce New York strip steak to exotic stir-fries, vegetarian curries, and the Woodstock Special (pesto pizza and a salad).

Wilderness recreation is all the rage in the Kootenays, especially in summer. The most popular local hike is up to an old miner's cabin called Slocan Chief Cabin in **Kokanee Glacier Provincial Park**. You can throw your sleeping bag on one of the bunks (mattresses provided), and cooking facilities are available for $10 a night. In winter, Slocan Chief is so popular that the price goes up an additional 5 bucks and accommodations are assigned by a lottery system. You need a group of 12 to reserve (money up front), and you must stay for the entire week. If the **Battleship Glacier** looming overhead looks familiar, it's because the mountains grace the label of the Kootenays' most famous beer, Kokanee lager.

To the west lie the even more wild and majestic **Valhallas**. A nice, easy trail leads the way along the edge of Slocan Lake. Although some hikers arrive by boat, the easiest way to the alpine trail is to drive 44 kilometers on good gravel road to the trailhead of Drinnon Pass and Gwillim Lakes. Watch for the blue parks sign at Passmore on Highway 6, and follow the arrows to the parking area. The trail to Gwillim Lakes is easy to follow and takes three hours (one way); once there, numerous alpine hiking options exist for experienced parties. Be aware that snow often lingers in the alpine basins until mid-July. For complete information on the trails in the Kootenays, contact the district office of BC Parks (Kokanee Creek Park, 4750 Highway 3A, Nelson, BC V1L 5P6; (604)825-4421).

Mountain biking is illegal within the perimeters of the provincial parks, but myriad logging roads in the region await adventuresome pedalers. Find out more (and rent a bike if needed) from Cool Sport (737 Baker Street, Nelson; (604)354-4674). You can obtain other outdoor gear (such as canoes and cross-country skis) from Snowpack (333 Baker Street, Nelson; (604)352-6411).

Due to its high elevation, **Whitewater Ski Area** gets prodigious dumps of snow, and the tree skiing attracts expert skiers from all over North America; (604)354-4944 or (604)352-7669 (24-hour snow report). Although "WH20" is smaller than nearby Red Mountain, few Nelson skiers would ever trade places. Call (604)354-4944 or (604)352-7669 for a 24-hour snow report. Cross-country ski trails begin at Apex Nordic Center, at the base of Whitewater's Mount Ymir. The warming hut is open for use all the time, and the trail fee is $5; contact the Nelson Nordic Ski Club (PO Box 486, Nelson, BC V1L 5R3).

The Kootenays' beauty isn't all superficial. At **Cody Caves Provincial Park** near Ainsworth, you can discover a subterranean passage crammed with stalactites. The logging road (accessible from Highway 31) is not suitable for low-clearance vehicles or those pulling trailers.

Sixty kilometers north of Nelson, on the shore of Kootenay Lake, backed by Kokanee Glacier Provincial Park and face to face with the pyramid-shaped peaks of the Purcells, rests **Kaslo**. Sitting in dry dock is the S.S. *Moyie*, a vintage stern-wheeler that logged over 2 million miles in its 50-year service on Kootenay Lake. Currently undergoing restoration, the *Moyie* was recently named a National Historic Site. If you're just passing through, stop at Rudolf's Pastries (416 Front Street, Kaslo; (604) 353-2250), but if it's a meal you're after, do as the locals do and eat at the Treehouse (419 Front Street, Kaslo; (604)353-2955). This neglected-looking place puts its emphasis on consistently good food (brown rice instead of white, housemade desserts, bulging burritos), happily surprising everyone who forks into one of the Sasquatch-sized dinners.

Slocan Lake slices between Kokanee Glacier Provincial Park and the awe-inspiring Valhallas. Three towns perch on the western shore of the

 *Side Trip*

On the way to Kaslo (from Nelson), take the Balfour ferry across Kootenay Lake. It's a pretty one-hour trip one way, and the **world's longest free ferry** ride. Don't miss **Ainsworth Hot Springs**, (604)229-4212, where for $5 you can explore a cave of piping-hot waist-deep water or swim in the slightly cooled pool (open 365 days a year).

deep blue lake: Silverton, New Denver, and Rosebury. The recreational opportunities in **Silverton** include fishing and trail rides. You can rent canoes from the Silverton Resort, (604)358-7157), and outfit yourself for the trail at Mistaya Outfitting, (604)358-7787.

The peaceful community of **New Denver** is home to a fascinating (and infamous) chapter in Canadian military history. During World War II, thousands of Japanese people living in Vancouver were declared "enemy aliens" and sent to internment camps in the British Columbia Interior. The **Nikkei Internment Memorial Centre** (306 Josephine Street, New Denver; (604)358-7288) was built as part of an historic redress settlement, and it's open for public viewing.

If your spirits need lifting after this somber memorial, hop in your car and drive up, way up, to **Idaho Lookout**, once used by the Forest Service as a fire tower. The view from Wildgoose Basin is not only stunning, it's one of the most colorful places in the province, courtesy of a brilliant carpet of alpine wildflowers that festoon the meadows in mid-summer. It's a suitable hike for kids, but don't forget the bug juice.

Back on Highway 6, **Rosebury** (population 50) is a bit hard to find, since the highway is now routed behind it. Once you find the town (start looking just north of New Denver), you'll have no problem finding the Wild Rose Cafe (Rosebury Loop Road, Rosebury; (604)358-7744). It's a pretty drive from Nelson, and for the past 12 summers, people have been dropping in at owner Andrea Wright's cafe to sit on the porch and enjoy the evening with some great Mexican food. Winter hours are limited, and reservations are suggested in summer.

Bubbling hot pools are common in the Kootenays. Ainsworth Hot Springs is the most famous—and the most commercial (and its cave is fun to explore); (604)229-4212. High atop the steep shores of Upper Arrow Lake (actually a very wide spot in the Columbia River) is the town of Nakusp; 12 kilometers up a dirt road north of town, you'll find the Nakusp Hot Springs, a wilderness swimming pool. In town, the bustling Lord Minto (93 5th Avenue, Nakusp; (604)265-4033), named after a paddle wheeler that once hauled supplies and passengers up and down Arrow Lake, stacks a juicy Greek burger with feta, onions, lettuce, and tomato.

You may feel caught in a time warp if you take the Kootenay Lake ferry from Balfour Bay to Kootenay Bay and follow Highway 3A to Creston. **Kootenay Forge**, (604)227-9466, is an authentic blacksmith shop where you can watch Kootenay artisans plying this forgotten trade. Farther south, look for a barn on the left that features custom-made straw brooms. Perhaps the most bizarre sight on all of Kootenay Lake is the **Glass House**, built from a half-million empty square-shaped bottles of embalming fluid. The grounds are beautifully landscaped, and visitors are welcome in the summer months.

Ornithologists from all over Canada come to the **Creston Wildlife Interpretive Centre**, (604)428-3259, to scope out the wetland habitat at the south end of Kootenay Lake. Watch for ospreys painstakingly building their nests on top of the pilings. Admission is free, and you can camp for a fee at Summit Creek. Stop for a steaming cup of java at the Kootenay Rose Coffeehouse in Creston, (604)428-7252, the only bistro east of Kelowna that roasts its own beans.

Over in the East Kootenays, **Cranbrook** is home to a plethora of strip malls complete with major department-store and grocery chains that draw shoppers from throughout the region. The **Canadian Museum of Rail Transportation** (1 Van Horne, Cranbrook; (604)489-3918) documents the history of what was once the railroad hub of this corner of British Columbia. Take the 30-minute guided tour ($4.50 for adults; 50 cents for children) through a railroad yard of elegantly restored Canadian Pacific Railway TransCanada passenger-train cars. A guide takes visitors through the cars. After the tour, English tea and scones are available in the dining car (Sundays only in the winter). Those willing to forgo the guide can view the cars from the platform outside for a buck less.

In some ways, **Kimberley** is like other Bavarianesque towns, with its chalet-style storefronts flanking a downtown pedestrian mall (called the Bavarian Platzl). Taped accordion music flows from the sizable wooden gazebo that sits squarely in the middle of this 3-block, brick-paved street. Kimberley has at least one unique attraction, though: Canada's largest cuckoo clock. For two bits, Happy Hans pops out of the clock window and yodels. Mountain High Bookstore (232 Spokane Street, Kimberley; (604)427-7014) has a creditable selection of books by Canadian authors. There's also a sprinkling of shops selling wood carvings, European crystal, and Austrian linens.

The sporting-crowd locals blow into the Snowdrift Cafe (110 Spokane Street, Kimberley; (604)427-2001), on the Platzl, for healthful foods: housemade whole-wheat breads, vegetarian chili and pizza, and fresh salads. Gardeners shouldn't miss the teahouse, greenhouse, and immaculately kept gardens on the grounds of Kimberley Hospital (260 Fourth Avenue, Kimberley; (604)427-2215. In summer, an English-style tea is taken at the teahouse.

At 4,000 feet, Kimberley (the highest incorporated city in Canada) boasts an alpine setting in which skiing dominates all other activities for nearly half the year. Appropriately, the Rocky Mountain summits that thrust skyward from across the valley are called **The Steeples**. Mark Creek gushes through downtown. Only a few kilometers up the hill from the Platzl, Kimberley Ski Resort has two triple chair lifts, a double, a T-bar, 35 mostly intermediate ski runs, and a stunning view of several mountain ranges in the vicinity; (800)667-0808. Daily lift tickets (sorry, no price breaks for weekday skiing) are $33 for adults (add $3, and you can ski from noon till 9pm). During the annual Spring Splash, the second weekend in April, lift-ticket prices are usually reduced. Package deals are available through area hotels and motels; call the ski resort for a list of participating establishments. The Kimberley Nordic Club's 26 kilometers of cross-country ski trails, an easy walk from the downhill resort, are varied and are groomed well into spring. About 3½ kilometers are lit for night skiing. Kimberley now maintains two 18-hole golf courses: Kimberley Golf Club, (604)427-4161, and the newer Trickle Creek Golf Resort, (604)427-5171, just down the mountain from the ski area.

Canadians are often accused of intentionally burying their past under a mound of modesty or misdeed, and their Western icons and myths are as likely to be from Hollywood as from Greenwood. Luckily, there's **Fort Steele Heritage Town**, a faithful re-creation of the 1890s Gold Rush town named after an officer of the North-West Mounted Police who was hired to defuse tensions between natives and new settlers. Though it's open year-round, it's most fun during the hustle and bustle of the summer months; (604)489-3351.

Eighteen kilometers west of Invermere, the ski area at **Panorama Resort** (Panorama Road, Invermere; (604)342-6941) features North America's second-highest vertical drop—4,300 feet. You can walk to the lifts at Panorama's own village—a sprawling establishment in the Purcell Mountains that contains two hotels, condos, two restaurants, a nightclub, and outdoor recreation aplenty. Eight well-maintained tennis courts, as well as horses, hiking trails, and river rafting on Toby Creek, relieve the resort from dependence on the winter ski trade. But ski season is still the time to visit. The snow is a deep powder (World Cup competitions have been held here), and if nature doesn't dispense enough of it, machines will. The hotel rooms are the best deal at the resort, but you can find even less expensive lodgings in Invermere. Wherever you stay, you're never more than a five-minute walk to the chair lifts. The cross-country trail network is exceptional.

At the northern tip of Kootenay country, **Revelstoke** serves as a base camp to some amazing ski runs in and around the Albert Icefields. Trouble is, you need a helicopter to get there. We're not about to list the heli-ski operations in this territory, but we will tell you that there are some great alpine cabins in Glacier National Park near Rogers Pass, where snow falls almost daily in winter. The cabins are open year-round for well-equipped backcountry skiers.

CHEAP SLEEPS

Angela's

1520 Spokane Street (PO Box 944), Rossland, BC V0G 1Y0
(604)362-7790

Angela is delightful, and if you can afford to pay full price you'll get the full treatment: a whopping breakfast, a fireplace in your room, and a soak in the hot tub. But if you happen to be a poor Australian ski bum (or an American one, or a Canadian one, for that matter), then she can probably work something out, as there are always extra foamies around. There are two bedrooms in the apartment on the top floor, which is well stocked with food and kitchen equipment. Groups often take over the whole joint. Plead your case or bring something to barter, and as long as it's not a holiday, you just might find yourself getting a very good deal.

Heritage Hill House

1345 Spokane Street (PO Box 381), Rossland, BC V0G 1Y0
(604)362-9697

It seems everyone in town has stayed here at one time or another, because it used to be a boardinghouse for seasonal employees. Upstairs (no wheelchair access) in this sprawling house are four simple, clean rooms, with two bathrooms down the hall. A fireplace warms you in the winter, and breakfast keeps you going all day.

Red Shutter

Red Mountain Road (PO Box 742), Rossland, BC V0G 1Y0
(604)362-5131

You don't walk to Red Mountain from here, you ski. Larry Williams and John Heintz have been running this slopeside bed and breakfast for over 18 years now, and they've got a good thing going. It's a comfy, kick-back kind of place; ask for the ski package and you'll get dinner too—and you can *still* call it a good deal. The best deal is a five–night package that includes breakfast, dinner, a place to sleep, and all applicable taxes for the unbeatable price of $330.

Scotsman Motel

Highway 3B and Highway 22 (PO Box 1071), Rossland, BC V0G 1Y0
(604)362-7364

It may be plain as Jane, but the Scotsman Motel has an outdoor hot tub that has cured a lot of sore muscles. All of the rooms are the right price (some even have their own kitchens). There's even a multiroom suite that sleeps 10 and may just be the best per-person deal in Rossland.

The Allen Hotel

171 Baker Street, Nelson, BC V1L 4H1 • (604)352-7573

The Allen Hotel is so pleasant and inexpensive, it's almost too good to be true. For 40 years the hotel was a boardinghouse that catered to miners and railway workers. Things changed drastically after the owners took a summer trip to Europe and, impressed with the quality of hostel accommodations there, decided to open a European-style hostel here in Nelson. Solo travelers may end up sharing a room with another guest, and everyone is free to use the communal kitchen and laundry facilities. The Allen is even air-conditioned—a real blessing on those hot July nights. A night's stay will cost $13.50 (IYH members) or $17.50 (nonmembers). Linens rent for $2 more.

The Alpine

1120 Hall Mines Road, Nelson, BC V1L 4E5 • (604)352-5501

The Alpine is the nicest little motel in town. The cheapest of the 30 rooms come in just under $50. Pay a little more, and you can slide into a room with a Jacuzzi.

Heritage Inn Bed and Breakfast

422 Vernon Street, Nelson, BC V1L 4E5 • (604)352-5331

In 1897, the Hume brothers decided that Nelson (then a bustling town of 3,000) needed a first-class hotel—so they built one. In a recent remodel, the hardwood floors and fireplace in the bar were rediscovered. Restoration is now complete, and almost everything but the hallways seems polished. The spacious rooms ($59) are decorated with floral prints, lace curtains, and four-poster beds. The Library Bar is the most comfortable meeting place in town, and the Boiler Room (a disco) and Mike's Place, with a big-screen TV, can be lively, especially on weekends. Breakfasts are ordinary fare, but the Sunday brunch continues to attract locals.

Park Place Bed and Breakfast

105 Park Street, Nelson, BC V1L 4K5 • (604)352-6981

Freshly cut flowers and canes of raspberries decorate the shared bathroom, and the shower is tiled with rock and slate at this delightful, whimsical home where Mike and Lana Hames have blended historic architecture with their personal touches. Skiers will find the imaginative and substantial breakfasts (including, perhaps, pastry shells filled with shrimp or veggies) more than enough to start the day. It's an easy 10-minute walk to downtown Nelson from Park Place's perch above the highway.

Lemon Creek Lodge

Kennedy Road (PO Box 68), Slocan, BC V0G 2C0 • (604)355-2403

Located between Nelson and Slocan is the Lemon Creek Lodge: part lodge, part cabins, and part tent and RV sites. Sociable types should choose one of the 10 lodge rooms, where reading nooks, oversized chairs, and family-style meals served to lodgers who come in groups encourage mingling. Cabins (with their own kitchens) are more private. If you don't like sharing your vacation with RVs, come in the winter, when cross-country skiing (right outside the front door) is routine. Owners Anna and Keith Kessler can organize trips, on mountain bikes or Sno-Cats, to ghost towns, hot springs, and remote mountain lakes. You can even pan for gold. Rates include breakfast.

Valhalla Lodge and Tipi Retreat

General Delivery, Slocan, BC V0G 2C0 • (604)365-3226

The Slocan Valley has always been a hideaway for earth-loving types, and it's only natural that one of the most environmentally friendly resorts in the Kootenays would be located here. Dean and Lynda Carter will pick you up by boat in Slocan and take you directly to their retreat, located right on the beach where Kutenai natives fished and camped for centuries. There's canoeing, hiking, and just plain relaxing on one of the most beautiful lakes in British Columbia. In the winter, the Carters take down their tepees and relinquish their spot to Mother Nature. There's a two-night minimum ($55 per night), and each tepee sleeps up to four people. No children under 16.

Loki Lodge

314 A Avenue (PO Box 1193), Kaslo, BC V0G 1M0 • (604)353-2684

You *could* go Sno-Cat skiing at Meadow Mountain, but such bliss will cost you a bundle, so instead consider Loki Lodge in Kaslo. Judith and Peter Chomitz have turned a former warehouse into a darn good place to stay. They provide five rooms (four have private baths) and a healthy breakfast around the big dining-room table. Use this as a launching pad to the beautiful British Columbia beyond, and return in the evening to a crackling fire and warm conversation.

Wing Creek Cabins

Box 1164, Kaslo, BC V0G 1M0 • (604)353-2475

This beautiful setting, 5 miles north of Kaslo, is where woodworker Karl Dietz built two special cedar cabins overlooking Kootenay Lake. Each handcrafted cabin (kitchens too) sleeps four and is enhanced by a fireplace and a verandah. There are two spare rooms in the annex. A 10-minute trek from the cabins ends at a private beach where you can swim, fish, or simply sit and do nothing. Extraordinary hikes wind through Fry Creek Canyon Provincial Park to the northeast.

Mountain Edge Resort Inn
930 Dogwood Drive (PO Box 98), Kimberley, BC V1A 2Y5
(604)427-5381

Though they're down the hill from the ski resort, these one-bedroom condos are still within a hardy walking distance of the lifts. Some units have views of the Rockies; all have a fireplace, TV, hideabed, and access to laundry facilities and sauna. Not all units have kitchenettes, and some are barely big enough to swing the proverbial cat, but the more deluxe accommodations have full kitchens.

Alpine Huts
Alpine Club of Canada (ACC), PO Box 2040, Canmore, AB T0L 0M0
(403)678-3200

Seventeen alpine huts are hidden away throughout the Kootenays and Rockies: standing at the corner of a wildflower meadow near Lake O'Hara, blanketed under meters of snow in Rogers Pass, or nested on a forested bench above Tokkum Creek. Access might require an easy 15-minute hike or a challenging 12-kilometer ski. Each hut is equipped with a Coleman stove, lantern, dishes, and extra foamies for sweet dreams. Many of the huts have wood stoves and rudimentary kitchens. A small fee is required. ACC members get reservation priority and discounts. Rates vary at all huts according to location and time of year.

 *Secret Campsites*

If you're a hardy camper and drive a 4 x 4, the best deal in the Kootenays (nay, in all of British Columbia) can be yours, courtesy of the province's largest landowner, the Ministry of Forests. Lands that are actively logged by private contractors are accessible via well-maintained gravel roads. The Ministry of Forests has built free campgrounds in areas of particularly high scenic or recreational value—on the shores of remote fishing lakes, for instance, or near the summit of alpine passes—but because the agency has very limited resources to patrol and collect garbage from these remote locations, it deliberately avoids putting out maps or pamphlets about them at Tourist Infocentres. Contact the BC Parks office in the Kootenays, (604)426-8563, for maps to the sites.

275

INDEX

285

LODGINGS INDEX

Ashland

Ashland Hostel, 50
Green Springs Inn, 50
Manor Motel, 50
*Palm Motel and
Houses, 50*
Timbers Motel, 51
Medford, OR
Royal Crest Motel, 51
Phoenix, OR
Phoenix Motel, 51

Bend

*Country Inn the City Bed
and Breakfast, 68*
Cultus Lake Resort, 68
*Mill Inn Bed and
Breakfast, 69*
Westward Ho Motel, 69
Sisters, OR
*Three Sisters Wilderness
Cabin, 70*

The Blue Mountains

Baker, OR
*Best Western Sunridge
Inn, 75*
*Powder River Bed and
Breakfast, 76*
John Day, OR
Dreamer's Lodge, 76
Prairie City, OR
Fireside Lodge, 76
Sumpter, OR
*Sumpter Bed and
Breakfast, 76*

Columbia River Gorge

(See also Hood River)

Bingen, WA
Inn at Bingen School, 158
Cascade Locks, OR
Scandian Motor Lodge, 59
Lyle, WA
Lyle Hotel, 157

The Dalles, OR
Colonial House, 59
White Salmon, WA
Orchard Hill Inn, 158

Gulf Islands

Gabriola Island, BC
Romney House, 228
Surf Lodge, 227
Galiano Island, BC
*Cliff Pagoda Bed and
Breakfast, 225*
Hummingbird Inn, 225
Sutil Lodge, 225
Ganges, BC
Tides Inn, 224
Mayne Island, BC
Springwater Lodge, 226
Pender Island, BC
Pink House, 224
Saltspring Island, BC
*Cusheon Creek Hostel,
224*
Saturna Island, BC
*Breezy Bay Bed and
Breakfast, 227*

ACTIVITIES INDEX

Northwest Cheap Sleeps
Report Form

Got a Tip? A find? A gripe? A fact?
Send us your Cheap Sleeps suggestions. Please be sure to include the address and
phone number, if convenient.

Name of place_____

Address_____

Telephone _____

Comments:

I am not concerned, directly or indirectly, with the management or ownership of
this establishment.

Name_____

Address_____

Phone_____ Date _____

Send to:
> Stephanie Irving
> Northwest Cheap Sleeps
> SASQUATCH BOOKS
> 1008 Western Avenue
> Seattle, WA 98104